FOR PEOPLE

LIKE ME

By

Mark Steven Hayes

©2026 Mark Steven Hayes. All rights reserved.

No part of this publication may be reproduced, distributed, or transmitted in any form or by any means, including photocopying, recording, or other electronic or mechanical methods, without the prior written permission of the publisher, Hambone Publishers, except in the case of brief quotations embodied in critical reviews and certain other non-commercial uses permitted by copyright law.

For permission requests, write to the author, addressed to:

Mark Steven Hayes

Dedication

I dedicate this book to my mother and father, whose unwavering hope was that one day the world would become a peaceful and prosperous place to live for all people everywhere. My parents were born at the beginning of the Great Depression and spent their teenage years witnessing the turmoil of a nation pulled into World War II. These formative years were marked by significant upheaval and uncertainty, and not long after the end of World War II, they also experienced the impact of the Korean War. The sequence of these major historical events played a substantial role in shaping their perspectives and their desire to make a better future for themselves and their children.

I am deeply grateful to my mother, who devoted her adult life to caring for our family. Through all the hardships she faced, particularly the many health challenges that marked her adult years, she remained steadfast in her commitment to us all. She loved each of her children unconditionally, and her strength and selflessness left an unforgettable mark on my life. I will always cherish the warmth and affection she gave me.

I am grateful to my father for his intelligence, wisdom, and unwavering fortitude. Throughout my life, he was always present in the most critical moments, offering support and guidance when I needed it most. His steadfast commitment to never giving up on me, even when I undeniably tested the limits of his patience as a father, has had a profound impact on my life. The resilience he demonstrated and the wisdom he shared have helped shape the person I am today.

When describing to others what it was like raising me, Dad used the following analogy: "Raising my son was like going fishing, and I was afraid that if I tried to reel him in, the line might break and he would be gone forever. So, I set the drag just tight enough to allow a little bit of line out at a time, keeping him on the hook until he was old enough to be on his own."

Privacy, Accuracy, And Intent Statement

In preparing this memoir, I have intentionally protected the privacy of individuals referenced throughout my story. To ensure confidentiality and respect for those involved, I have omitted or altered certain names and identifying details. This approach is consistent with best practices for safeguarding personal information and is intended to prevent any unauthorized disclosure of private facts.

I further acknowledge the psychological concept known as the "objectivity illusion," which recognizes that personal beliefs and biases may unconsciously influence one's perception and recollection of events. While I have made every reasonable effort to present the facts truthfully and accurately, I recognize that my narrative is inevitably shaped by my own experiences and memory. Where minor adjustments have been made, they serve solely to improve the clarity and enjoyment of the narrative, without distorting the essential truth of the events described.

This memoir is a work of personal reflection and remembrance, and it would be incomplete or misleading if it excluded significant experiences, including those that may be painful or challenging. The stories herein are carefully constructed from my own recollections, and I have strived to remain faithful to the substance of what occurred. My intent in sharing these accounts is to honor the legacy of my family and those who have influenced my life, while also inspiring others to preserve their own histories for future generations. By documenting these experiences, I hope to provide a meaningful record for descendants who may one day seek to understand their heritage and find value in these stories.

TABLE OF CONTENTS

Why Tell My Story 1
Chapter 1 Why Oildale 7
Chapter 2 Wilson House 18
Chapter 3 Green House 27
Chapter 4 Highland Knolls House 68
Chapter 5 High School 82
Chapter 6 Freedom Ride 106
Chapter 7 Eighteen 121
Chapter 8 Young Marriage 126
Chapter 9 The Oil Patch 147
Chapter 10 Strange Tales 163
Chapter 11 Time To Fly 187
Chapter 12 An Unexpected Opportunity 198
Chapter 13 An Expat Life 207
Chapter 14 The Land of Smiles 223
Chapter 15 A Cohesive Life and Living "Sabai-Sabai" 240
Chapter 16 Retirement and Reflection 280

For People Like Me

Why Tell My Story

My name is Mark Steven Hayes. I don't know why my first name is Mark; only official venues and strangers use it. Mom and Dad always called me by my middle name, "Steve," short for Steven. For years, I asked my parents why they chose "Mark" as my first given name, but always addressed me as Steve. Their response was always the same: "I don't know." This answer always amused me, especially considering my parents would never accept such a childish response from me, or from any of my siblings.

In consolation, when I answer the phone and hear someone on the other end say, "Hello, Mark?" I automatically know it's a sales call of some sort, certainly not a friend or someone I know, and I can hang the phone up without giving it another thought. (It's the telemarketer's secret handshake.) It doesn't matter all that much, except the world tends to address people by their first name. And because of this, when people ask me why I don't go by Mark, I can't just say "I don't know," like my parents. Instead, I produce a simple reply: "middle child, middle name." Then I continue to say, "My friends call me Steve, and you can Mark it on the calendar, Mark it on the wall, or Mark it any way you like, just don't Mark me late for dinner."

For people like me, perhaps it takes a slightly brighter light to reveal the ingenuity that quietly waits within, eager to emerge when the time is right. I never considered myself one who was destined for greatness. I had no aspirations to do anything specific with my life and learned to roll with the punches as they came, sometimes ducking, sometimes just hoping the punch would miss. I didn't create any masterpieces of art, invent groundbreaking technologies, or amass a significant financial legacy that might shape the future or influence generations. Instead, I started out grounded in the practical abilities of using my two hands to develop reliable skills long before I began to make sense of my sometimes uncertain and bewildering mind.

At times I had a feeling like there were two angels sitting on opposite shoulders, an angel of good and an angel of less than good, both whispering their arguments in my ears. I most definitely struggled with some elementary-level undiagnosed learning disability that was associated with attention and hyperactivity, perhaps Attention Deficit Hyperactivity Disorder (ADHD). In those days, "ADHD" was just a fancy way of saying, "Why can't you sit still for five minutes?" or "How did you lose your homework again?" Teachers accused me of "Not Having An Interest In School," which, to be fair, was only half true, I was extremely interested in anything that wasn't school. If there had been a gold medal for daydreaming, I'd have been on the podium, probably wondering how I got there.

But when it came to sports, any sport, I generally excelled above most others my age, and even a couple of years older. Apparently, my brain was like a high-performance engine: just don't ask it to remain idle. Give me a ball, a bat, or a finish line, and suddenly all that "excess energy" became a superpower. I could focus on the game with laser precision.

Because of my learning issues, I came to believe that I wasn't as smart as other people, until I started working in the oil patch. That's when I discovered where all the other people with learning disabilities hung out, and my true nature for learning. Turns out, if you put me in a place with moving parts, real problems, and the occasional explosion risk, I could focus just fine. I went through life without taking medications, unless you count recreational meds or coffee, which I consider both to be coping strategies.

If ADHD has taught me anything, it's that life isn't about fitting into someone else's mold. Sometimes, you just need to find the right sandbox, and maybe check your pockets for missing homework before you leave.

People have always told me I was lucky, a lucky person. Yet, hearing these words often left me feeling indifferent, as I didn't view myself in the same light. Luck, as I have come to understand it, is a far more nuanced companion than most people realize. It is not the whimsical force that bestows its favor on a chosen few while leaving others in the shadows. Rather, it is woven into the fabric of our daily existence, often disguised as a fleeting moment, a chance encounter, or a decision made in the quiet solitude of our own thoughts.

I have learned that luck favors those who are present, those who pay attention to the subtle signals that life offers and who are willing to act, even when the outcome is uncertain. It is not enough to wait for fortune to knock at your door; sometimes, you must build the door yourself and stand ready to open it when opportunity arrives. In this way, luck becomes less a matter of chance and more a testament to resilience, courage, and the quiet determination to keep moving forward, no matter how unpredictable the journey may be.

So, when people call me lucky, I smile and accept their words with gratitude, knowing that luck, in my experience, is not a matter of fate, but a reflection of the choices we make and the risks we are willing to take. It is the reward for showing up, for saying yes when it would be easier to say no, and for believing that something good can come from even the most uncertain beginnings. In the end, perhaps we are all lucky, if we only have the eyes to see it and the heart to claim it as our own.

Friends and family have asked me why I decided to write this book, the answer is simple. I loved listening to the stories my parents shared about their experiences growing up, the relatives they knew, and the folklore passed to them through the generations. I was always captivated by these tales, which sparked a deep curiosity and a desire to learn more about my ancestors and the worlds they inhabited.

On my father's side, the family lore spins a tale as winding as the rivers themselves. The first Hayes in our clan, Robert, is said to have sailed from Ireland and washed up somewhere in the Carolinas, though, as with all good legends, the details are a bit foggy, perhaps intentionally so. According to the stories passed down, Robert didn't just settle in; he became a ship's captain, ferrying "unscrupulous goods" up and down the Ohio, Mississippi, and Wabash Rivers. Whether he was a daring entrepreneur or a river rogue is anyone's guess, but I like to think he had a knack for finding opportunities where others saw only muddy water.

Robert's legacy, however, didn't end with his own adventures. He had a son, Peter, whose rebellious streak would make any modern teenager proud. As the story goes, Peter and his father had a falling out, no small feat when your father commands a ship. At sixteen, Peter jumped ship (literally) somewhere along the Wabash in southern Illinois. He wandered inland, found work as a stable boy on a plantation, and promptly fell in love with the owner's daughter. When she became pregnant, the family orchestrated what's politely called a "shotgun wedding", a tradition that, I suspect, has saved many a family from scandal and many a young man from a swift exit.

Listening to these stories as a child, I was always full of questions, most of which, to my frustration, no one could answer. The details were slippery, the facts blurred by time and retelling. I found myself longing for something more enduring than folklore, a written account, a tangible record that could anchor these family legends for future generations. As is often the case with families who lived by the river's current, there was nothing in writing. Just stories, drifting from one generation to the next, waiting for someone to finally put pen to paper.

My mother's side of the family always carried a quiet pride in their Native American Cherokee heritage, a pride that, as a child, I found both mysterious and magnetic. The stories they shared about my Grandpa Chester, born in 1905 and described as half Cherokee and half English, were tinged with wonder and a hint of reverence. According to family lore, his mother was either descended from, or somehow related to, a Cherokee chief. The tales grew even more poignant when I learned that her ancestors had endured the Trail of Tears, a chapter of history that, even as a boy, I sensed was both tragic and profound.

Life, as it often does, took unexpected turns. Grandpa Virgil took Grandma Beulah to Washington State, where my Grandpa

Chester was born. But the journey didn't end there. Eventually, they returned to Oklahoma and, after having several children, parted ways. What happened next still surprises me every time I recall it: after her divorce, Great Grandma Beulah met a good man who wished to marry her. Fearing he might turn away if he knew the full size of her family, she made the heartbreaking decision to place two of her children, including my grandfather, into an orphanage on an Indian reservation. It's a choice that, even now, humbles me with its complexity and the quiet courage it must have taken.

But fate, it seems, had a sense of mercy. Not long after marrying her new husband, William, the truth came out, thanks to a mutual friend. Rather than turning away, William took Grandma Beulah to the reservation, retrieved the two children, and raised them as his own. That act of acceptance and forgiveness is a reminder of the humanity that threads through even the most difficult family stories.

Yet, for all the vividness of these tales, I was never able to find written records to substantiate them. None of my ancestors kept diaries or documents, just stories, passed from one generation to the next, growing softer and blurrier with time. That absence of written history became, for me, both a source of frustration and inspiration. It's what moved me to write my own memoirs, hoping that by putting pen to paper, I might offer a lasting testament to my journey and encourage those who come after me to do the same. In sharing our stories, however ordinary or extraordinary, we connect future generations through the fragile, beautiful thread of memory.

The stories collected in this book are intended to give readers a candid peek behind the curtain, into who I am, and the wild, unpredictable environment and experiences that shaped me throughout my life. Through these accounts, I hope to convey not just the innocence and wonder of my childhood (think: sticky fingers, scraped knees, and the occasional ill-advised adventure), but also the confusing, transformative years of adolescence, and onward into early adulthood, culminating in that pivotal, heart-thumping moment when I finally left behind the familiar comforts that had defined my life up to a crucial turning point. That decision, made with more hope than certainty, led me to seek new opportunities and possibilities that ultimately shaped my future and carried me to places I'd never imagined, some of them delightful, some of them, well, let's just say "character-building."

There's an old saying that "every picture tells a story, but not every story paints a picture." I find this especially fitting for myself, as I've never thought of my storytelling as possessing the kind of dazzling ingenuity or artistic flair that could whisk someone away on a mystical journey through the imagination. In fact, if you're looking for a literary magician, you might want to check the next tent over. Still, I must admit, there were moments when I was tempted to travel to the land of my great Irish ancestors just to kiss the Blarney Stone, hanging upside down, hoping its legendary charm might bless me with a gift for more colorful and engaging storytelling.

If you find yourself surprised by what you read, know that I am too. Life, after all, has a way of tossing in plot twists when you least expect them. My hope is that, in sharing these stories with humility and a dash of humor, you'll see not just the events, but the humanity behind them, the stumbles, the laughter, the lessons learned, and the gratitude for every unexpected turn. After all, for people like me, the best stories are the ones that remind us we're all just doing our best, one surprise at a time.

Chapter 1
Why Oildale

My parents' story began in 1948, when fate brought them together at a soda shop while they were both attending college in southern Illinois. At the time, Mom was diligently pursuing a nursing degree, and Dad was wrestling with the complexities of petroleum engineering. Their first meeting sparked an immediate and undeniable connection, one of those moments where the universe seems to wink and say, "Just wait, you two have no idea what's coming."

As is often the case with young couples in love, my parents chose to set aside their academic pursuits and focus on building a life together as husband and wife. Their commitment to one another quickly led to the start of their family. Nine months after exchanging vows, they celebrated the arrival of their first child, a daughter named Angela Kaye.

The joy and excitement of parenthood grew at a pace that would make any grandparent's head spin, and just eighteen months later, they welcomed their second child, a son named David Alan. With Kaye and David, my parents' young family began to take shape, each new addition strengthening the bonds between them and deepening their commitment as they embarked on the grand adventure of raising a family together. If they ever wondered what they'd gotten themselves into, they certainly didn't let on, at least not until the third child arrived and the real surprises began.

Dad grew up in a lively household with two brothers and one sister, which meant there was never a dull moment. But among this spirited bunch, it was his older brother Jerry who managed to rewrite the family script. Jerry, ever the trailblazer, packed up and headed west to Tulare, California, a place so far from home it might as well have been the moon, at least to the rest of the family.

Jerry's phone calls home were legendary. He painted California as a land where the sun always shone, the jobs grew on trees, and the beaches were so beautiful you'd forget all about the mosquitoes back in Illinois. He described the local economy as "booming," the scenery as "breathtaking," and the climate as "welcoming," which to be honest, sounded suspiciously like a travel brochure. The rest of the family couldn't help but wonder if Jerry was living in paradise or just had a wild imagination.

Inspired, Mom and Dad started to dream of California themselves. It wasn't just Jerry's stories that got them thinking, it was the promise of new opportunities, a fresh start, and maybe, just maybe, a chance to escape the endless cycle of shoveling snow. So, in the spring of 1951, they packed up their hopes, a few suitcases, and set off to follow Jerry's footsteps. Little did they know their journey would be filled with surprises, a healthy dose of humility, and enough humanity to fill a moving van. And if they ever doubted their decision, they could always blame Jerry, after all, he started it.

Although California's famous beaches to the west and the celebrated wine country to the north held undeniable appeal, my parents made a different choice. Instead of chasing sunsets on the Pacific or sipping their way through Napa, they set their sights on Oildale, a modest unincorporated town perched across the Kern River from Bakersfield.

Why Oildale? Well, Bakersfield's reputation as the capital of California's oil and gas industry played a starring role in their decision. Dad, with dreams (and perhaps a little bit of stubbornness) in his pocket, set out to build a career in the petrochemical industry. He soon landed an entry-level position with Standard Oil Company, proof that sometimes fortune favors those willing to get their hands a little greasy. Not long after, he was offered and accepted a position with Union Oil Company as a draftsman, marking the official beginning of his professional journey in California. Who knew that a leap of faith across a river would lead to a life filled with unexpected adventures, a few oil stains, and more than a handful of stories worth retelling?

In July 1952, while my mother was five months pregnant with her third child, our family received a rather dramatic welcome to California, courtesy of Mother Nature herself. A powerful earthquake, clocking in at a whopping 7.3 on the Richter scale, rattled the region near Tehachapi, just thirty-seven miles east of Oildale. Although I was still safely tucked away in my mother's belly, this seismic spectacle marked my very first (and most literal) shake-up in life. I suppose you could say I arrived with a bang, though thankfully, not the kind that required a hard hat.

This was the strongest quake to hit California since the infamous San Francisco disaster of 1906, and it left my parents wide-eyed and a little shell-shocked. For two Midwesterners trying to build a new life far from home, the event was a sobering reminder that California wasn't just about sunshine and opportunity, it came with its own set of surprises, some of which could rearrange your furniture without warning. The earthquake underscored the risks of their westward adventure and tested their resolve, adaptability, and, I imagine, their ability to keep a straight face while the ground did its best impression of a roller coaster.

Four months after the quake, Mom gave birth to a healthy baby boy, her third child. In her eyes, he was the most beautiful baby she'd ever seen. That baby was me, and with a healthy set of lungs and all ten fingers and toes accounted for, my parents bundled me up and brought me home. Little did they know, their "beautiful healthy son" would soon prove to be a bit of a wild card. The so-called "Terrible Twos" gradually gave way to the complexities and independence of a "Threenager," that magical age when a child's favorite word is "No!" and their favorite activity is testing the limits of parental patience.

This is when my parents first realized I didn't fit so neatly into the mold of their previous parenting experiences. If they were hoping for a repeat performance of their earlier children, I was happy to surprise them with my own script. Over the next fifteen years, I helped Mom and Dad embark on an unpredictable journey filled with trials, surprises, and the occasional need for a deep breath (or maybe a stiff drink).

I consistently challenged their preconceived notions, refusing to simply adopt their viewpoints or fit neatly within the boundaries they had previously known. My determination to forge my own path often manifested in a defiant independence, leaving little room for concern about meeting traditional expectations. If there was a rule, I was likely to ask, "Why?", and if there was a boundary, I was probably already halfway over it.

With each passing year, Mom and Dad found themselves navigating a new realm of reality, one that, at times, must have felt like they were traversing the twilight zone and beyond. The experience redefined their approach to parenting, requiring adaptation, patience, and a willingness to embrace the unknown as they sought to support a child intent on living life according to his own rules. Looking back, I can only imagine the number of times they wondered if there was a manual for raising a free spirit, or at least a warranty they could check. But through it all, we learned together that sometimes the best surprises in life come from the ones you never saw coming.

Just as my parents resigned themselves to the fate of raising a child such as me, our family grew by two tiny heartbeats, twice the love, and, let's be honest, probably half the sleep. But that's okay, because Mom and Dad knew every yawn would be worth every moment of laughter, every special cuddle, and every little hand that wrapped around their fingers. Michael Dale and Patricia Ann were proof that life's greatest blessings sometimes come in pairs. The twins were both surrounded with gentle care, endless compassion, and laughter that filled every corner of our world. The best part about this set of twins is how easy it was to tell them apart.

I always felt like Oildale was the kind of place where you could walk into a honky-tonk wearing muddy boots, a cowboy hat, and a church bulletin in your back pocket, and nobody would bat an eye.

The town had a reputation for being rough-and-tumble, sure, but it was also a patchwork quilt of personalities: rednecks, roughnecks, cowboys, farmers, truckers, outlaw bikers, and churchgoers all stitched together in one big, noisy family. If you ever wondered what it was like to see a cowboy and a biker argue over who made the best chili, Oildale was the place to find out. And let's be honest, the only thing more unpredictable than the weather was how folks settled their disagreements, sometimes with a handshake, sometimes with a wrestling match, and occasionally with a pie to the face (humility comes in many flavors).

For outsiders, Oildale could feel a bit like stepping into the wild west, including the tumbleweeds, and with plenty of colorful characters. Newcomers learned quickly that earning acceptance meant surviving a few raised eyebrows and maybe a friendly prank or two. The Kern River marked the town's boundary, and crossing it was almost like passing through customs: you needed a good reason, a sense of humor, and maybe a spare tire. Most folks who ventured across the river had a mission, usually involving one of the honky-tonk bars, where the jukebox played everything from Hank Williams to Buck Owens, or the Bakersfield Speedway, where the cars went fast, and the stories got even faster.

Whether you were chasing the thrill of the racetrack or just hoping to catch the bakery man before he ran out of donuts, Oildale's attractions were as much about the people as the places. And if you ever found yourself lost, don't worry, the locals would set you straight, probably with a story that started with, "Back in my day..." and ended with a laugh. In Oildale, surprise was always just around the corner, and if you couldn't laugh at yourself, someone else would do it for you.

Community life in Oildale was so tightly woven with the petrochemical industry that even the local bakery probably had a "crude oil special" on the menu. Most businesses in town existed to keep the oil patch humming, or at least to keep the workers caffeinated and their trucks running. As for the population, no one really knew the exact number, census takers probably got lost in the tule fog or distracted by the bakery man's donuts, but I'd wager there were no more than 20,000 souls, give or take a few who wandered in and never left (or never found their way out).

Education in Oildale was a community affair. The town boasted a single high school, two junior highs, and four elementary schools. That meant if you misbehaved in first grade, your reputation could follow you all the way to graduation. The teachers knew your siblings, your parents, and probably your dog's name. It was the kind of place where you couldn't get away with much, unless you were really clever, or your grandma was on the PTA.

Highway 99, affectionately known as the "trucker's highway," sliced through the west end of town. It was more than just a road; it was Oildale's main artery, pumping in opportunity and the occasional lost tourist from Los Angeles all the way up to Red Bluff. The constant rumble of semitrucks was the town's unofficial soundtrack, occasionally interrupted by the honk of a horn or the clatter of a dropped wrench.

Family road trips north on "99" to visit our cousins in Tulare were legendary events. They didn't happen as often as I would have liked, probably because my parents needed a week to recover from the last one, but when they did, they were unforgettable. The journey was always shrouded in tule fog, a dense, low-lying mist that wrapped the highway in a ghostly, Halloween-like embrace.

Highway 99 was a parade of semitrucks, each one a potential source of childhood delight. My siblings and I would press our faces to the car windows, arms pumping in the universal "pull the horn!" gesture, hoping to coax a mighty blast from the truckers. When a driver obliged, the resulting honk was so thunderous it could rattle your fillings, and your parents' nerves. That booming sound was the highlight of every trip, a small thrill that made the endless miles and sibling squabbles fade into the background. Looking back, I realize those moments were pure magic: a blend of surprise, shared humanity, and the humility of knowing that, in the grand scheme of things, we were just kids in the backseat, hoping for one more honk before the fog rolled in again.

For People Like Me

People used to be a whole lot more tolerant and considerate than they are nowadays. As a boy, I only had one telephone in the house, and it operated on a party line shared with neighbors. This early design meant that phone conversations were not always private, and sometimes you could tell if someone was listening in on your phone conversation. Using the telephone came with its own set of etiquette, and before making a call, it was customary to lift the receiver and check if a neighbor was already using the line.

As one can imagine, the problem with the party line was that there was always someone talking on the phone. If our call was urgent, we had to politely ask the person on the line to end their call so we could use the phone. Of course, even after the neighbor ended their call, they might continue listening in, curious about the reason for our interruption. Despite the frustrations one experienced at times, I don't recall any neighbors fighting over the phone line, but it's easy to imagine the kind of arguments or conflicts that might arise in today's world if people were required to share a single phone line with others in their neighborhood.

The expectation that I memorize our family's telephone number was not just a casual request, but a true necessity instilled by my parents. Knowing the number meant that, in the event of an emergency, I had the means to reach home and connect with my family. There was never an acceptable excuse for not using it, especially if I ever found myself in a place other than where I had said I would be. This simple act of memorization was one of the first lessons in responsibility and self-reliance that my parents taught me, ensuring that I always had a way to contact them and reinforcing the importance of accountability from a very young age.

Oildale wasn't just a town, it was a living, breathing stage where the daily cast of characters made every street feel like a friendly sitcom. The bustling neighborhoods had their own set of local celebrities, and none were more beloved, or more essential, than the Postman, the Milkman, the Bakery Man, and the Ice Cream Man.

The Postman was our unofficial town crier, striding through the neighborhood in full uniform, sometimes with a hat perched just so, as if he'd stepped straight out of a Norman Rockwell painting. He carried a leather bag that looked big enough to hold a week's worth of secrets, and he delivered the mail with the precision of a Swiss watch. Unlike today's impersonal mailbox clusters, our Postman brought letters right to the door, or, if you were lucky, through a mail slot that doubled as a built-in alarm for napping dogs. If you ever wondered what trust sounded like, it was the gentle clatter of mail landing in the catcher behind the door.

Then there was the Milkman, a hero in a white cap and a company truck, braving the wilds of Oildale to deliver glass bottles of fresh milk to every porch. He was the original recycling champion, collecting empties with a nod and a wink. In our neighborhood, milk theft was unheard of; the only thing more sacred than your own milk was your neighbor's, and if you ever ran out, you simply borrowed a bottle with a solemn vow to repay by tomorrow.

But the real excitement came with the musical parade of the Bakery Man and the Ice Cream Man. The Bakery Man's truck was a rolling concert hall, announcing his arrival with a cheerful tune that could make even the grumpiest Dad leap from his recliner. I would race outside, sometimes on my bike, sometimes barefoot, orbiting the truck like a hungry satellite. Donuts and pastries were the currency of happiness, and if I managed to convince Mom to buy a treat, I felt like I had won the lottery.

The Ice Cream Man, though, was the undisputed king of summer. On those sweltering afternoons, the jingle of the ice cream truck was the call to arms for every kid within earshot. His truck was a treasure chest on wheels, packed with candy, popsicles, and enough ice cream to cool off the entire block. His jingle was the siren song of childhood, growing louder as he approached.

I would dash outside barefoot, or in flip-flops, waving my coins like flags of victory. The Ice Cream Man, a hero in a white cap, would greet us with a knowing smile, fully aware that he was about to make our day. All it took was a couple of nickels or a dime to embark on a grand childhood adventure, one where the quest for a simple treat became a mission worthy of the bravest explorer. But if I were lucky enough to have a quarter in my pocket, I felt like I'd struck gold and ascended to the very gates of heaven. The arrival of the Ice Cream Man was nothing short of a neighborhood festival, especially in our town, where the sun seemed to have a personal vendetta against cool weather.

Looking back, it's clear that these neighborhood figures weren't just delivering mail, milk, or sweets, they were delivering moments of surprise, kindness, and connection. They reminded us that life's simple pleasures are often the sweetest, and that a little humility (and maybe a donut) goes a long way in bringing people together.

Living in Oildale was never dull, our small town sat close enough to Edwards Air Force Base that, on any given morning, you might be jolted out of your cornflakes by the sound of the X-15 rocket slicing through the sky. For me, each sonic boom was a free thrill ride. Windows rattled, dogs barked, and for a split second, everyone wondered if the dishes would survive. The grown-ups tried to act nonchalant, but you could see them checking for cracks in the walls. The sheer force of those booms left a mark on our memories, after all, not every town gets its own impromptu percussion section courtesy of the space race.

But it wasn't just about the X-15. Oildale's residents were hooked on the unfolding drama of space exploration. Families gathered around their TVs, eyes wide, following every satellite launch and mission update. The promise of reaching beyond our little patch of earth was enough to make even the most skeptical neighbor pause and dream a little. I personally listened intently to the voices of the early astronauts describe their experiences while orbiting the Earth, sharing with the world the sights they witnessed and the emotions they felt.

These broadcasts captivated me, drawing me into the unfolding story of human exploration beyond our planet. When the first astronauts set foot on the moon, I was glued to the television, watching in awe as history was made before my eyes. The moment they filmed the now-famous words, "one small step for man, one giant leap for mankind," it was utterly hypnotic. The sense of wonder and possibility was overwhelming, and I felt fortunate to witness such a pivotal milestone in human achievement.

On rare summer evenings, the sky over Oildale provided its own spectacular show. Brilliant colors would burst across the horizon, illuminated by the streaking debris of a failed rocket or space satellite that had exploded at the edge of space. I remember standing there, neck craned, mouth agape, trying to guess whether the dazzling display was courtesy of NASA's latest experiment or just another piece of space junk making its final curtain call. The grown-ups would shake their heads and mutter about "the risks of progress," but for me, it was pure magic, a reminder that even when things go sideways up there, humanity keeps reaching for the stars, undeterred by the occasional cosmic blooper.

The first home I ever knew was affectionately called "the White House." It wasn't the presidential kind, but a cozy cottage village where my family landed when I was born. I can't claim any vivid memories of living there, unless you count Dad's legendary habit of driving us by the cottages and retelling, for the hundredth time, how he painted every last one just to pay our rent. If there's a Hall of Fame for creative problem-solving, Dad would have a plaque right next to the paint cans.

Soon enough, we packed up and moved to the "Wilson House" on Wilson Avenue in the Beardsley district. This place holds a special spot in our family lore because it's where the twins, Mike and Patty, made their grand entrance. The Wilson House wasn't just a roof over our heads, it was the backdrop for some of our earliest shared adventures, sibling squabbles, and the kind of chaos that only a growing family like mine might appreciate.

Next up was the "Green House." If you've ever wondered what monsters sound like tiptoeing down the hallway at night, try combining the steady hum of a swamp cooler, a train rumbling by, and my father's infamous snoring. To my young mind, it was a symphony of eerie noises, equal parts comfort and mild terror. We lived in the Green House longer than any other home in Oildale, and it became the stage for most of our family's daily routines and memories. If walls could talk, these would probably ask for earplugs.

Our final stop in Oildale was the "House in Highland Knolls," perched in the last housing tract on the north end of town. We stayed there through my middle school years, a time marked by Dad and Uncle Russ building a brick wall around the backyard and seeding grass in every yard within sight. It was a period of growth, not just for the lawn, but for all of us.

Looking back, each home wasn't just a place to sleep; it was a chapter in our story, stitched together by belonging, humbleness, and the kind of compassion that comes from learning to laugh at yourself, and occasionally at Dad's snoring. No matter what house we lived in, my father had a unique way of rousing us children from our beds each morning, by singing a silly tune: "Up in an atom, out on the job, work like the devil, all day long." Not even pulling my pillow tightly against my ears with the covers over my head could drown out his waking call. If NASA ever needs a new alarm system for astronauts, I'd suggest Dad's morning serenade, guaranteed to launch anyone out of bed faster than a rocket on a caffeine binge.

Despite all the stories, good or bad, that people may have heard about Oildale, I have no unpleasant memories from my childhood there, at least none that weren't of my own making. Whenever my siblings and I reminisce about our years in Oildale, our conversations often revolve around the different homes we lived in, but the soundtrack was always the same: laughter, love, and a whole lot of rock 'n' roll. Each residence held its own unique significance and left distinct impressions on our family's narrative, but music, and my sister's infectious enthusiasm, made every house feel like home.

Chapter 2
Wilson House

The Wilson House was a gentle reminder that true comfort isn't measured in square footage, but in the memories made within its walls. Small and unassuming, this older home welcomed you with three sturdy steps leading to a covered front porch, a perfect spot for watching summer storms roll in or waving to neighbors passing by. Inside, the main room greeted you on the left, bathed in soft light from two windows: one framing the lively street, the other offering a glimpse of the neighbor's garden. The front bedroom, just to the right, also looked out onto the street, its window a portal for morning sunshine and the laughter of children playing outside.

From the heart of the house, a cozy dining area with a cheerful side window sat beside the kitchen, where sunlight poured in from windows overlooking both the backyard and the side of the house. This made even the simplest family meals feel special, as if the world outside were joining in. A hallway off the kitchen led to the bathroom and second bedroom, both tucked away for privacy and quiet. At the end of the hall, two doors waited: one opening back into the family room, the other leading to the back porch, a place of simple magic.

The back porch was home to an old-fashioned wash tub, complete with a scrub board and rollers, where laundry days became moments of togetherness. Clothes hung on the backyard line would flutter in the breeze, filling the air with the scent of sunshine and soap. Though the Wilson House was pieced together from distinct memories, every detail, no matter how small, added to its faithful charm. It was a place where warmth lingered in every corner, and where the ordinary became extraordinary simply because it was home.

My earliest memory in the Wilson House sparkles in my mind like a treasured gem, set on a late September morning in 1955. The air was thick with anticipation and childlike excitement as my family awaited the arrival of the twins, my younger brother Mike and sister Patty, coming home from the hospital for the very first time. We lived in the Wilson House then, a place that seemed to hum with life and possibility, and although I was just two months shy of my third birthday, the details of that day remain etched in my heart with remarkable clarity.

I remember the sky being overcast, a gentle gray blanket that made the world outside feel cozy and close. My siblings, Kaye and David, and I darted back and forth between the two front windows, each of us vying for the best vantage point, our little feet pattering with excitement, our eyes wide with curiosity, eager to catch the very first glimpse of the twins' arrival. The energy in the house was electric, as if every wall and floorboard were holding its breath along with us.

Through the window of my memory, I can still see Dad parking a black car on the street in front of our house. He didn't own that car, it was borrowed from a friend, a neighbor, or maybe a colleague, because times were tough and buying his own wasn't an option. Yet, there was no sense of lack, only resourcefulness and hope.

Dad stepped out, walked around to open the door for Mom, who sat cradling Mike and Patty in her arms. With gentle strength, he took each twin from Mom, one at a time, careful and loving, and carried them together into the house. After laying the twins safely in the crib they would share, Dad returned to help Mom out of the car, escorting her up the stairs and into our home. I can still see the soft, gentle smile on my mother's face as she stepped out, Dad holding her securely by the arm, their love and partnership shining through even the simplest gestures.

That morning, the world felt new and full of promise. As a young child, I didn't realize then that our baby brother Mike had been born severely clubfooted, nor could any of us have understood the challenges that lay ahead. All I knew was the joy of family, the warmth of togetherness, and the magic of welcoming new life into our home. It was only later that Mom and Dad would gently explain to us that Mike would need corrective surgery and special braces to help him learn to walk, a lesson in resilience and hope that would shape our family's journey for years to come.

Looking back, I cherish the excitement, the curiosity, and the love that filled that day. It was a moment that glowed with warmth and character, a testament to the strength of family and the beauty of small beginnings.

I don't remember if Grandma arrived at our house before or after the twins, but she entered like a gentle whirlwind, her presence a blend of nurturing care and quiet determination. She came to help Mom regain her strength after a difficult childbirth, stepping in to manage the house and wrangle the three of us older kids while Mom focused on the newborn twins. Whether or not I can truly picture Grandma bustling around our home, or if my mind has stitched together this memory from years of family storytelling, hardly matters. What's certain is that her visit became legendary in our family lore.

Every afternoon, after lunch, Mom would retreat for a well-earned nap with the twins, trusting Grandma to keep the rest of us in line. Grandma's strategy was simple: she'd gather us together and declare it was time for everyone to take a nap, hoping to transform the house into a sanctuary of peace and quiet. My older sister Kaye and brother David, ever the model children, would obediently settle down and drift off as instructed. I, on the other hand, saw nap time as the opening act of my daily adventure.

Instead of lying down, I'd launch into a full-scale game of "Catch Me If You Can," darting through the house with the energy of a caffeinated squirrel. I'd weave through the main room, dash into the dining area, zip through the kitchen, and race down the hallway, always with Grandma in hot pursuit. She'd chase me, her laughter and gentle pleas trailing behind, never quite catching me but never giving up either. It was a dance of wills, a test of stamina, and I suspect a secret source of amusement for her.

Dad, ever the observer, once remarked that Grandma "wasn't holding the brightest candle in the room" because she kept chasing me until she was completely worn out. He even suggested she could just close a door to make her job easier. But as I've grown older (and perhaps a bit wiser), I've come to suspect that Grandma was far cleverer than Dad gave her credit for. I think she let me run wild on purpose, knowing that by the time I finally collapsed, I'd nap soundly for at least an hour, giving her, and the rest of the household, a much-needed break. Maybe Grandma's candle shone brighter than anyone realized, lighting our home with patience, humility, and a quiet sense of humor that made even the wildest days feel safe and loved.

It was after Grandma had packed up her gentle whirlwind of care and returned home that one of my most memorable stories at the Wilson House unfolded. My older sister Kaye shared her recollection of sleeping in a small bed set up in the dining area next to the kitchen, a detail that pairs closely with my own understanding of how and why she ended up there.

I remember the three of us older kids, Kaye, David, and I, shared the front bedroom, at least for a while. Kaye had a double bed, while David and I claimed the bunk beds, one stacked atop the other, creating a rickety skyscraper. Eventually, the arrangement changed, and Kaye's bed was exiled to the dining room, a diplomatic move to separate the boys from the girls. But before that, our bedroom was the stage for some of our wildest antics.

One night, while Dad was absorbed in his favorite television shows in the front room, we transformed our shared bedroom into a makeshift playground. David and I, fueled by the kind of energy only kids possess, pushed Kaye's double bed up against the bunk beds. The result? An impromptu jungle gym. We chased each other in circles, scrambled up the ladder, and took turns leaping from the top bunk onto Kaye's mattress, bouncing off with the kind of reckless joy that made us erupt in laughter every time we landed. The room was alive with our excitement, each jump more daring than the last, our giggles echoing through the house like a pack of mischievous monkeys.

Then came my turn, the grand finale. I climbed to the top bunk, took a deep breath, and launched myself into the air. For a split second, I felt like an Olympic gymnast. But as I landed, there was a sound that could only mean trouble: a sharp crack, followed by the unmistakable thud of the bed frame crashing to the floor. Suddenly, the room was silent. You could have heard a pin drop, or, in our case, the sound of Dad's footsteps approaching.

Dad entered, his face a mix of concern and the weary patience of a man who'd seen it all. There I was, sitting perfectly still on Kaye's broken bed, stunned by what had just happened. David and Kaye stood nearby, each with a silent finger pointed in my direction, the universal sibling signal for "It was him!" Even though we'd all been part of the fun, the evidence was clear, and it was obvious who would be held responsible for the mishap.

Looking back, I can't help but laugh at the sheer chaos of that night. There's a certain humility in realizing that sometimes, the best-laid plans (or the wildest leaps) end with a crash, and a lesson learned. If nothing else, I discovered that being the youngest sometimes means being the fall guy, but it also means having the best stories to tell. And as for Dad, I'm sure he secretly admired our creativity, even if it meant another repair on the honey-do list.

This next tale is one of those stories my mother recounted so often that, over time, I've lost track of where genuine memory ends and where her loving retellings begin. Who among us doesn't have a sweet tooth? From my earliest days, I was irresistibly drawn to anything sugary, my curiosity for sweets matched only by my knack for noticing exactly where Mom and Dad stashed the candy. While the treats weren't exactly hidden, my parents did their best to keep them safely out of reach, tucking them away on high shelves they believed were beyond the grasp of little hands. But for a child with a vivid imagination and a determined spirit, the allure of forbidden candy was as powerful as any treasure map promising adventure.

Fueled by both appetite and ingenuity, I hatched a plan worthy of a young explorer. I dragged a kitchen chair across the linoleum, climbed atop it, and then hoisted myself onto the countertop, a precarious perch that would have made any circus acrobat proud. Balancing carefully, I began stacking whatever objects I could find, each one bringing me closer to the summit where the candy bowl awaited. I don't recall ever being caught red-handed, but I can only imagine the look of shock on Mom's face if she'd walked in to find her child teetering atop a makeshift tower, fingers poised above the prize.

After that escapade, my parents, concerned for both my safety and their dwindling candy supply, moved the sweets to a new hiding spot: a shelf above the refrigerator. This, they believed, was truly out of reach. Most children would have accepted defeat, but I was not most children. My parents had underestimated just how resourceful and stubborn a determined child could be when the quest for candy was at stake.

The adventure didn't end there. During afternoon nap time, while Mom rested with the twins and my siblings drifted off to sleep, I would lie in wait, listening for the gentle rhythm of the household settling into quiet. When the coast was clear, I'd slip out of bed, tiptoe into the main room, and push a chair up to the front door. With the stealth of a seasoned escape artist, I'd climb up, unlock the door, and set off on my next expedition, a solo trek to the little neighborhood market a block and a half away. The store was a familiar outpost, and I knew exactly where the candy was kept. The owner, who knew my family well, would always oblige my request for a treat, but not without first calling Mom to let her know her wayward adventurer was at the store again and needed to be picked up.

Looking back, I can't help but laugh at the blend of mischief and innocence that colored these escapades. There's humbleness in realizing how much patience and understanding my parents, and the community, showed a child whose curiosity sometimes outpaced caution. My "naughty but clever persistence" became a running joke in our family, and I suspect Dad installed more than one extra lock on the door, each one a silent testament to the ongoing contest of wits between parent and child.

Reflecting on these moments now, I see more than just a quest for candy. I see the humanity in a small community that looked out for its children, the concern of parents who balanced discipline with love, and the humor that softened the edges of childhood rebellion. Most of all, I see the seeds of adventure, ingenuity, and resilience, qualities that, in one form or another, have shaped my journey ever since.

My final memory of life in the Wilson House is painted with the innocence and curiosity that only childhood can offer. We lived next door to a family of four, their two boys forming a sort of parallel universe to my own siblings, one about my sister Kaye's age, the other just a bit older than me. Their father, a pioneer in his own right, decided he wanted to be the first in the neighborhood to have a stucco house. For us kids, this was nothing short of a spectacle. We watched with wide-eyed fascination as he measured and cut wood, nailed it with the precision of a craftsman, and layered paper and wire mesh like he was building a fortress. The driveway became a stage for his evening and weekend performances, and sometimes my Dad would join in, lending a hand when he wasn't at the golf course. To us, these grown-ups were magicians, conjuring something new out of sweat and determination.

I couldn't tell you how long it took them to finish that first side of the house because time, for a child, is measured in adventures, not hours. But I do remember the warm summer evening when Dad and the neighbor finally stepped back, admiring their handiwork with the quiet pride of men who'd wrestled order from chaos. Their satisfaction was palpable, a moment of accomplishment that seemed to glow in the fading light.

The next morning, riding high on their success, Dad and the neighbor decided the occasion called for a celebration, a round of golf at their favorite course. It was a well-deserved break, and perhaps a little reward for surviving the trials of home improvement. But as fate would have it, their absence set the stage for a different kind of creativity, one fueled by the boundless curiosity and mischief of two young boys with tricycles and too much free time.

At some point, one of us, memory blurs the culprit, but I suspect we were equally guilty, reached out and touched the freshly applied stucco. To our young minds, it was like play-dough, soft and inviting, begging to be explored. What began as a tentative poke quickly escalated into a full-blown artistic collaboration. Over the next few hours, we transformed the side of the house into our own masterpiece, drawing pictures and carving patterns in the still-soft stucco. We were so engrossed in our "artwork" that we stripped away the stucco as high as our little arms could reach, leaving behind a patchwork of doodles and bare spots, a mural of innocence and mischief, painted in the language of childhood.

I will never forget the look on my Dad's face when he came home that evening and saw what we had done. Shock and disbelief mingled with a kind of weary resignation, the universal expression of a parent confronted by the unpredictable genius of their offspring. Through the side window, I watched as Dad spoke to our neighbor, apologizing with genuine humility and promising to help repair the damage.

That evening, I learned a lesson about actions and consequences, delivered not with anger but with the steady hand of a father who understood that mischief is often just curiosity in disguise. The aftermath of our adventure resulted in a well-deserved punishment, a spanking on my bare backside, a moment that stung more in memory than in pain.

Yet, even as I nursed my wounded pride, I couldn't help but reflect on the altruism of it all: the way grown-ups and children alike stumble through life, making messes, cleaning them up, and laughing at the surprises along the way. And if nothing else, I learned that every masterpiece, no matter how fleeting, comes with its own story, and sometimes, a little humility is the best brushstroke of all.

Chapter 3
Green House

The summer after my fourth birthday was a turning point for our family, a time when the ordinary became extraordinary. Moving into the "Green House" wasn't just about changing addresses; it was the start of a new adventure, brimming with possibility and the thrill of discovery. The house itself, with its three cozy bedrooms, single bathroom, and one-car garage, might have seemed modest to outsiders, but to us, it was a world waiting to be explored.

As we stepped through the front door, the living room welcomed us like an old friend, and the hallway ahead promised countless stories yet to unfold. The dining room and kitchen, tucked to the right, quickly became the heart of our home, where laughter echoed, meals were shared, and the simple act of being together felt like a celebration. The kitchen's side door opened onto a covered patio, a magical space shaded by a wall of ivy that climbed over wooden latticework, offering both privacy and a touch of whimsy.

Just beyond, a sturdy tree cast its shade over the backyard, where a brick barbecue grill and a wide clothesline stood ready for family gatherings and sun-dried laundry, each detail adding to the tapestry of our new life. The garden wrapped around the house, bursting with fruit trees, bananas, lemons, and limes, each one a small treasure waiting to be picked. The sun shone brightly on moving day, and the air was electric with excitement.

Mom and Dad moved with purpose, carrying boxes and memories, transforming the unfamiliar into a place of comfort and belonging. It didn't matter that the house wasn't brand new; what mattered was the sense of freedom and togetherness it offered, a space where we could grow, play, and simply be ourselves.

Even amid the excitement of that very first day, my older brother and I found something to raise Cain over. Sibling rivalry in our house was practically a contact sport, a blend of competition, chaos, and the unspoken rule that no grudge could outlast the next round of hide-and-seek. My older brother, David, and I were locked in a perpetual contest for supremacy; I was convinced that the universe had shortchanged me in the birth order lottery.

Our battles were rarely about anything important; a sideways glance, a missing toy, or the last cookie could spark a skirmish worthy of a Saturday-morning cartoon. Yet, for all our wrestling and wild chases, we never truly hurt each other, at least, not in any way that left a mark for more than a day.

If blood was ever drawn, it was usually thanks to our older sister Kaye, who, as the reigning authority in our parents' absence, had her own unique approach to conflict resolution. Kaye's method was swift and effective: she'd swoop in, talons at the ready, and break up our scuffles with a well-placed swipe of her sharp fingernails. The result? A quick end to the chaos and a mutual understanding between David and me that challenging Kaye's rule was a losing proposition. In the absence of Mom and Dad, she was judge, jury, and, occasionally, executioner.

The day in question began like any other, with David and me circling each other like boxers waiting for the bell. I can't recall what sparked the chase, maybe a borrowed baseball glove, maybe just a look, but soon David was after me, his threats echoing around the stucco house. He was older and bigger, but I had the advantage of speed and a knack for zigzagging just out of reach. My agility was my secret weapon, and I relished the thrill of the pursuit, darting around corners and doubling back, always just a step ahead. The more I eluded him, the more his frustration grew, a classic case of sibling rivalry fueling both our engines.

We must have circled the house once or twice, the excitement building with each lap, until fate (and a poorly placed patch of rough stucco) intervened. As I rounded the back patio, I stubbed my big toe so hard that a chunk of skin tore away, sending me tumbling to the ground in a dramatic display of agony. There I was, clutching my wounded toe and howling like a banshee, while David, sensing victory at last, closed in for the final tag. But just as he was about to claim his prize, our father appeared, drawn by the commotion. With the perfect timing of a sitcom dad, he separated us before things could escalate, restoring order to our wild afternoon.

Looking back, I see more than just the rivalry and the roughhousing. There was excitement in the chase, humanity in the way we always forgave each other, and humility in the lessons learned, sometimes the hard way, about limits, laughter, and the bonds that held us together. And if there's a moral to the story, it's this: in the grand arena of sibling rivalry, it's not about who wins or loses, but about the memories made, the scars earned, and the stories we'll tell for years to come, preferably with a little humor and a lot of heart.

The same year, during autumn before my fifth birthday, was a season of sniffles and stubborn colds, the kind that lingered just long enough to worry a mother's heart. Sensing something more might be at play, Mom decided it was time for a doctor's visit, a mission of love disguised as a routine checkup. Our family car, a "Pink" 1956 Ford Fairlane, was a rolling time capsule from an era when seat belts were more suggestion than standard. None of us ever wore them, and I suppose we trusted in luck, love, and Mom's careful driving to keep us safe.

That afternoon, I climbed into the front passenger seat, blissfully unaware of the adventure ahead. Sleep claimed me almost instantly, the gentle hum of the engine and the warmth of Mom's presence lulling me into dreams. Suddenly, the car jolted to a bumpy stop, rousing me from my nap in a fog of confusion. Still half-asleep, I did what any self-respecting four-year-old might do, I assumed we'd arrived at the doctor's office, reached for the door, quickly opened it, and started to get out.

What happened next was a testament to maternal reflexes and unconditional love. In a flash, Mom's hand shot out, grabbing me by the back of my pants and yanking me back into the seat. With the agility of a circus performer and the nerves of a fighter pilot, she managed to close the door, keep one hand on me, and the other on the steering wheel, all while navigating the car over the railroad tracks at Norris and Airport Drive. Only then did I realize, as Mom's voice trembled with relief and exasperation, that we were not at the doctor's office at all. We'd narrowly avoided a tumble onto the tracks, and I'd nearly made my grand exit into the middle of nowhere.

Once we finally arrived at the doctor's office, I underwent a thorough examination. The verdict: my tonsils had overstayed their welcome and needed to go. The surgery was scheduled at Mercy Hospital in Bakersfield, the very place where Mom worked as a nurse's aide. For many kids, a hospital stay might spark anxiety, but I was oddly excited, perhaps buoyed by the knowledge that Mom's friends would be there, watching over me like a flock of kindly guardian geese.

From the moment I arrived, I was enveloped in a cocoon of care. Nurses and aides, many of whom knew me, stopped by with smiles, gentle words, and the kind of reassurance that only comes from people who genuinely care. Their kindness transformed what could have been a frightening ordeal into something almost comforting, a reminder that even in sterile hallways, humanity and warmth can shine through.

The day of my surgery remains vivid in my memory. As I was wheeled into the operating room, someone placed a mask over my face and asked me to count to ten. I barely made it to five before drifting off, surrendering to the unknown with a child's trust. When I awoke, I was greeted by gentle smiles and soothing voices, the kind that make you believe everything will be all right. And then, the ultimate reward: as much Jell-O as I could eat. In that moment, Jell-O wasn't just a dessert, it was a symbol of comfort, love, and the sweet relief of knowing I was safe, cared for, and deeply cherished.

Looking back, I see more than just a medical adventure. I see a mother's fierce devotion, a community's quiet support, and the humility of a child who learned, sometimes the hard way, that life's bumps and near-misses are often softened by the hands that catch us. And if there's a lesson in all of this, it's that love, laughter, and a little bit of Jell-O can turn even the scariest moments into stories worth telling.

The twins were just 18 months old and spent most of their time living in the playpen, mostly because of brother Mike's extraordinary challenges. Born with clubbed feet, Mike faced a daunting path from the very start. At just two years old, he underwent corrective surgery, a moment that filled our family with both hope and deep concern. When Mike returned home, his tiny legs were encased in casts stretching from his feet to his hips, held together by a single stabilization bar. The sight was both heartbreaking and humbling, a vivid reminder of the fragility and resilience of childhood.

In those early days, our parents embodied the purest forms of love and kindness. With unwavering patience, they worked alongside Mike, gently encouraging him to stand, to move, and to believe in his own strength. Their care was not just physical, it was emotional, nurturing his spirit through every painful struggle and small victory. Each attempt to roll over, each effort to stand, was met with gentle hands and words of encouragement, reflecting a deep humanity and humility that shaped our family's bond.

As time passed, Mike was fitted with special shoes and braces, his progress marked by perseverance and quiet celebration. The wall in our home became his security blanket; as long as his finger touched its surface, he could shuffle forward with determination, step by step. We watched with awe as he gradually weaned himself from the wall, each milestone celebrated not just as a triumph over adversity, but as a victory of love and community. The day Mike no longer needed his special shoes was a moment of pure joy, a celebration of resilience, kindness, and the collective support that carried him through.

Yet, Mike's journey was far from over. Not long after his physical recovery, our parents discovered he had been born with perforated eardrums, resulting in significant hearing loss. This new challenge brought fresh waves of concern but also deepened our family's compassion. Despite the frustration and anger that sometimes accompanied his struggles, Mike remained gentle and kind-hearted, never allowing hardship to harden his spirit. His humility and quiet strength inspired all who knew him, reminding us that true humanity is found in how we respond to life's trials.

Reflecting on Mike's story, I am reminded of the enduring power of love, care, and perseverance. Our family's journey was marked by moments of concern and humility, but also by countless acts of kindness and celebration. Through every challenge, we learned that the greatest victories are not measured by what we overcome, but by the love and humanity we share along the way.

Looking back, I'm convinced my parents enrolled me in kindergarten early not because I was a prodigy, but because my younger brother Mike required more hands-on attention, and, let's be honest, I was already running circles around the house like a caffeinated squirrel. Most kids started school after their fifth birthday, but I was nearly three months shy of the cutoff, making me the youngest and possibly the most clueless student in the class. Adventure, it seemed, was already calling my name.

At the time, a brand-new elementary school was rising just down the street, but it was still a hard-hat zone, so I had to ride a school bus clear across town. My older brother and sister went to the same school, but they rode a different bus, and in a twist worthy of a sitcom, I never saw them at school all year. It was as if we were living parallel lives, separated by the mysterious forces of bus schedules and classroom assignments.

In those first weeks, Mom was my personal bodyguard, walking me to the bus stop each morning and meeting me after school to escort me home. Eventually, she decided I was ready to brave the wilds of suburbia alone, a decision that, in hindsight, was either a testament to her faith in me or her desperate need to remain with Mike and Patty.

I was always the first kid at the bus stop, fueled by the thrill of early-morning freedom and the hope of squeezing in a few rounds of tag before the bus arrived. But then, she appeared. Her name is lost to history, but her image is burned into my memory: a red dress with delicate lace, standing out like a rose in a field of dandelions. From that day on, my usual antics faded into the background. I'd drift over to her, quietly reach for her hand, and together we'd wait for the bus, two tiny romantics in a world of peanut butter sandwiches and nap time.

Boarding the bus was a covert operation worthy of a spy novel. I'd head straight to the back, wait for the wheels to start rolling, then execute my signature move: crawling under the seats, dodging stray shoelaces and the occasional wad of gum, until I found her. I'd pop up beside her, take her hand, and ride to school in silent triumph. When we arrived, I'd slither back under the seats to the rear, making it look like I'd been there the whole time. On the way home, I'd repeat the ritual, a pint-sized Houdini with a heart full of hope.

We almost never spoke. Words weren't necessary. Everyone at the bus stop knew she was my girlfriend, and my friends respected the unspoken code: no teasing, unless you wanted a punch in the arm. In the grand theater of childhood, this was my first taste of love, pure, awkward, and utterly sincere.

Now, with the benefit of hindsight, I can laugh at the drama I conjured from a simple bus ride. There was excitement in every morning, adventure in every crawl beneath those seats, and a kind of humanity in the way we all silently agreed to let a shy kid hold hands with his first crush. If there's a lesson here, it's that first love doesn't need grand gestures or flowery speeches, sometimes, it's just a quiet hand to hold on the way to kindergarten, and the courage to risk a punch in the arm for what matters most.

First grade was a whirlwind of new beginnings and daily adventures. The newly built elementary school, with its twin buildings stretching side by side, felt like a world divided, one for the little kids, one for the older, wiser crowd. My sister Kaye, already a fourth grader, vanished each morning into the mysterious back building, a place with its own playground and rules. I rarely glimpsed her during the day, and that distance made her seem both close and impossibly far away. My brother David, a third grader, was just across the way, but he guarded his circle of friends like a fortress. To him, I was the pesky little brother, always eager to tag along, always just a step behind.

But I was undeterred. The schoolyard was my arena, and every morning, as the sun climbed over the rooftops, I threw myself into the chaos of kickball with the older kids. The thrill of the game, the thud of the ball, the rush of running bases, the shouts and laughter, was pure excitement. I was younger, but I was quick, and I played with a fierce determination that caught the captains' eyes. Being picked early for a team, ahead of older kids, felt like a secret victory, a badge of honor I wore with pride. Even if David rolled his eyes, I knew I'd earned my place. Sibling rivalry was alive and well, but beneath it was a current of respect, one I hoped he'd notice, even if he'd never admit it.

Lunchtime brought its own adventures. After wolfing down my sandwich, I'd race to the field, kicking the ball with friends, savoring the freedom of those golden midday moments. But just before the bell, I always took the time to check on my girlfriend since kindergarten. She was gentle, quiet, and preferred the sandbox to the rough-and-tumble games. I felt a protective urge toward her, a kind of innocent, fierce love that made me want to keep her safe from the world's small cruelties.

One day, I found her in tears, sand tangled in her hair, her face streaked with hurt. Johnny, a classmate, had dumped a handful of sand on her, and the sight of her crying ignited a flash of anger in me. Without thinking, I charged at Johnny, fists flying, driven by a need to defend her honor. The scuffle was brief but intense, my heart pounding with a mix of rage and righteousness. The teacher's whistle cut through the chaos, and suddenly I was being pulled away, my hands still clenched, my cheeks burning with emotion.

I didn't understand why I was the only kid marched to the principal's office. Standing there, I felt a confusing mix of pride and frustration. I was punished, three sharp whacks from the principal's paddle, a note sent home to my parents. But even as I rubbed my sore backside, I held my head high. I had stood up for someone I cared about, and in my young mind, that mattered more than any punishment. Johnny never bothered her again.

Looking back, I see that day as more than just a childhood fight. It was a moment shaped by adventure, love, respect, anger, and the instinct to protect. And now, with the wisdom of years, I reflect on how those early experiences, both the triumphs and the consequences, helped shape the person I would become.

When autumn rolled around, and the leaves all began to fall, our front yard would transform into a wonderland of crunchy color. We'd grab our rakes, some of us more enthusiastically than others, and corral those leaves into one gigantic pile, a mountain of gold and red just begging for trouble. Then, like a pack of giggling daredevils, we'd take turns launching ourselves into the heap, arms flailing, laughter echoing through the crisp air. Each leap sent a flurry of leaves skyward and, occasionally, a lost shoe or two. Hours would slip by as we dove, tumbled, and sometimes disappeared completely beneath the leafy avalanche, only to pop up with twigs in our hair and grins on our faces. Looking back, I'm convinced those leaf piles held some kind of magic, capable of turning ordinary afternoons into endless adventures, and even making chores feel like the best kind of mischief.

The anticipation of Halloween in our house was electric, a current of excitement that built all day as we carved mischievous faces into pumpkins and set them aglow on the porch, their flickering grins promising adventure. The air itself seemed to shimmer with possibility, as if the night were holding its breath, waiting for dusk to fall and the magic to begin. Our costumes, chosen with care and a dash of sibling rivalry, transformed us into pirates, ghosts, or wild animals, each disguise a ticket to a world where the ordinary rules no longer applied.

Instead of the usual Halloween-themed bags, we armed ourselves with oversized pillowcases, lured by the legend that our neighborhood was a treasure trove for the bold and the clever. There was a sense of fun and friendly competition in the air: who would collect the most candy, who would find the rarest treat, who would dare to knock on the house with the creaky gate and the mysterious, flickering light? The allure of the unknown pulled us from house to house, our laughter echoing through the crisp autumn night as we darted from porch to porch, our hearts pounding with the thrill of the chase.

But beneath the excitement, there was always a whisper of danger, a reminder that the night belonged to more than just children and candy. Shadows stretched long across the lawns, and every rustle of leaves or distant bark of a dog could send a shiver down your spine. My parents, with a love both fierce and gentle, made sure to remind us to be careful, their last-minute instructions a shield against the unpredictable.

I was five years old the first time I was allowed to go trick-or-treating with my siblings, Kaye and David. The air was electric with excitement, my heart pounding as I watched them dart ahead, their costumes fluttering in the cool autumn breeze. The night was alive with mystery, shadows danced across lawns, and every porchlight seemed to promise adventure and a treasure trove of candy. I could barely contain myself, eager to break free and join my siblings in the thrill of Halloween.

Just as I was about to sprint across the street to catch up, my mother's voice rang out, a sudden, urgent call that cut through the night. In that instant, her instinct became my lifeline. I stopped abruptly, turning to see what she wanted, and at that very moment, a car with no headlights and no driver rolled silently past, gliding through the darkness before crashing down the street. The danger was real, immediate, and invisible until the last second. Had I not paused, I would have been struck by that runaway vehicle, my story might have ended before it truly began.

Looking back, I realize how lucky I was that Mom called out to me at the exact right time. Her love and compassion, her unwavering vigilance, saved me from what could have been my last Halloween. The memory humbles me still, reminding me that sometimes, the smallest acts of care can change the course of a life.

From an early age, my parents instilled in me not only the importance of caution but also the deep love and care that shaped our family's approach to safety. Their warnings about strangers were never just rules, they were acts of protection, rooted in a desire to keep me safe from harm. They spoke of the "boogie man," not to frighten, but to teach me that danger sometimes wears a friendly face, and that vigilance is an act of self-respect as much as self-preservation.

As I began walking to and from school on my own, their lessons echoed in my mind. The school was only a block away, and unless it rained, I made the journey alone. One afternoon, I encountered a moment that would stay with me for life, a test of both the wisdom my parents had shared and my own ability to act with humility and humanity in the face of uncertainty. A car pulled up beside me, and inside was a woman who appeared kind and well-dressed, her smile warm and inviting. She offered me candy and a ride home, her tone gentle, almost maternal. Yet, beneath her pleasant demeanor, I sensed the subtle danger my parents had warned me about. With a polite "No, thank you," I declined, choosing caution over comfort, and continued on my way, alert and aware.

The woman returned over the next few days, her friendliness never wavering. At first, my youthful innocence saw only kindness, not threat. But as the encounters repeated, I shared my experience with my mother. Her response was swift and protective, an embodiment of parental love in action. Together, we sat in the principal's office, recounting the events to ensure everyone was aware, and that no child would face danger alone. For the next month, my mother drove me to and from school each day, and I never saw that woman again.

Looking back, I am humbled by the care my parents showed, grateful for the compassion that guided their choices, and reflective on how love is often expressed through the quiet, everyday acts that keep us safe. Their warnings about strangers were not just about fear, they were about empowering me to make wise decisions, to honor the trust placed in me, and to recognize that humility and vigilance are gifts we give ourselves and those we love. I am forever grateful for the protection and wisdom my parents offered, and for the chance to carry those lessons forward, honoring the legacy of care that defines our family.

Our house was just a block and a half from the regional airport, a magical proximity that transformed ordinary days into extraordinary adventures. Living so close meant the sky itself became our playground, and the world of aviation unfolded right outside our door. Each time the crop dusters took off and landed, their engines rumbling low over the fields, it was as if giants were tiptoeing across the horizon. We'd watch, wide-eyed and breathless, as these daring pilots skimmed just above the ground, their planes dancing with gravity in a spectacle that never failed to fascinate us. The thrill of seeing them up close, feeling the vibrations in our chests, and imagining ourselves in the cockpit was pure childhood excitement.

But the airport's true treasures lay beyond the crop dusters. Along the fence, an impressive lineup of vintage military planes stood like silent sentinels of history. Their weathered fuselages and gleaming propellers whispered stories of distant wars and heroic journeys. My friends and I would press our faces to the chain-link fence, captivated by the sheer size and mystery of these old aircraft. We'd invent wild tales about their missions, picture ourselves as brave pilots, and marvel at the craftsmanship that had carried these machines through time.

Once a year, the airport transformed into a festival of flight, drawing crowds from all around for the legendary air show. The highlight was always the arrival of the Blue Angels, their jets slicing through the sky in breathtaking displays of speed and precision.

The roar of their engines, the impossible maneuvers, and the shimmering trails left behind were enough to make even the most stoic grown-ups gasp in awe. For us kids, it was pure entertainment, a real-life superhero show where the sky was the stage.

The day was packed with excitement: planes of every shape and size taking off and landing, skydivers leaping from thousands of feet above, their parachutes trailing colorful flares that painted the sky with streaks of light. The parachutes were the classic military kind, floating gently and steadily to the ground, adding a touch of nostalgia and drama to the spectacle. And then there were the family tours, climbing up a ladder to explore the interiors of different planes, running our hands over the controls, and imagining the adventures that awaited. One unforgettable year, I even had the chance to sit inside a Blue Angels jet. That moment, surrounded by dials, switches, and the promise of flight, fueled my fascination with airplanes and made me believe that anything was possible.

Not all the air shows could be seen with the naked eye. Some arrived as thunderous surprises, the X-15 test jet project, which flew overhead a few times each week. Every time the X-15 broke the sound barrier, it announced its presence with a sonic boom so powerful it rattled every window in our house. The shockwave would make the dishes tremble and the dogs bark, and for a moment, it felt like the whole world was holding its breath. We'd laugh, duck, and then race outside, hoping to catch a glimpse of the jet streaking across the sky. Even when we couldn't see it, we could feel its presence, a reminder that the boundaries of possibility were always being pushed just above our heads.

These experiences, woven together with the excitement of local air shows, fueled my growing fascination with jets. My interest became so intense that Mom would sit down with me to help write letters to several U.S. Air Force bases. We'd carefully craft our requests, politely asking for photographs and literature about their aircraft. The anticipation was half the fun, coming home from school, hoping to find a large yellow envelope waiting in the mail. Opening those envelopes to discover new photos and information was like unwrapping a treasure chest, each piece deepening my enthusiasm for aviation and sparking new dreams of flight.

Looking back, I realize how lucky I was, not just to witness these spectacles, but to share them with family and friends. The airport wasn't just a place for planes; it was a place where imagination soared, where humility was learned in the face of awe-inspiring machines, and where humanity was found in the shared excitement of a community coming together. The fun we had, the stories we invented, and the dreams we nurtured all became part of the tapestry of my childhood.

Growing up as a rambunctious kid was nothing short of an epic adventure, the terror of the neighborhood, as some put it. Each morning, before the sun had even finished stretching its golden arms across the sky, I was already wide awake, charged with restless energy and an irrepressible sense of anticipation for whatever wild possibilities the day might bring. The world, in those early hours, felt brand new and brimming with promise. I'd step outside, the cool air tingling on my skin, and let the chorus of birds serenade me into action. For me, dawn wasn't just a time, it was an invitation to seize the day with both hands and a fearless heart.

Weekends were my personal festival of freedom. I'd leap onto my bike and carve wild circles in the middle of the street, my shouts echoing through the neighborhood like a rallying cry for adventure. "Come on out!" I'd holler, undaunted by the occasional grumpy parent who'd bellow from a window, "Hey, kid! Shut up and go home!" Their protests were just background noise to my mission. If one house didn't yield a playmate, I'd pedal to the next, my enthusiasm undimmed, my independence unshaken. I suppose, in hindsight, I was a bit of a neighborhood alarm clock, one that didn't come with a snooze button.

Sure, my boundless energy and knack for mischief sometimes landed me in hot water. But I wasn't a troublemaker at heart, just a kid with a wild imagination and a stubborn streak of curiosity. Looking back, I can see why some folks might have pegged me as a real-life Dennis the Menace. Still, there was always a thread of humility woven through my escapades; I never set out to cause harm, only to squeeze every drop of fun from the day.

One morning, just after sunrise, I set out on what I thought would be a routine quest for camaraderie. I hopped on my trusty bike and zipped down the street to my friend's house, eager to summon him for another round of early-morning adventure. But fate, as it often does, had other plans. Instead of my friend, his dog, a beast with a purple tongue and a bark that could rattle windows, came tearing around the corner. With a fearless (or perhaps foolish) grin, I tried to outpace the canine missile. My legs pumped like pistons, but the dog was faster. In a flash, it caught up and sank its teeth into the back of my left knee, leaving me with a badge of honor (and a fair bit of blood) to show for my valor.

Now, pride is a funny thing. Even as pain shot through my leg, I refused to cry in front of the other kids. I was determined to be tough, to wear my wounds like a medal. But as soon as I was within earshot of my parents, all that bravado melted away. I let out a scream that could wake the dead, hoping for a little sympathy, and maybe a hero's welcome. My dad, ever the realist, was less than impressed. He scolded me all the way to the doctor's office for a tetanus shot and again on the ride home, his frustration mixing with a father's quiet concern. After we returned, he marched over to my friend's house to settle things with the dog's owner. Whatever was said behind closed doors must have worked because Dad came home unscathed, no dog bites for him, just another story for the family archives.

Reflecting on those wild mornings, I see more than just a kid on a bike. I see the fearless pursuit of fun, the stubborn independence that refused to be tamed, and the humility that comes from learning, sometimes the hard way, that even the boldest adventurers need a little help (and a tetanus shot) now and then. There's a certain humanity in these memories: the way parents worry, the way friends forgive, and the way a neighborhood, for all its quirks, becomes a stage for growing up. And if there's a lesson in all this, it's that life's greatest stories are born from the courage to chase the sunrise, the humility to laugh at your own missteps, and the wisdom to know that every scar is just another chapter in the grand adventure of being a kid.

My endless days of terrorizing the neighborhood did end when the doors locked me in for the night. Even when I laid my body down for the night, my mind was alive with dreams, vivid, cinematic, and brimming with the kind of detail that makes the line between sleep and waking feel paper-thin. As a child, my nights were not mere escapes from the day, but thrilling adventures, each dream a new chapter in an epic saga where I was both hero and humble student of my own imagination.

One extraordinary chapter began with a surge of excitement: I found myself able to draw energy straight from the air, gathering it in my palms until they tingled with invisible power. With a leap of faith, and a child's boundless courage, I lifted off the ground, floating above the world, the wind of possibility beneath me. But this was no effortless glory; to stay aloft, I had to keep "flapping" my hands, channeling fresh energy, much like a bird must keep beating its wings. The thrill was electric, and when I awoke, the memory was so real, so exhilarating, that I could hardly wait for nightfall, eager to return to that realm where I was both the adventurer and the architect of my own destiny.

The next night, the adventure continued, my dream picked up exactly where it had left off, as if the story had been waiting for me. I became the conductor of my own symphony, orchestrating the events, learning to master the art of flight. With each dream, I grew braver, more skillful, and soon, I was not alone. I taught my siblings to float, and together we soared through the dreamscape, a band of young explorers reveling in the glory of our shared nighttime adventures. There was honor in leading them, and humility in realizing that even in dreams, the greatest joy comes from sharing the journey with others.

What stands out most, even now, is the clarity with which I understood the source of these dreams. Their inspiration was rooted in a real-life discovery: the mysterious "chi energy" I felt when I pressed my palms together, a tingling force that sparked my curiosity and set my imagination ablaze. That simple experiment became a wellspring of wonder, fueling not just my dreams, but a lifelong fascination with the hidden energies that connect us all.

But not every night was filled with triumph. The scariest dream I ever had was a lesson in fear, humility, and the strange ways our minds test us. One night, as I lay in bed, waiting for sleep, I heard a shuffling from the closet, a sound that prickled my skin with dread. The closet door slid open, and out stepped a circus clown, his painted face both comical and terrifying. He moved with eerie silence, raising a finger to his lips, a gesture that demanded secrecy and sent a chill down my spine. I was paralyzed, caught between the urge to flee and the stubborn pride of a child determined to appear asleep. The clown, fully aware of my act, inspected my brothers, then returned to me, repeating his silent warning before slipping back into the shadows of the closet. I lay frozen, fear and exhaustion wrestling within me until sleep finally claimed me.

The next morning, driven by a mix of adventure and anxiety, I searched the closet for hidden doors or secret passages but found nothing. The world was unchanged, but I was not. I recounted the tale to my father, who assured me with gentle humor that it was "just a dream" and urged me to let it go.

Yet, the memory of that clown, equal parts terror and mystery, remains with me, a reminder that even our darkest dreams can teach us about courage and vulnerability. They were lessons in adventure, in the thrill of discovery, and the honor of teaching others. They taught me to laugh at my own fears, to reflect on the boundaries between reality and imagination, and to cherish the simple, glorious truth that every night brings a new chance to learn, to lead, and to dream again.

Every year, our elementary school threw an open house that felt like the Oscars for kids, minus the red carpet, but with plenty of construction paper and Elmer's glue. Parents would parade through the halls, peeking into classrooms as if they were touring a museum of questionable art, nodding politely at macaroni mosaics and science projects held together by hope and Scotch tape. Teachers would stand by, valiantly trying to convince everyone that little Johnny's volcano was a sign of future greatness, not just a baking soda disaster waiting to happen.

It was the open house of my third grade, a night that would start with excitement and end with a plot twist worthy of a sitcom. That morning, our class was buzzing as we assembled our finest work: math sheets with more eraser marks than numbers, spelling tests that looked like I'd invented a new language, and an art project that, if you squinted, might have resembled a dog. Or a cloud. Or possibly a pizza.

That evening, I marched into the classroom with Mom and Dad, feeling like a VIP and a nervous wreck all at once. My teacher gave her speech about the curriculum and her hopes for us, while I stood by my desk, ready to unveil my "masterpieces." I opened my folder with all the drama of a magician revealing a rabbit, except my rabbit was a stack of homework that had survived the bottom of my book sack.

I watched my parents' faces as they flipped through my work, hoping for a smile or at least a nod that said, "Well, at least you tried." Then, out of nowhere, my teacher appeared. She started off with a gentle voice, telling my parents how much she appreciated my effort and what a good kid I was. Suddenly, she burst into tears, real, honest-to-goodness tears! For a split second, I thought, "Wow, my handwriting really is that bad."

Through her sobs, she confessed she didn't know what she was going to do with me. The room went silent. My parents looked at me, then at each other, probably wondering if they should start a college fund or a bail fund. Dad, always the problem-solver, suggested I go outside and play with my friends, possibly to give everyone a chance to recover. On the drive home, things were quiet. Dad gently told me I'd need to put in extra effort from now on. Looking back, my parents were just as confused as I was. Sometimes, grown-ups don't have all the answers either, especially when their kid's teacher has a meltdown at open house.

My parents discovered my eyesight was 20/300, a number that meant the world was a blur unless it was right in front of my nose. They were stunned; after all, I was a talented ballplayer, and no one understood how I could catch, throw, and hit the ball so well, let alone see the blackboard. What they didn't realize was that my passion for sports fueled an in-depth concentration, a kind of mind-over-matter that emerged whenever I was truly interested. The doctor explained that this intense focus, driven by genuine enthusiasm, had somehow helped me compensate for my poor vision, a small miracle in itself.

Wearing glasses let me see the world more clearly, but they didn't magically fix my struggles in the classroom, a place that didn't spark my interest. Learning was still difficult. I'd read a sentence, forget it, and have to read it again, and again, hoping the words would finally stick. Writing was even tougher. Composing more than a few lines felt impossible, and my attempts were, by any measure, horrific. I watched other kids breeze through their work, wondering why it was so easy for them and so hard for me. Even with glasses, the world of learning remained a maze, and I often felt lost inside it.

Looking back, none of us had any clue what ADHD was. If you'd asked me, I'd have guessed it was a new brand of sneakers or maybe a secret code for "kid who can't sit still." It's almost comical that neither my teachers nor my parents suspected I was wrestling with it. I mean, I was the kid who could turn a simple math worksheet into an origami swan before recess and who thought "focus" was just the name of a camera brand. However, when you put me on the ball field, I became the leader, the captain, the one who called the plays and scored all the points.

The Summers weren't just hot, they were legendary. The sun didn't just shine; it attacked, turning the asphalt into a sizzling griddle that threatened to fry your feet if you dared cross barefoot. Shoes weren't just footwear; they were survival gear. If you forgot your tennis shoes or thongs, you had two choices: sprint like your life depended on it, or risk hopping across the street like a panicked cartoon character. I usually chose the latter, and let's just say my feet learned humility the hard way.

Sidewalks? Not in our neighborhood. We blazed our own trails, cutting across front lawns like miniature explorers on a quest for cooler ground. The grass was our oasis, soft, forgiving, and a whole lot less likely to leave you with blisters. It didn't matter if Mrs. Johnson gave us the stink-eye for trampling her petunias; we were on a mission, and nothing could stop a determined pack of kids in search of adventure.

But the real magic happened at the high school swimming pool, which doubled as the local recreation hotspot. That pool was more than just a place to cool off, it was our summer headquarters. I took swimming lessons, learned to glide through the water, and quickly earned a reputation as the kid who could out-swim just about anyone (except maybe the lifeguard, who was basically Aquaman). The pool was divided into two zones: the splash-and-play lanes, where chaos reigned, and the deep end, reserved for the brave souls who dared to conquer the diving boards. No flips or back dives allowed, apparently, the grown-ups thought we were a little too enthusiastic about testing gravity. Still, leaping off the high dive felt like flying, and every jump was a lesson in courage (and occasionally, humility, when you belly-flopped in front of your friends).

On days when the pool was off-limits, we became masters of improvisation. Water balloon fights erupted in backyards, garden hoses transformed into weapons of mass soaking, and running through sprinklers became an Olympic sport. If someone set up a slip-and-slide, it was game on, and no one stopped until the plastic was shredded and the grass underneath looked like a mud-wrestling pit. We even invented our own skimboards from leftover plywood, turning soggy lawns into makeshift surf zones. Of course, convincing parents to let us flood their yards was a lesson in negotiation, and more than once, our best arguments were met with a firm "not a chance." Still, we never stopped trying.

Building forts was another favorite pastime. We scavenged for materials, old boards, blankets, cardboard boxes, and transformed them into secret hideouts. Each fort was a headquarters for our wildest schemes, a place where imagination ruled and every stick could be a sword, every shadow a lurking dragon. The excitement of constructing these hideaways was matched only by the pride we felt showing them off to our friends, even if the roof leaked and the walls wobbled in the breeze.

Our creativity didn't stop at architecture. We engineered rubber band guns from whatever we could find, popsicle sticks, clothespins, and a healthy disregard for parental warnings. These homemade contraptions fueled epic battles around the neighborhood, with rubber bands zipping through the air and laughter echoing down the street. Of course, we had our own code of honor: no aiming at faces, and definitely no shooting at the family dog (except for the dog that bit me behind the knee). Slingshots were another staple, and our competitions tested not just our aim, but our humility, since missing the target was always met with good-natured teasing.

The neighborhood itself was a treasure trove. Fruit trees of every kind lined the streets, and picking fresh fruit became a daily ritual. Bananas, cherries, plums, peaches, nectarines, apples, oranges, nature's bounty was ours for the taking, and we never had to look far to satisfy a sudden hunger. Grapes and berries grew wild on backyard vines, and the thrill of discovering the ripest fruit was only surpassed by the joy of sharing it with friends. Sometimes, our enthusiasm got the better of us, and we'd sneak over the fence behind our house to snatch a few grapes from the neighbor's carefully guarded rows. He was a vigilant farmer, and catching us in the act was almost a sport in itself, a lesson in humility and a reminder that adventure sometimes comes with a side of mischief.

McCray Park wasn't just a patch of grass in the middle of our neighborhood, it was our childhood kingdom, a place where adventure, laughter, and a little bit of chaos reigned supreme. The tall trees stood like gentle sentinels, wrapping us in shade and making every game feel like a secret mission. In one corner, a modest baseball backstop waited patiently for us to transform it into the epicenter of our "over the line" battles. Sure, the field was small, but that only made our games more creative, and the competition more fierce. Every hit, every catch, every wild throw was met with shouts of triumph and groans of good-natured defeat. If you wanted to see humility in action, just watch a kid strike out and then immediately challenge everyone to a rematch.

Sometimes, we'd sprawl out on our backs in the grass, inching toward the nearest tree like stealthy explorers. Suddenly, a squadron of blackbirds would swoop down, wings flapping and voices squawking, determined to defend their nests from our giggling invasion. It was a dramatic showdown, us versus the birds, and even though we never won, we always walked away with a story to tell and a new appreciation for the art of retreat. There was a kind of joy in those moments, a reminder that sometimes the best adventures are the ones that end with a little surprise and a lot of laughter.

Just a few blocks away, the local recreation center beckoned with its own treasures. There were plenty of activities on offer, but for me, nothing compared to the bumper pool table. That table was my personal arena, and I loved it with the passion of a true competitor. Of course, access was limited, timing was everything. If you didn't show up early, you'd find yourself waiting in line, plotting your strategy and sizing up your opponents. But when it was finally your turn, the excitement was palpable. Every shot was a chance for glory, and every miss was met with good-natured ribbing from friends. Bumper pool wasn't just a game, it was a lesson in patience, humility, and the fine art of pretending you meant to bank that shot off three cushions.

At home, our parents had their own system for keeping us in line. When it was time to come inside, Mom or Dad would step out and call our names with the authority of seasoned drill sergeants. If we were too far away to hear, one of us would be dispatched as a messenger, a noble quest to fetch the others home. We always knew where we were supposed to be, thanks to Mom's meticulously marked calendar hanging on the kitchen wall. Every significant occasion was written down, ensuring there was no confusion about where we needed to be or when. It was understood: home in time for lunch, dinner, and definitely before the sun set. There was a certain humanity in those routines, a gentle structure that kept us safe, loved, and just rebellious enough to keep things interesting.

On especially hot summer days, Mom enforced the lunch rule with the precision of a general. We'd come home, sweaty and sunburned, and she'd greet us with simple but comforting meals, peanut butter and jelly sandwiches, or my personal favorite, grilled cheese, paired with glasses of punch or Kool-Aid that tasted like pure happiness. Sometimes, after lunch, I'd stretch out underneath the swamp cooler in the hallway with one or two of my siblings, soaking up the cool air and taking a short nap to recharge before heading back outside. It was a moment of pure joy, a pause in the day that reminded us that fun, excitement, and a little humility were always waiting, just around the corner.

Two doors down from my house lived one of my closest friends, a true partner in mischief. Together, we transformed ordinary afternoons into epic adventures, inventing games and daring each other to push the boundaries of what was possible. One day, as our gang gathered for a high-stakes round of hide and seek, my friend leaned in with a conspiratorial grin and whispered about a secret hideout so ingeniously concealed that it seemed to exist outside the laws of discovery.

The house between ours belonged to an elderly couple, quiet as shadows. We'd glimpse them only occasionally, tending their garden, shuffling to the store, or hanging laundry in the backyard. Their home, like all the houses on our block, had a generous crawl space beneath it, a mysterious underworld that beckoned to our imaginations. My friend had stumbled upon the entrance, and with the stealth of seasoned spies, we crept over, hearts pounding, careful not to be seen or heard as we slipped into the darkness.

Inside, the crawl space felt like another realm. Dust motes danced in the slivers of light, and the air was thick with the thrill of secrecy. We hollowed out a small chamber, just big enough to sit and peer out through the access door, feeling like explorers in a hidden fortress. Over time, our ambition grew: we dug a trench to one side, piling the displaced earth into corners, expanding our domain until we could almost stand upright. Every scrape of dirt, every muffled giggle, was a test of our stealth and nerve.

But danger lurked beneath the fun. We knew, in the back of our minds, that we were trespassing on forbidden ground. The risk only added to the excitement, each day in the fort was a gamble, a dance with discovery. One day our luck ran out when the neighbors called in a professional to inspect the crawl space. The trench was found, and the alarm was raised. The owners, realizing the peril, had the trench filled in to prevent any structural collapse. Our secret lair was lost, sealed off forever.

I remember overhearing my Dad and the neighbor discussing the incident, their voices tinged with concern. They spoke of how the house could have collapsed, how our innocent adventure had skirted real danger. As kids, the possibility of disaster never crossed our minds; we were too caught up in the thrill of the game. We kept our secret for decades, never admitting our role.

Thirty years later, over a glass of wine, I finally confessed to my dad. To my surprise, he didn't scold me or say he'd suspected me all along. He just smiled and said he wasn't surprised. Maybe he understood that for kids with wild imaginations, a little danger was part of the fun, and that sometimes, the best stories are the ones you're brave enough to tell.

As you can tell, my life was a whirlwind of endless fun and excitement, but beneath the laughter and adventure, there was always a spark of mischief ready to ignite. I wasn't just the kid who colored outside the lines, I was the one who drew new lines just to see if anyone would notice. If there was a rule, I saw it as a personal invitation to test its limits. Whether it was sneaking an extra cookie when no one was looking, orchestrating elaborate pranks on my siblings, or mimicking my father's every move (right down to his most colorful language), I seemed to have an uncanny knack for finding trouble, and, more often than not, inviting it to stay for dinner.

My mischievous streak wasn't just a phase; it was a way of life. I relished the thrill of pushing boundaries, even when it meant risking a swift slap to the back of my head or a stern lecture about "respect." Sometimes Dad would say strange things to me like, "You're going to end up just like your Uncle Don", but who was Uncle Don? I never met him. Anyway, the more I was scolded, the more determined I became to carve my own path. Each reprimand only fueled my sense of defiance, transforming me from a playful trickster into a master of creative rebellion. I learned early on that if you're going to get in trouble, you might as well make it worth the price of admission.

Through it all, I developed not just a mischievous way of looking at the world, but a stubborn defiance that refused to be tamed. I challenged authority, questioned expectations, and found a certain satisfaction in outsmarting the very people trying to keep me in line. Looking back, I realize that my mischief wasn't just about breaking the rules, it was about discovering who I was, one harmless act of rebellion at a time.

This next story baffles even what the most defiant minds can fathom. Down the street from my childhood home, beyond the elementary school, sprawled a forbidden kingdom: the sumps. These old oilfield lands, ringed with barbed wire and punctuated by stern "Danger: Do Not Enter" signs, were more than just off-limits, they were a psychological gauntlet for every kid in the neighborhood. The warnings were clear, but the real deterrent was unspoken: if Dad ever found out you'd been inside, punishment was guaranteed.

Curiosity, however, is a force that rarely yields to caution. The sumps were a mystery wrapped in danger, their history stretching back to the 1920s and 30s, when they held the toxic leftovers of the oil industry, crude, chemicals, and drilling mud. By the time we came along, they were environmental headaches, but to us, they were a wild frontier. The berms, ten feet high, were both barrier and invitation, and inside, each sump was encircled by its own earthen wall, like a series of secret fortresses.

Despite the risks, we couldn't resist. Armed with BB guns and a thirst for adventure, we'd sneak in, building tumbleweed forts and shooting at imaginary foes. Some kids had mini-bikes and go-karts, and the dusty trails became our racetrack. The excitement was electric, a blend of camaraderie and the thrill of getting away with something we knew was wrong.

Inside the sumps, the ground was treacherous, a thick, tar-like substance that clung to anything it touched. Sometimes, we'd spot the bones of unlucky cows, their skulls half-submerged in the black ooze. Determined to claim these macabre trophies, we'd drag old boards across the tar, engineering makeshift bridges with the ingenuity of desperate explorers. The plans, like those of mice and men, often failed: the tar was too deep, the bones too stuck, and more than once, someone would slip, earning a telltale stain on their shoes, a mark that had to be scrubbed away before facing parental inspection.

One weekend, driven by the familiar tug of defiance, I told Dad I was heading to the school to shoot hoops. Basketball in hand, I played just long enough to make my alibi believable, then slipped away toward the sumps. Halfway through the barbed wire, I caught movement out of the corner of my eye, Dad's car, with my older brother David beside him, unmistakably pointing me out. The realization hit like a punch: I was caught, red-handed, and punishment was inevitable.

But here's where psychology and stubbornness collided. Faced with certain consequences, I made a split-second decision: if I was going to be punished anyway, I might as well finish what I started. I pretended not to notice them, crawling through the fence and over the berm, determined to play it cool. I imagined a dramatic chase, a tense standoff, a battle of wits and wills. Instead, when I peeked out from my hiding spot, I saw Dad quietly drive away. The game had changed; he would simply wait for me to come home, knowing I'd have to face him eventually.

The walk home was heavy with dread, each step a rehearsal for the confrontation to come. Dad led me into the bedroom, his tone calm but resolute. "Were you in the sumps?" he asked, a question that felt like a trap, since we both knew the answer. Here, the battle of wills reached its peak. I denied it, stubbornly sticking to my story, refusing to yield even as the tension built. Dad pressed harder, seeking a confession, but I dug in, determined not to break.

He told me, with a heavy heart, that this was going to hurt him more than it hurt me. As the belt fell, I resolved not to let the punishment break my spirit. We both knew the truth, and through the pain and tears, I stood my ground.

Looking back, humility and psychology color the memory. I was making my Dad suffer along with me, him struggling with his emotions and me receiving the wrath of his belt. I sometimes wonder: if he understood this was going to hurt him worse than me, why was he set on punishing himself? Maybe things might have ended differently had Dad addressed the situation head-on, if he'd simply acknowledged that we'd seen each other and asked why I hadn't turned back. Maybe I would have replied with something foolish, like "I don't know," but at least it would have opened the door to a real conversation, rather than the stubborn denial and tense standoff that actually occurred.

In the end, the sumps were more than a forbidden playground, they were a crucible for testing boundaries, learning the psychology of risk and consequence, and discovering the limits of defiance. The failed plans, the excitement, the battle of wills, and the eventual humility all became part of the tapestry of growing up, a lesson in how even the most carefully laid schemes can unravel, and how sometimes, the greatest growth comes from facing the truth, even when it hurts.

A part of growing up in Oildale brought its own set of juvenile challenges, and learning how to navigate the street was an essential part of daily life. In a place where the rules were often unwritten and the pecking order was established around the neighborhood, you quickly discovered that avoiding trouble was an art form, and sometimes, standing your ground was a necessity. Personality and popularity could serve as a kind of invisible shield, letting certain kids sidestep conflict with a well-timed joke or a confident swagger. But for most of us, the only reliable way to stay safe was to be willing to defend yourself, even if your knees were knocking and your heart was pounding like a jackhammer.

One of the most common forms of humiliation inflicted by the older kids was called "pantsing." This wasn't just a prank, it was a full-contact sport. A group of bigger kids would swoop in, tackle a defenseless kid to the ground, and yank their pants down to their ankles, leaving them exposed and red-faced in front of those watching. If the victim was particularly disliked, the older kids might go further, removing their pants entirely and leaving them in nothing but their underwear, or, in the worst cases, even less. Sometimes, in an especially cruel twist, the pants would be paraded down to the schoolyard and run up the flagpole for everyone to see, a makeshift banner of someone else's embarrassment.

Fortunately, I never witnessed either of my brothers experience this, and it certainly never happened to me because I would fight back. Maybe it was luck, maybe it was the way I learned to stand my ground with a mix of stubbornness and humility. I wasn't the biggest or the strongest, but I figured out early on that if you could take a joke at your own expense, and maybe dish one back, you could earn a kind of respect that kept you out of the worst trouble. I did see pantsing happen to other kids from time to time, and I'll admit there were moments when I had to fight the urge to laugh along with the crowd. But I was never involved as a participant in such acts. There was a line I wouldn't cross, even if it meant risking my own place in the social food chain.

Looking back, I can't help but reflect on the strange logic of childhood justice. Regardless of whether these actions were right or wrong (and let's be honest, they were mostly wrong), the reality was clear: you had to be someone the bigger kids would physically respect to avoid becoming the target of their jokes and pranks. It wasn't about being the toughest kid on the block, but about carrying yourself with enough grit, or enough humor, to make them think twice. Sometimes, a quick comeback or a well-placed laugh could defuse a situation faster than a clenched fist.

There was also a kinder side to living in our neighborhood, which usually came in the form of pretty girls. It's impossible to forget the day that special letter arrived in the mail. I was in the fifth grade, still wearing the dust and sweat of a school ball game, when I walked through the door and found Mom standing there, grinning from ear to ear. My older brother and the twins were gathered at the door, each wearing huge smiles as Mom handed the envelope to me. The envelope itself was light pink, heavily scented with perfume, and sealed with a prominent red lipstick kiss, a detail that, to a fifth-grade boy, felt both thrilling and mortifying.

Overwhelmed with embarrassment, I did what any innocent kid would do: I hid the letter in my secret spot, waiting until I was certain no one was watching before daring to open it. Inside, I discovered two full pages of the sweetest words a boy could ever hope to read, written by the most popular and prettiest girl in my class. She'd adorned the pages with pink lipstick kisses and sprayed them with perfume, making the gesture even more special.

At that age, love was a mystery, something you heard about in songs or saw in movies but never expected to find in your own mailbox. My heart raced as I read her words, a blend of excitement and disbelief swirling inside me. Was this real? Or was it some elaborate joke? I'd never noticed her glancing my way, and the possibility that she might actually like me seemed almost too good to be true.

Because of this uncertainty, I chose not to mention the letter to anyone. I carried the secret with a mix of pride and humility, unsure whether to believe in my own good fortune. Eventually, the girl approached me and asked if I had received her letter. I admitted that I had and told her I liked it a lot. But innocence and honesty got the better of me, and I couldn't help but ask if she had to embarrass me in front of my whole family by mailing the letter to my home.

That moment marked my first lesson in miscommunication with girls, a lesson delivered with the gentle sting of humility. I never had the chance to hold her hand or maybe share my first kiss, one that would have been with the prettiest girl in school. Looking back, I can't help but smile at the humor of it all: the pink envelope, the lipstick kisses, the perfume, and the way my family conspired, knowingly or not, to make the moment unforgettable.

Now, with the benefit of years and perspective, I see that story not as a missed opportunity, but as a perfect snapshot of childhood innocence. It was a time when love was simple, when embarrassment was fleeting, and when the greatest adventures could arrive in the mail, sealed with a kiss. And if I ever find myself doubting the magic of those early years, I remember that letter, and the lesson that sometimes, the sweetest moments are the ones that leave us blushing, laughing, and grateful for the chance to feel something new.

I think it was when I was in the fifth grade that I first started to question some things outside of the playground, such as being part of a generation that regularly participated in "duck and cover" drills. These drills were not just a routine, but a sobering reminder of the uncertainties of the world around me. At the sound of the school bell emitting three short blasts, every student instinctively dove under their desks, knees pulled tightly to their chests, arms wrapped over their heads, and hands shielding their eyes. We remained curled in that position, waiting for the signal that it was safe to emerge. Only when the "all clear" bell sounded were we permitted to return to normal activity. Looking back, it's humbling to realize how commonplace and serious these drills were for children at the time, how we accepted them without question, trusting the adults around us to keep us safe, even as the threat of nuclear disaster loomed over our young lives.

The seriousness of those times was reflected not only in our daily routines but in the collective mood of the nation. The 1960s were marked by a series of shocking and traumatic events that deeply affected the American people. I witnessed the nation collectively fall to its knees in disbelief and sorrow as the assassination of a young and popular president played out on television screens across the country. This president, who had recently protected America from the threat of nuclear missiles positioned just within range by an adversary, became a symbol of hope and strength. His sudden and violent death sent waves of sadness, fear, and anger throughout the nation.

Just five years after this tragedy, the country suffered another devastating loss with the assassination of the greatest leader of the civil rights movement. The impact of his death was profound, bringing feelings of grief and outrage to communities already struggling for equality and justice. That same year, the younger brother of the previously assassinated president became a candidate for the presidency. His campaign brought hope to many who were still mourning the loss of his older sibling and yearning for positive change amid the unrest. However, this hope was shattered when he too was shot and killed, adding another layer of heartbreak to an already tumultuous era.

The back-to-back assassinations of two influential leaders from the same family deepened the nation's sense of grief, uncertainty, and sorrow, leaving an indelible mark on the collective memory of the American people. Although the government provided official explanations for these senseless murders, every account seemed to leave unanswered questions and unexplained gaps. These ambiguities fueled numerous conspiracy theories that persist even today, as people continue to search for the truth behind the events that shaped a generation.

Reflecting on those years, I am struck by the humility that comes from living through such turbulent times as a child. We were taught to respect the gravity of the moment, to find comfort in routine, and to lean on each other when the world felt uncertain. In those moments under our desks, we learned not only about fear, but about resilience, the kind that comes from facing the unknown with courage, and the humility to accept that some things are beyond our control.

Sports was the one area where I gained personal recognition, appreciation, and positive feedback from my parents and others. My love for sports ignited at a very early age, transforming ordinary evenings into thrilling adventures right in our living room. I can still picture myself, a wide-eyed kid perched on a pillow on the hardwood floor, utterly captivated as my Dad worked his magic with our modest black-and-white TV. Every game, whether it was football, basketball, baseball, or boxing, became a shared quest, a battle of giants that filled our home with electricity and anticipation. The room would erupt with cheers and groans as we rooted for victory or consoled each other in defeat, our voices blending into a chorus of excitement that brought us closer together.

Back then, we didn't have the luxury of crystal-clear reception. Instead, we relied on rabbit ear antennas, which Dad would wrap with tin foil in a daring act of resourcefulness, determined to pull in every possible channel. Adjusting those antennas became a family ritual, a mini-adventure in itself, each of us taking turns, laughing and shouting directions until the picture sharpened and the game came to life. These moments weren't just about watching sports; they were about teamwork, problem-solving, and the thrill of overcoming obstacles together.

The arrival of the first color console television was nothing short of a revolution. Suddenly, the games exploded with vibrant hues, and the action felt even more immediate and exhilarating. We celebrated the new rooftop antenna as if it were a trophy, knowing it would bring us even more epic showdowns and unforgettable memories. Despite having only three channels, every evening felt like a new adventure, with the whole family gathered around, united by our love for the game and for each other. Even when there wasn't a ball game on, we cherished the programs we watched together, finding joy and connection in the simple act of sharing the moment.

Looking back, those nights were more than just entertainment, they were the foundation of our family's bond. The excitement of each game, the adventure of chasing a better signal, and the laughter that echoed through our home created a tapestry of memories that I carry with me to this day. In those moments, I learned that the real magic of sports isn't just in the competition but in the way it brings people together, turning ordinary days into extraordinary adventures.

My passion grew from watching sports on TV to playing sports, all sports, any sport, just as soon as my little legs allowed. In elementary school, I was usually chosen as team captain, whether it was football, basketball, or baseball. Baseball was nothing less than America's sport in those years. I played the position of catcher on my baseball team, a role that demanded not just quick reflexes and constant vigilance but a healthy dose of grit and improvisation. Behind the plate, I was always in the thick of the action, ready to spring into motion at a moment's notice.

My glasses, however, had other plans. I tried wearing them under my catcher's mask, but they were forever getting in the way, especially when I had to yank the mask off in a hurry to chase a pop fly or make a play at the plate. The glasses would shift, wobble, or get knocked loose, turning every crucial moment into a blurry adventure. So, I produced a solution: before each inning, I'd slip my glasses into my back pocket, since there was really nowhere else to put them.

Of course, this plan had its own pitfalls. More than once, I'd forget about those glasses until I slid into a base or collided with another player charging home. The result? Broken frames, sometimes the corner of one of the arms, sometimes the frame holding a lens. My parents simply couldn't afford to keep replacing my battered glasses, so I learned to improvise. I became a master of the art of patching, wrapping the damaged frames with tape until they looked less like eyewear and more like a science project held together by hope and determination.

Before long, I was recognized as the kid who always wore glasses patched with tape, a badge of resourcefulness and humility. I'm certain there's at least one class photo out there where I'm sporting those famously mended glasses, a testament to my knack for making do and finding humor in the everyday challenges of growing up.

I formed a strong partnership with our pitcher, whose unpredictable sidewinder pitch kept batters guessing. Off the field, our friendship was built on respect and compassion. His sidewinder pitch was legendary among our teammates, but what truly set him apart was the quiet resilience he carried off the field. I remember the modest bungalow where he lived with his mother, tucked away on the edge of our neighborhood, I could see my friend's house from the schoolyard. I'd hear the sharp crack of a bullwhip against a tree, a sound that sent most kids running. The man outside, shirtless, stern, and intimidating, was a fixture in their lives, none of us kids were ever allowed inside their home.

No matter what was happening at his house, my friend always knew he had a place at ours. My parents never hesitated to set an extra plate at the table, and even though I forgot to ask permission, they welcomed him with open arms. Those dinners were more than meals, they were a refuge, a chance for him to laugh and relax, and for me to feel the warmth of true camaraderie. Sometimes he and his mother would vanish for weeks, but like clockwork, he'd reappear just in time for baseball season, ready to pick up where we left off as if no time had passed at all.

One year, when Dad surprised me with a brand-new glove, I didn't hesitate, I handed my old one to my friend. I knew he needed it, and the look of gratitude in his eyes said more than words ever could. On the field, we were unstoppable, a pair of scrappy kids who understood each other's strengths and weaknesses, who covered for each other when the game got tough.

Those seasons weren't just about winning games; they were about learning what it meant to show up for someone, to offer support without judgment, and to find family in unexpected places. Even now, I carry those lessons with me, grateful for the friendship that helped to shape a small piece of who I am.

Some memories linger in our minds, even when they defy explanation. One afternoon, while I was in the midst of a school baseball game, an unfamiliar man approached the ball diamond. He cheered for my team, but his words seemed to be meant just for me, comments that felt oddly personal, as if he knew me in ways I couldn't understand. I stole glances at his face, searching for recognition but found only confusion. There was no memory to anchor him in my life, no familiar warmth, just a stranger's gaze that left me unsettled. He stayed for only a couple of innings before quietly slipping away, leaving behind a strange emptiness.

That evening, the house was filled with the low hum of my parents' conversation. I overheard my Dad mention, almost as an afterthought, "He was back in town again and asking for money." The words hung in the air, heavy with a sadness I couldn't quite name. Curious, I asked who they were talking about, and Dad explained it was his younger brother, my Uncle Don. Suddenly, the pieces fell together, the man behind the backstop, the stranger who seemed to know me, was family. I recounted the encounter, and Dad confirmed that it was probably Uncle Don.

That day marked the only time I ever saw my Uncle Don, at least as far as I can remember. There's a bitter irony in that: family, so close in blood, can feel like a stranger in the heart. According to Dad, Uncle Don had the potential to accomplish anything, he was talented, smart, and considered handsome, a true ladies' man. Yet, despite these gifts, he struggled with self-pity over something that happened between himself and his father, and eventually turned to alcohol, which ultimately took control of his life. The worst part of it was that I learned that my father looked at me as though I was like my Uncle Don.

It's a story tinged with sadness and confusion, a man who could have been anything, who instead became a fleeting shadow on the edge of a baseball field. The irony is sharp: the gifts that should have lifted him up became lost in the fog of regret and addiction. And yet, there is hope in the telling. The memory lingers, not just as a cautionary tale, but as a gentle reminder that even the briefest encounters can shape us. In the end, perhaps the greatest hope is that we learn from the stories left behind and find the courage to reach for connection, even when it feels out of reach.

During the summer, our house buzzed with the electric energy of Little League Baseball. All three of us boys, and my sister Patty, devoted ourselves to the game, transforming ordinary evenings into a whirlwind of practices, games, and unforgettable moments. The ballpark became our second home, and Dad, ever the reliable coach and chauffeur, would finish work and, without fail, pile us into the car for another night under the stadium lights. Those drives were filled with laughter, anticipation, and the kind of playful banter only siblings can muster. The routine was more than just a schedule, it was a cherished ritual, a source of excitement and unity that stitched our family together.

On the field, I thrived in the heat of competition. Whether pitching, catching, or darting between third base and shortstop, I relished the challenge of switching positions, sometimes two or three in a single game. Every season, I was honored to be selected for the all-star team, a badge of pride that fueled my drive to improve. One year, I pitched a nine-inning masterpiece, allowing only a single hit. The thrill of nearly clinching victory was palpable, but fate had other plans: that lone hit soared over the fence for a home run, costing us the game. The sting of defeat was real, but so was the camaraderie and respect among teammates. We learned that sometimes, the most memorable victories are found in the effort, not just the scoreboard.

Patty, my younger sister, was a force to be reckoned with. Whenever we organized sandlot games and I was captain, I'd pick Patty for my team, often before several of the guys. The boys grumbled, but the reason was simple: Patty played ball better than many of them, even those older and bigger. Her determination and skill made her a formidable competitor, and her presence on the field was a testament to the power of drive and grit. She didn't just keep up, she set the pace, inspiring everyone to raise their game.

Patty once confided that, although Dad coached most of her teams and helped her develop, it was my relentless practice sessions that made the greatest impact. I pushed her to scoop up grounders and catch for me during pitching drills, never letting her slack off. Hearing her say that flattered me, but honestly, I never thought about it that way. For me, it was simple: you give your best, whether it's a game or just practice. The joy was in the effort, the teamwork, and the shared drive to improve.

Dad was the heart of my sports journey. He didn't just coach, he taught me the fundamentals, blending clear instruction with constructive feedback and a healthy dose of humor. His coaching style was equal parts wisdom and wit, always ready with a joke when the pressure mounted. Looking back, I realize Dad found as much joy in coaching as I did in playing. The mutual excitement, the lessons learned, and the laughter shared created lasting memories that shaped not just my skills but also my character.

Those summer nights at the ballpark were more than just games, they were a celebration of teamwork, competition, and family. I tasted victory and learned humility in defeat. I discovered compassion in encouragement, drive in practice, and humor in every misstep. And through it all, I built a foundation of memories that still bring a smile, reminding me that the true win is in showing up, giving your all, and enjoying the ride with the people who matter most.

Some things didn't seem to have an end but carried on throughout the entire year, like scouting. It wasn't just another extracurricular, it was the glue that held us all together, a shared adventure that transformed ordinary days into unforgettable memories. From ages eight to twelve, my family dove headfirst into both boys' and girls' scout groups, fueled by a spirit of fun and a commitment to each other that made every moment count.

Our time as scouts was a wild ride of camping trips and hikes, each outing bursting with excitement and the thrill of discovery. Picture us scrambling through the woods, laughter echoing as we raced to set up tents, or gathered around a crackling campfire, roasting marshmallows for s'mores and swapping stories beneath a sky ablaze with stars. Those evenings weren't just about snacks, they were about family, teamwork, and the kind of togetherness that only comes when you're all in it for the adventure.

We learned practical skills with a dash of humor, tying knots that sometimes looked more like spaghetti than rope but always left us feeling accomplished. Every challenge, whether it was conquering a steep trail or figuring out how to keep the campfire lit in the rain, became a lesson in resilience and resourcefulness. And if someone tripped over a tent stake, you could bet other troops would be there to help up, and tease them about it for weeks.

One of our favorite traditions was the legendary bottle hunt. Armed with boundless energy and a competitive spirit, we'd scour the neighborhood for empty bottles, turning what could have been a chore into a full-blown treasure hunt. The excitement of finding a hidden stash was matched only by the joy of cashing in our loot at the local store. That hard-earned money wasn't just pocket change, it was the fuel for our troop's Christmas Day parade float, a masterpiece built with teamwork, creativity, and a healthy dose of sibling rivalry.

Building the float was a family affair, with everyone pitching in, painting, decorating, and sometimes arguing over whose idea was best. In the end, it didn't matter whose vision won out; the real victory was seeing our creation roll down Chester Avenue, a testament to what we could accomplish together. And if the float wobbled a little or the decorations fell off, we'd just laugh and call it "custom engineering."

Every year, we looked forward to the epic potluck picnics organized by our scout group. Dozens of families would descend on the park, tables groaning under the weight of homemade dishes, desserts, and enough punch to fill a swimming pool. The air buzzed with excitement as kids and adults battled it out in baseball, football, and volleyball matches, where the only rule was to have fun (and maybe let the grown-ups win once in a while).

For those less inclined to sports, there were alternative activities, like seeing who could eat the most brownies or inventing new games on the spot. But the highlight was always the Pinewood Derby races. Scouts poured their hearts into carving and decorating their cars, hoping for glory in categories like fastest, best-looking, and even "most likely to fall apart before the finish line." The friendly rivalry and laughter made every race a celebration of creativity and camaraderie.

Our family's scout experience was supercharged by close friendships with three or four other families. Summer league baseball brought us even closer, and frequent backyard gatherings became the backdrop for legendary cookouts. Grilling burgers and hot dogs was just the warm-up, the real magic happened when someone broke out the homemade ice cream, a treat so good it could silence even the rowdiest crowd.

As night fell, the energy only ramped up. We kids would play outside until the stars came out, sleepovers turning into backyard campouts where we'd spread blankets on the grass and gaze up at the constellations. The anticipation built as we waited for Dad's thunderous snoring, the unmistakable signal that the coast was clear for late-night adventures. Once the grown-ups were out, we'd sneak through the neighborhood, giggling and daring each other to explore the quiet streets. Looking back, it's a wonder we never ran into a police car, maybe they were too busy enjoying the peace and quiet we left behind.

Scouting wasn't just about badges or skills, it was about excitement, fun, and the kind of family support that turns ordinary moments into extraordinary memories. Through every challenge and every laugh, we learned the true meaning of commitment, humanity, and humor. And if you ever hear a story about a parade float that almost fell apart or a midnight adventure under the stars, you'll know it was just another chapter in the wild, wonderful saga of our family.

Music also played a central role in my upbringing, and early rock 'n' roll was the heartbeat of my childhood. My love for music wasn't just a personal passion, it was a family affair, especially with my older sister. We shared endless days of joy listening to bands like the Beach Boys, whose harmonious melodies and catchy rhythms filled our home and shaped my taste in music. My sister's portable record player, not much bigger than a schoolboy's lunchbox, was our prized possession. We'd huddle around it, swapping records and playful banter, sometimes arguing over which song deserved to be played next. She had a knack for picking the perfect tune for any mood, and I always admired her musical intuition, even if I pretended to groan when she chose a ballad over a rock anthem.

Everything changed, though, when the Beatles arrived on the scene. Their fresh sound and unique hairstyle swept over the country, bringing longer hair and a new cultural energy to the public. I remember how the girls, my sister included, reacted to them, jumping up and down, screaming their devotion in a way that seemed almost unbelievable at the time. The excitement was palpable, and a new musical revolution was underway. I teased my sister mercilessly about her Beatles obsession, joking that she'd marry Paul if he ever showed up in Oildale. She'd roll her eyes and threaten to replace my transistor radio with a mop if I didn't stop, but we both knew it was all in good fun.

Rock 'n' roll music was my constant companion, day and night, and my handheld transistor radio was never far from my side, serving as my gateway to the latest hits and chart-topping songs. But the real magic was sharing those moments with my sister, singing along, laughing at our off-key harmonies, and inventing dance moves that would have made even the Beatles blush.

Chapter 4
Highland Knolls House

Dad established himself in the petrochemical industry as a highly skilled design draftsman. During our last year living in the Green House, he set up a makeshift home office in the living room, using a folding table to handle his drafting work. I remember watching him spread out blueprints and technical drawings, his hands moving with practiced precision as he transformed lines and symbols into the foundations of real-world projects. The quiet focus he brought to his work fascinated me; even as a child, I found myself drawn to the tools of his trade, the mechanical pencils, the rulers, the stacks of tracing paper that seemed to hold endless possibilities.

His dedication to his craft was more than just a means to support our family; it was a window into a world of creativity and problem-solving. I often sat nearby, peppering him with questions about what he was designing, how the machines worked, and why certain details mattered so much. Dad never brushed me off; instead, he'd patiently show me how a simple change in a drawing could alter the outcome of an entire project. Those moments sparked a lifelong curiosity in me about how things are built and how ideas become reality.

This arrangement continued until he secured office space downtown, where he launched his own drafting business and began taking on design projects outsourced by local petroleum companies. His business quickly showed promising returns, and the early success gave my parents the confidence to purchase a new home. Before long, they became first-time owners of a brand-new house. Looking back, I realize that my Dad's journey, from makeshift home office to successful entrepreneur, was more than just a story of professional achievement. It was a lesson in perseverance, ingenuity, and the quiet pride that comes from building something lasting, both for his clients and for our family.

Moving into the House on Kevin wasn't just a change of address, it was the launchpad for a whole new chapter of excitement and joy for our family. Picture this: a three-bedroom, one-and-a-half-bath home with a two-car garage, perched at the far north end of Oildale in the Highland Knolls housing tract. The exterior was painted in cheerful blue and white, crowned with a pebble rock roof so bright it could probably be seen from space (or at least from the Bakersfield Speedway down the road). Walking through the front door, you'd be greeted by a layout that practically invited fun, turn right for the kitchen and dining area (the heart of family feasts and sibling snack raids), or head straight into the main room, an open floor concept that connected everyone, whether you were plotting your next prank or just trying to sneak a cookie before dinner.

The dining area had a secret weapon: a door to the garage, perfect for quick escapes when Dad started sweeping the backyard dirt (yes, with a broom, he was determined to win the war against pebbles). Down the hallway, three bedrooms and the main bathroom were organized like a well-oiled machine, ensuring privacy for plotting, dreaming, and the occasional sibling rivalry.

But the real magic was outside. The neighborhood's community pool was a beacon of excitement, drawing families together for splash-filled afternoons and cannonball competitions. Just across the two-lane highway, a three-par golf course offered easy access for aspiring golfers (and for us kids, a place to hunt for lost balls and maybe a little mischief). The Bakersfield Speedway was within walking distance, adding a dash of adrenaline to our weekends, nothing says "family bonding" like cheering for demolition derby cars and pretending you're the next racing legend.

Our house's location was legendary: on the opposite side of the infamous sumps, which meant we were just far enough from school to make every morning a mini-adventure. The move brought a whirlwind of new routines. My sister Kaye was already conquering high school, David was navigating the wilds of eighth grade, and the twins and I continued our elementary school escapades, with me in sixth grade and the twins three grades behind. Each of us was charting our own course, but together, we were a team, sometimes rowdy, sometimes rebellious, but always united by the joy of discovery and the humor that comes from surviving family life.

The first year we lived in the Kevin House brought a home improvement project that quickly became a family legend. Dad, with the help of my Uncle Russ, decided to build a brick fence around our backyard, a task that, in theory, sounded straightforward but, in practice, became a masterclass in teamwork and humility. David and I, the youngest recruits, were assigned the crucial job of hauling bricks from the driveway to the work site. While our muscles may have been small, our enthusiasm was mighty, and we learned that even the simplest tasks matter when everyone pitches in.

As we worked side by side, we discovered that building a fence was more than stacking bricks, it was about learning from others, laughing at mistakes, and celebrating small victories (like not dropping a brick on our toes). Dad and Uncle Russ, ever patient, did their best to show us the finer points of building brick walls (and it kept David busy long enough to keep him from chasing after me for not doing my share).

Before Dad could plant grass, he became obsessed with preparing the soil. We often joked that he was losing his mind, watching him sweep the bare dirt with a broom as if he were auditioning for a new kind of gardening show. The sight of Dad determinedly chasing pebbles blown down from the roof became a running gag in our family. We'd tease him, "Careful, Dad, you'll sweep us up next!" But beneath the humor was a lesson in attention to detail and pride in a job well done.

In time, our collective efforts paid off. Grass, grown from seed, eventually covered both the front and back yards, transforming our house into a true home. Looking back, it wasn't just the fence or the lawn that made the Kevin House special, it was the teamwork, the humility to learn from each other, and the laughter that echoed through every step of the process. And if you ever need advice on brick fences or sweeping dirt, just ask, our family has plenty of stories, and a broom or two to spare.

A shadow of sadness lingers when I recall the little black dachshund we had as a family pet. Her name escapes me now, perhaps it was Cleo, short for Cleopatra, but what remains clear is the sense of misfortune that seemed to follow her, as if she shared the fate of the Egyptian Sphinx that lost its nose.

Cleo's arrival in the family is a mystery; I never knew how she came to be with us, nor do I remember what ultimately became of her. What I do remember, painfully, is that she was never truly given a fair chance to become a beloved member of our household. From the very beginning, Cleo struggled to fit in. Her incessant barking grated on Dad's nerves, and his frequent yelling frightened her so deeply that she would cower and urinate on the spot, a small creature overwhelmed by fear and confusion.

Dad, for all his strengths, was never particularly good with dogs. He treated them more like farm animals than cherished companions, and Cleo bore the brunt of his strict approach. She was forbidden from entering the yard while Dad tried to cultivate new grass, his fear that she might ruin it condemning her to spend her days confined to the hot, lonely garage. The garage itself became a battleground, cleaned at least twice a day to keep up with the mess, always with the expectation that the car would be parked inside, leaving little space for Cleo to feel at home.

Even inside the house, Cleo's world was limited. She was allowed only in the dining and kitchen areas, where the linoleum floor made cleaning easier. But even then, someone had to be with her at all times, as if she were a burden rather than a friend. The restrictions piled up, and the message was clear: Cleo was never truly welcome. She was a presence on the margins, longing for warmth and acceptance, but always kept at a distance.

Looking back, I can't help but feel a deep empathy for Cleo. She was a small soul, misunderstood and isolated, yearning for the simple joys of belonging, a gentle touch, a kind word, a place to call home. I hope, with all my heart, that we eventually found her a good home, somewhere she could finally be loved as she deserved. But the truth is, Cleo never really had a chance to become a true part of our family, and that knowledge still brings a quiet ache, a reminder of how easily the vulnerable can be overlooked, and how important it is to offer compassion to those who need it most.

I was lucky enough to have a cast of characters straight out of a coming-of-age movie living just a stone's throw away. Two of my closest friends were girls from our street. One, whom I admired with all the subtlety of a lovesick puppy, lived just a couple of houses up. I'd find any excuse to pass by her place, returning a lost baseball, borrowing a cup of sugar (even though I had no intention of baking), or just "accidentally" riding my bike a little too slowly past her front yard. The other was my confidante and partner in crime, living two doors up from the entrance, strategically positioned near the community pool, a detail that made her house the unofficial headquarters for summer mischief.

Then there was the girl who'd once sent me a love letter in fifth grade, a pink, perfumed envelope that nearly caused me to faint from a combination of embarrassment and delight. She lived just behind us, so close that, with a running start and a bit of reckless optimism, I could vault over our back fence and land in the corner of her yard. I'm not saying I was a regular backyard Olympian, but I did have a few grass stains that told the tale.

My social circle didn't stop there. Some friends were classmates, others were teammates from the local sandlot, and a few were new faces who brought with them the holy grail of childhood transportation: minibikes and go-karts. The kids with these mechanical marvels lived in a house that backed up to the infamous sumps, a forbidden zone ringed with barbed wire and "Do Not Enter" signs. But with a minibike and a little nerve, we could zip straight into the sumps from their backyard, our parents none the wiser. If there were a neighborhood award for creative rule-bending, we would've taken home the trophy (and probably spray-painted it for good measure).

The neighborhood itself was a living, breathing construction zone. New houses sprang up like mushrooms after a rainstorm. As soon as the crews packed up for the day, we'd swarm the unfinished frames, turning them into our own jungle gyms. We'd climb rafters, balance on beams, and invent games with rules that changed every five minutes, usually to favor whoever was "it" at the time. Looking back, it's a miracle we didn't end up with more splinters, but we wore our scrapes and bruises like badges of honor.

There was excitement in every day, amusement in every mishap, and a sense of humanity in the way we all looked out for each other, even if it meant covering for a friend who'd "accidentally" tracked mud through someone's freshly poured foundation. And through it all, there was always laughter, sometimes at ourselves, sometimes at each other, but always with the kind of joy that only comes from being a kid in a neighborhood where the next adventure was just a backyard away.

On weekends during the summer months, just before dusk, I was always on high alert for the electrifying rumble of motorcycles, a sound that sent a jolt of anticipation straight through my bones. Somewhere in the nearby foothills, a legendary outlaw motorcycle club made their home, and to a kid like me, their choppers were nothing short of mechanical marvels. The chrome gleamed, the engines thundered, and every time those bikes rolled into town, it was as if a parade of mythic heroes had descended from the hills, bringing with them an air of wild possibility and a dash of danger.

I'd perch myself at the edge of the street, heart pounding, hoping to catch a fleeting glimpse of these modern-day cowboys as they cruised by, their engines roaring like a stampede. The spectacle was mesmerizing, each bike a beast, each rider a character straight out of an action movie. And oh, the drama they brought. The otherwise sleepy evenings would suddenly crackle with energy because everyone knew: when the bikers rolled into town, it was only a matter of time before the local honky-tonk bars erupted into full-blown, glass-shattering, table-tipping barroom brawls. It was as if the universe itself had scheduled a showdown for our entertainment.

But the excitement didn't end there. Later that night, the same bikers would tear back out of town, engines howling, with police cars in hot pursuit, red and blue lights flashing, sirens wailing, the whole scene straight out of a Hollywood chase sequence. I'd watch in awe as the chaos unfolded, marveling at the sheer audacity of it all. It was as if the town itself had been transformed into a living, breathing action set, and I had a front-row seat.

Our neighborhood was perfectly situated for witnessing this adrenaline-fueled spectacle. Just past our housing tract stood the legendary Bakersfield Speedway, and across the highway loomed Suicide Hill, a name that alone promised adventure. That hill became my personal throne, my vantage point for all things thrilling. I'd scramble to the top, breathless with anticipation, and from there, I could watch the car races on the weekends. My absolute favorite was demolition derby night, when battered old cars became gladiators, smashing and crashing in a glorious display of mayhem. The crowd would roar, the dust would fly, and I'd be grinning ear to ear, convinced I was witnessing the greatest show on earth.

And as if that weren't enough, Suicide Hill also offered the perfect perch to watch the police chase the outlaw motorcycle club out of town. Picture it: the sun setting, engines roaring, sirens blaring, and me, just a kid on a hill, soaking in every wild, wonderful, and hilarious moment. Those summer evenings weren't just thrilling; they were legendary, each one a story waiting to be retold with a twinkle in my eye and a laugh in my heart.

Seventh grade drifted by almost like a blur, marking the start of a particularly awkward and uncertain chapter in my life. I remember feeling a strange mix of anticipation and anxiety as I watched my classmates seem to mature overnight, growing taller, stronger, and more confident, while I felt stuck in place, as if I were waiting for my own transformation to catch up. That sense of being left behind gnawed at me, making every day feel like a test of patience and self-acceptance. I was acutely aware of my differences, and that awareness sometimes made me shrink into myself, questioning whether I'd ever fit in or find my stride.

But even in the haze of those memories, one day stands out with electric clarity, a day that pulsed with energy, excitement, and the wild spirit of exploration. My friend, whose family owned a minibike, and I decided to venture into the sumps, a forbidden patch of land that seemed to call out to our restless curiosity. The air was thick with possibility, and we felt invincible, fueled by the thrill of doing something daring and just a little bit reckless. We'd gotten our hands on a couple of firecrackers, convinced that a little mischief would add some spark to our adventure.

What happened next was anything but ordinary. The moment one of the firecrackers ignited a fire in the dry grass and tumbleweeds, panic surged through us like a jolt of electricity. The flames leapt higher, and in that instant, all our bravado vanished, replaced by a raw, urgent need to fix what we'd started. Our hearts pounded as we tore off our shirts, beating at the flames with every ounce of energy and desperation we could muster. The wind, mercifully, was still, and our frantic efforts paid off: we managed to extinguish the fire before it could spiral out of control or draw the attention of the law.

That day, I earned my stripes as a firefighter, albeit in a way that was anything but conventional. More importantly, I learned a lesson that burned itself into my memory: never play with fireworks in an open field, especially one covered in dry grass and tumbleweed. The experience humbled me, reminding me that excitement and exploration come with real risks, and that sometimes the most important thing you can do is own up to your mistakes and act with responsibility.

By the time I reached eighth grade, I was standing just over five feet tall and weighed no more than ninety pounds. Meanwhile, many of the boys around me shot up three to ten inches taller, their confidence growing with every inch. For the first time, I felt my self-confidence slipping away, especially as I watched others surpass me in the sports I cared about so deeply. Yet beneath the uncertainty and humility, there was a quiet determination, a belief that even if I didn't fit the mold, I could still carve out my own path, one adventure at a time.

Oildale had a Jack Frost football team for seventh- and eighth-graders that competed in a league with teams from the surrounding areas of Bakersfield. I wanted nothing more than to play on that team, the desire was almost overwhelming, burning inside me like a secret hope I was afraid to voice aloud. Yet beneath that longing, a gnawing fear crept in: what if I wasn't good enough? Each practice was a test, not only of my physical abilities, but of my courage to face my own limitations.

Despite my passion for football and my deep desire to be part of the Jack Frost team, I quickly became aware of my shortcomings. I knew I was quick on my feet and had a strong ability to read the field, often anticipating plays and reacting swiftly. But as the season wore on, it became painfully clear that my size and strength simply weren't enough to allow me to compete at the level I wanted. That realization hit me hard, stirring up a storm of frustration and self-doubt. I watched my teammates, bigger, stronger, more confident, move with an ease I envied, and I couldn't help but feel small, both in body and spirit.

Fear began to take root, whispering that I might never measure up. My confidence faltered, and I found myself hesitating, second-guessing every move. The anger I felt was directed inward, at my own body for betraying me, at my mind for letting doubt creep in, and at the unfairness of wanting something so badly yet feeling powerless to achieve it. Still, I kept showing up, determined to prove to myself that I belonged, even if only in spirit.

One evening during practice, I was playing defense as the middle linebacker. I was just about to make a tackle when I was unexpectedly blocked from the side, and a player fell across the back of my legs just as the ball carrier and I collided. The impact bent me backward over the person on my legs, knocking the wind out of me and leaving me with sharp pain around my ribs. For a moment, fear overwhelmed me, was I broken?

Dad decided to take me to the doctor to get checked out. After taking X-rays, the doctor found that my rib cage had shifted slightly, though thankfully no bones were broken. Despite not being a starting player, I was sidelined for the remainder of the season to allow my ribs to heal. The humiliation of sitting out, watching others play the game I loved, was a bitter lesson in humility. I had to accept my limits, recognize my own vulnerability, and learn that sometimes strength isn't measured by how hard you hit, but by how you get back up after being knocked down.

Every junior high school in the San Joaquin Valley buzzed with anticipation as the Optimist Club, an elite group reserved for eighth-grade boys, prepared to welcome its next generation of leaders. As the school year drew to a close, the air was electric with excitement and possibility. As seventh graders, full of hope and determination, we watched as the club's graduating members deliberated over nominations. For a week, our names were discussed, our actions weighed, and our character evaluated. The process was rigorous, demanding not just talent or intelligence, but the courage to stand out, the confidence to inspire others, and the humility to lift up those around us.

Membership in the Optimist Club was more than a badge, it was a call to lead with integrity and optimism. To be chosen meant you had shown true leadership, whether through athletic triumphs, academic effort, or simply by being the kind of person who made others believe in themselves. When my name was announced as one of the new members, I felt a surge of pride and gratitude. It was a moment that demanded both excitement and humility: I knew I was stepping into a role that would challenge me to be my best, not just for myself, but for my peers.

The club's basketball team was legendary, competing fiercely against schools throughout Bakersfield and the neighboring towns.

On the court, I found my true calling. Though my academic achievements were modest, my passion for basketball burned bright. As point guard, I embraced the responsibility of orchestrating plays, reading the game, and creating opportunities for my teammates. Each match was a test of courage and confidence, moments when I had to trust my instincts, rally my team, and stay humble enough to learn from every win and loss. The thrill of competition was matched only by the camaraderie we shared, knowing that our success depended on each of us giving our all.

After practice, our group, players and cheerleaders alike, would walk home together, laughter echoing down the sidewalks. We'd stop at Foster Freeze or A&W, savoring cold drinks and swapping stories, our spirits high from the day's adventures. These walks were more than just a routine; they were a celebration of friendship, resilience, and the simple joy of belonging. In those moments, I realized that true confidence comes from lifting others up, and that humility is found in the gratitude we share for the journey itself.

As my parents began to loosen the reins and grant me a taste of freedom, I found myself stepping into a world brimming with new possibilities and adolescent wonder. One of the most exhilarating milestones was being allowed to attend parties at friends' homes, some of which, to my delight (and my parents' mild horror), were blissfully unchaperoned. These gatherings were more than just social events; they were electric laboratories of self-discovery, where the air pulsed with the promise of adventure and the sweet, awkward anticipation of firsts.

It was at these parties that I stumbled into the intoxicating joy of dancing to rock 'n' roll music. The beat seemed to pulse right through my sneakers, and for a few glorious minutes, I could almost forget how self-conscious I felt about my two left feet. There was a wild, amorous excitement in the air, a sense that anything could happen when the right song came on, and the living room lights were dimmed just enough to blur the edges of embarrassment.

And then, of course, there was spin the bottle. The mere mention of the game sent a collective shiver of nervous laughter around the circle. I remember the bottle's slow, suspenseful twirl, the way my heart would leap into my throat as it wobbled and pointed, sometimes at the prettiest girl in the room, sometimes at my best friend (which, let's be honest, was a different kind of panic). The first time the bottle landed on me, I tried to play it cool, but I'm pretty sure my face turned the color of a ripe tomato. The kiss itself was a clumsy, blink-and-you'll-miss-it affair, but in that moment, I felt like I'd just been initiated into a secret society of the brave and the bashful.

Those parties were a crash course in the art of growing up. I became acutely aware of the subtle, mysterious changes in the way the girls looked and acted. Suddenly, the girls I'd known since grade school seemed to glow with a new kind of confidence and allure. Dancing to romantic songs brought a rush of feelings I wasn't quite prepared for, excitement tangled with awkwardness, hope laced with humility. I fumbled through slow dances, stepping on toes and apologizing with sheepish grins, learning that sometimes the best way to handle embarrassment was to laugh at myself and keep moving.

Looking back, I realize those nights were less about perfect moves and more about the courage to show up, to risk a little humiliation for the chance at connection. Each awkward moment, each burst of laughter, was a small victory, a sign that I was stumbling, with as much grace as I could muster, into the wild, wonderful territory of coming of age.

During my eighth-grade year, our family faced significant financial hardships as Dad's business began to struggle. Near the end of the school year, Dad accepted a position with an oil company in Long Beach, California. This decision marked the beginning of a profound transition for our family, as my parents put our house up for sale and began planning to relocate so we could be closer to

Dad's new job. Until the house sold, we had to adjust to a new way of life marked by tight budgets and simple meals. Beans and rice became staples at our dinner table as we managed to live from paycheck to paycheck, a daily reminder of the necessity to adapt and persevere with humility.

Transportation also presented new challenges. With only one car in the family, Mom needed it to commute to her job each day, so she would drive Dad to the bus station on Sunday evenings. From there, Dad would take a bus to Long Beach, where he temporarily lived in an apartment hotel while working. He would spend one or two weeks away from home before returning on Friday evenings to spend the weekend with us, only to head back to work at the start of the new week. This demanding schedule required our family to rely on resilience, cooperation, and mutual respect, honoring the sacrifices each member made to support one another through uncertainty.

Beneath the surface of these practical adjustments, I was gripped by a growing sense of uncertainty and fear about what the future might hold. The familiar rhythms of our lives, our home, our neighborhood, the friends and routines I'd always known, suddenly felt fragile, as if they could vanish at any moment. Each evening, as we gathered around the dinner table, I could sense the quiet worry in my mother's voice and the unspoken questions that lingered in the air: Would the house sell? Would Dad's new job be enough? What would life be like in a new city, surrounded by strangers?

I tried to hide my anxiety, but it crept into my thoughts at night, making it hard to sleep. I wondered if I would fit in at a new school, if I'd be able to make new friends, or if our family would ever regain the sense of stability we'd lost. The uncertainty was unsettling, and for the first time, I realized how quickly life could change, and how powerless I felt to control what might come next.

During this period, I realized that if I wanted to go anywhere, whether it was a trip to the movies, buying a new record, or simply enjoying a burger and a cherry cola with friends, I would have to earn the money myself. The cost of food was low at the time, and I fondly remember a small hamburger stand across from the school where, during lunch hour, a cheeseburger and a Coke could be purchased for just twenty-five cents.

To make ends meet, I occasionally earned a few coins by cutting lawns or pulling weeds for neighbors, and sometimes by collecting range balls at the golf course across the highway. Despite my efforts, most days my pockets remained empty, and money was always in short supply. These experiences instilled in me a deep sense of humility and respect for the value of hard work, and a greater appreciation for the simple necessities that sustain us.

I began my high school journey as a freshman in Oildale. However, a significant change occurred when our house finally sold one month before Thanksgiving in 1966. Shortly thereafter, we moved to Huntington Beach, California, a transition that would profoundly disrupt my life and leave me facing a couple of challenging years ahead. Through these changes, I learned that honoring the journey means embracing both the hardships and the growth they bring, and that true humanity is found in the way we support and uplift each other during times of need.

Chapter 5
High School

When our family left Oildale, the impact on my brothers and sisters was immediate and profound. They felt as though they had been transported to paradise, awakening on the sunny shores of Huntington Beach. The town's rustic charm and proximity to the ocean made living there exhilarating for all of us. However, beneath the surface of excitement, I struggled with my own feelings of loss and disconnection. Leaving behind the friends I had grown up with was far from easy, and the unfamiliar beach community only amplified my sense of isolation.

I was young, immature, and insecure, suddenly without a single friend to turn to except for those I could reach by letter, which quickly became my lifeline to the world I'd left behind. (Let's just say, if there had been frequent flyer miles for mail, I'd have earned a free trip back to Oildale.) The environment around me was strikingly different from everything I was used to, and I realized it would take considerable time to adjust. Even the way people dressed stood out to me.

The boys at school all wore Levi jeans, a clothing staple I had never owned. Instead of polished wingtip shoes, they favored brushed leather chukka boots worn without socks. Their shirts were colored T-shirts with pockets, never tucked in, in contrast to my neatly pressed plaid shirts layered over white T-shirts, always tucked in. Hairstyles were another marked difference, with most boys wearing their hair long, some letting it grow even longer, while I was confined to an Ivy League cut no longer than an inch on top and shorter on the sides, which was the rule of the house for as long as I was under my Dad's roof. (I sometimes wondered if Dad was secretly running a boot camp for barbers.)

The transition to my new high school was overwhelming from the start. The student body was nearly double the size of the school I had come from, and I didn't know a single person. The feeling was much like standing at a busy crosswalk, watching cars speed by in a blur, unable to move for fear of being swept away by the unfamiliar pace and crowd. This sense of isolation shaped my entire freshman year, as I focused on quietly attending classes and retreating home as soon as the final bell rang. (If there had been a medal for "fastest exit from campus," I'd have been a contender.)

Once I arrived home, I'd blitz through my homework with the single-minded focus of someone escaping a burning building, because, let's be honest, the real prize was waiting for me outside. The moment I finished the last scribble, I'd grab my basketball and head down the street to the local elementary school, my own little sanctuary of freedom. There was something magical about stepping onto that empty court: the world's noise faded, and suddenly, it was just me, the ball, and the echo of my sneakers on the blacktop. The open space felt infinite, like I could run forever, or at least until dinner.

Shooting hoops alone was my therapy, my meditation, and my ticket to forgetting the confusion and anxiety of being the new kid in town. Each swish of the net was a tiny victory, a reminder that even if I didn't know anyone's name yet, I could still nail a free throw from the top of the key. The solitude wasn't lonely, it was liberating. Out there, I could breathe, move, and let my energy fly in every direction. If the ball bounced off the rim and rolled off the court, I'd chase it down like a wild dog, grinning at the absurdity of it all.

But the best part? Freedom has a way of attracting company. After a while, a couple of kids who shared my love for the game wandered over, drawn by the sound of bouncing rubber and the promise of a little friendly competition. They invited me to join in for two-on-two or three-on-three matches, and as the weeks passed, more boys started showing up, like moths to a porch light, or maybe like kids to the only decent hoop in town.

Before long, we had enough players for full-court games, and the energy on that playground was electric. The court became our arena, our stage, and our comedy club all at once. We played hard, laughed harder, and in those moments, the sense of isolation melted away, replaced by the simple joy of belonging, even if it was just to a ragtag crew of future benchwarmers. Looking back, those afternoons were more than just games. They were my first taste of real freedom in a new place, a chance to carve out my own space, let loose, and enjoy something I loved with every ounce of energy I had.

Looking back, I realize how small and uncertain I felt during those first months. My struggles seemed insignificant compared to the excitement my siblings experienced, and I often wondered if my discomfort was simply a sign of weakness. Yet, in those moments of loneliness, I learned to appreciate the value of humility, recognizing that my pain was real, but not unique. Many others have faced similar upheavals, and my journey was just one among countless stories of adaptation and growth. I am grateful for the letters that kept me connected to my old life, which helped strengthen my acceptance of vulnerability. The experience taught me that loss and separation, though painful, can foster resilience and a deeper understanding of myself and others.

With my freshman year drawing to a close and the promise of my first summer in the beach community shimmering on the horizon, I found myself at a crossroads between the familiar and the unknown. Eager not to drift aimlessly, I enrolled in summer school, a move that, in hindsight, was equal parts ambition and a subtle attempt to avoid getting hopelessly lost in this new world of sand and surf.

At just fourteen, I signed up for driver's education, a rite of passage that combined the thrill of classroom theory with the white-knuckle reality of navigating unfamiliar streets.

Each lesson behind the wheel felt like a mini-adventure: one moment, I was gripping the steering wheel with the intensity of a racecar driver; the next, I was sheepishly apologizing for a slight miss in parallel parking. Still, every cautious turn and hesitant merge gave me a growing sense of independence, a small victory in a landscape where everything else felt so new.

Outside of school, I was determined to embrace the beach life, even if I wasn't entirely sure how to go about it. The truth is, I was still a bit shy, more likely to watch the surfers from a safe distance than to charge into the waves myself. Securing a ride to the beach was a quest in itself, often requiring the negotiation skills of a seasoned diplomat. When those efforts failed (which was often), I'd settle for my own company music blaring and a basketball in hand. Shooting hoops became my anchor, a familiar rhythm that steadied me as I tried to make sense of my new surroundings.

I approached each day with a mix of humility and curiosity, quietly observing the locals as they navigated the beach walkways with effortless cool. I admired the young people with their sun-bleached hair, easy laughter, and the way they seemed to know instinctively which taco stand had the best fish tacos. I, on the other hand, was still figuring out how not to get sand in my shoes, or worse, in my nachos.

Looking back, I realize that my early days at the beach were less about making a splash and more about learning to wade in slowly, toes first, with a healthy dose of self-deprecating humor. I didn't become a beach legend overnight, but I did discover that sometimes the best adventures begin with a little uncertainty, a lot of humility, and the willingness to laugh at yourself as you stumble (sometimes literally) into a new chapter of life.

My sophomore year drifted in and out of my life like a lazy beach fog, one moment thick with possibility, the next gone before I could catch my breath. After school, I took on the noble responsibility of babysitting a young boy and his sister who lived just two doors down. For a teenager, this was a golden ticket: a little pocket money, a dash of independence, and the thrill of being trusted with someone else's most precious cargo.

The boy, all of seven years old and brimming with that wild after-school energy, would drop off his books at home, then make a beeline to my house so we could walk back together. His sister would arrive soon after, and for the next couple of hours, I was the captain of their ship, keeping the peace, doling out snacks, and occasionally refereeing sibling squabbles until their Mom returned and handed me my hard-earned pay.

But one afternoon, the routine shattered. The boy showed up at my door, his face pale and his eyes wide with a fear that instantly sobered me. He was shaking, his words tumbling out in a rush as he explained that he'd just encountered a stranger inside his house. My heart leapt into my throat. Suddenly, I wasn't just a babysitter, I was the first responder, the adult in the room, and for a split second, a terrified kid myself.

Without a moment's hesitation, my Mom sprang into action, her instincts as sharp as ever. She grabbed the phone and dialed the police, her voice steady even as my hands trembled. The officers arrived in record time, sweeping through the house with the kind of calm authority that made me want to stand a little taller. Once they'd checked every room and declared the house safe, they turned to the boy and praised his bravery, calling him courageous for how he'd handled himself in the face of real danger. I could see the pride flicker in his eyes, even as the adrenaline still buzzed through him.

Later, as we pieced together what had happened, the story unfolded with all the drama of a Hollywood thriller. The boy had come home, wandered past the hallway toward the kitchen for a drink of water, and there, at the far end of the hall, stood a complete stranger, clutching his father's rifle. The air must have crackled with fear. But instead of freezing, the boy's instincts kicked in. He dashed into the kitchen, grabbed the biggest butcher's knife he could find, and, channeling every action hero he'd ever seen, hurled it at the intruder. The man dodged the knife, then bolted through the back bedroom and out the very window he'd used to break in, vanishing before anyone could stop him.

When the police surveyed the scene, they were genuinely impressed. The tip of the knife was bent, and there was a fresh dent in the doorknob at the end of the hall, a silent testament to the boy's quick thinking and surprisingly strong arm. I couldn't help but joke later that if baseball didn't work out, he might have a future as a knife thrower (though hopefully not in similar circumstances).

After that harrowing day, the rules changed. The children were given strict new instructions: from now on, they were to come directly to our house after school and stay put until a parent came home. No detours, no solo adventures, just safety, routine, and for all of us, a little more peace of mind.

It was around midyear of my sophomore year that the world outside my window seemed to tilt on its axis. The political temperature in America was rising, and I felt it, not just in the headlines or the music, but deep in my bones. The counterculture movement swept across the nation like a tie-dye tidal wave, and I was right there, caught in its undertow. As a young, impressionable teenager, I was both a witness and a participant, swept up in a storm of public passion and private confusion.

I remember feeling a strange mix of excitement and uncertainty. The world was changing rapidly, and I was desperate to belong to something bigger than myself, even as I struggled to figure out who I was. There was a kind of naïve hope in the air, a belief that a young generation could change the world with music, protest, or even just the right words. But there was also fear, and a sense that the ground beneath us was shifting in ways none of us could fully understand.

I found myself slowly making friends with guys in my neighborhood, drawn to their effortless cool and independence. Many of them seemed to move through the world with a confidence I envied, while I often felt like an outsider, peering in through a window I wasn't sure how to open. One friend in particular had already run away a time or two and served time in juvenile detention. He was experienced well beyond his age, carrying a kind of world-weariness that both fascinated and unsettled me. Yet, I saw the good in him too, a reminder that people are rarely just one thing.

Something inside me was stirring, a quiet but persistent urge to carve out my own space, to assert a bit of independence in a world that often felt dictated by the rules and routines of adults. Privacy at home was nonexistent, so when I needed space, I'd slip away to the nearby liquor store. The store had a reputation for selling cigarettes to minors, and I'd usually pick up a bottle of RC Cola and hang out for a short while. Smoking cigarettes became my early act of quiet rebellion, a small but significant way to test boundaries and experience a taste of autonomy away from the watchful eyes of parents and teachers. Each visit to the store was a subtle declaration that I was beginning to make my own choices, even if they were small ones.

Music became my anchor and my guide. The Rolling Stones, Jimi Hendrix, Cream, Buffalo Springfield, and the Doors were more than just background noise, they were the soundtrack to my confusion and my coming-of-age desire for change and self-expression. But it was Bob Dylan's music and words that resonated most deeply with me. I felt a connection to his messages, even as I struggled to understand my own place in the world. His lyrics gave voice to my empathy and concern for others, and to the sense that something was fundamentally wrong with the way things were.

At home and in the community, the Counterculture movement, Civil Rights movement, and Anti-Vietnam War movement were everywhere, on TV, in the music, and in the worried looks exchanged by parents at the dinner table. Young people everywhere united with activists, chanting "turn on, tune in, and drop out," and even the Women's Liberation movement had joined in, burning brassieres as a symbol of defiance. Antiwar songs blared from radios, and college students staged sit-ins and love-ins, hoping to change the world with peace signs and poetry. The establishment, caught off guard, responded with tear gas and batons, and sometimes, heartbreakingly, with violence that left scars on the nation's soul.

I felt the weight of these times personally. I was passionate about the causes I saw on TV, but also naïve, unsure how to channel my feelings into action. I was confused by the contradictions around me: the call for peace met with violence, the promise of freedom shadowed by fear. I was excited by the possibilities, but also anxious about where I fit in. My empathy for others grew as I watched friends and family struggle with the same questions, and my concern for the future was real, even if I didn't always know how to express it.

Rebellion became part of my identity, not just in the cigarettes I smoked or the music I played, but in the way I questioned authority and sought out my own truth. As opposition to the war grew, young men began burning their draft cards in protest, while some fled to Canada, where they remained until receiving pardons in 1977. In 1969, the Selective Service System introduced the draft lottery as a new way to conscript soldiers. My eighteen-year-old brother drew a low number in the lottery and was immediately drafted into the Army, where he served for two years, including one year in Vietnam. The reality of war came home to me in a way that was both personal and profound, deepening my sense of empathy and my concern for those I loved.

Too young to join in, my rebellion came on Friday nights, when I'd meet up with the guys to share a few beers or some cheap rotgut wine before heading out to attend the school's ballgame. After the game, the evening would continue at the sock-hop, a school dance held in the gym, where the only thing stiffer than my dance moves was the punch. Despite the lively atmosphere, I always felt out of place at these events.

My shyness kept me from asking any of the girls to dance, even though I was interested. Instead, I spent most of the night wandering around with my hands shoved deep in my pockets, feeling awkward and wishing I were somewhere else, but not quite ready to head home either. If you'd been there, you might have spotted me casually leaning against the bleachers, looking cool, like a glass of ice water. Occasionally, I'd muster up the courage to make eye contact with a girl across the room, only to panic and immediately study my shoes as if they held the secrets of the universe.

Still, those nights taught me something important: sometimes, the best stories come from the sidelines. And hey, if there's ever a reunion for the "Wallflowers' Hall of Fame," I'll be the one in the corner, waving, just as soon as I work up the nerve.

As my circle of friends expanded, so did the boundaries of my teenage mischief. Suddenly, I found myself swept up in a whirlwind of new experiences, some exciting, some questionable, and all of them tinged with the kind of rebellious spirit that only adolescence can muster. It wasn't long before someone introduced me to marijuana, and I'll admit, I took to it with the enthusiasm of a kid discovering a secret candy stash. Compared to the harsh burn of cheap booze, weed felt like a ticket to relaxation, and, more importantly, a way to blend in when I often felt like an outsider at the party of life. Turns out, I wasn't alone; plenty of us "cooler misfits" were just looking for a little peace in a world that seemed determined to keep us on edge.

Of course, curiosity (and maybe a dash of peer pressure) led me to dabble in other substances making the rounds. I tried "bennies", amphetamines that promised to turn me into the Energizer Bunny, and "reds," those infamous barbiturates that could knock out a horse. The result? Let's just say my brief foray into the world of uppers and downers taught me that not all adventures are worth repeating. I quickly realized I preferred my highs mellow and my lows, well, not quite so low. So, I left the harder stuff behind and stuck to the occasional joint, content to keep my mischief on the lighter side.

All the while, my parents remained blissfully unaware of my extracurricular activities, chalking up any odd behavior to the usual "growing pains" of adolescence. In their defense, I did my best to keep my escapades under wraps, though, looking back, I'm not sure how convincing I really was. The local police, for their part, seemed equally naïve. There were more than a few officers who couldn't tell a stoned teenager from a sleep-deprived one, which worked out just fine for us. Marijuana was so cheap back then that a handful of us could scrape together ten bucks and walk away with an ounce, enough to keep the whole gang giggling and philosophizing about the meaning of life until someone's Mom called us in for dinner.

The summer after my sophomore year was a wild cocktail of "official" schoolwork and "unofficial" beachside education. Sure, I signed up for a couple of classes, just enough to keep the adults off my back, but let's be honest: my real major was Advanced Beach Studies, with a minor in Sunburn Management and a PhD in Dodging Parental Supervision.

Every day, the beach called my name like a siren with a surfboard. Belly boarding? Check. Body surfing? Double check. Watching the girls? Let's just say I was a dedicated observer of the local scenery. And if I wasn't catching waves, I was catching the latest trends in the head shops, where the only thing thicker than the incense was the haze of questionable life choices.

Getting to the beach was its own adventure, a logistical puzzle worthy of a NASA launch. If my parents or friends couldn't give me a ride, I'd stick out my thumb and hitchhike, armed with nothing but optimism and the kind of confidence only a teenager with questionable judgment can muster. Every ride was a roll of the dice: would I end up in a rusty VW van with a guy named Moonbeam, or squeezed between two retirees who thought "surf's up" was a weather report?

My choices that summer were, let's say, "bold", the kind of bold that makes parents reach for the Tylenol and wonder where they went wrong. My folks tried everything to bridge the growing gap: heart-to-hearts, stern lectures, even the classic "I'm not mad, just disappointed." But at that age, their words bounced off me like sunscreen on a slip-and-slide. I was fluent in the ancient teenage art of selective hearing, if it wasn't about the beach, it didn't register.

Looking back, I realize I was living life at full throttle, with the windows down and the radio blasting. It was reckless, impulsive, and absolutely unforgettable, the kind of summer that leaves you with stories, sunburns, and just enough wisdom to know you probably shouldn't try it again (but you're glad you did).

In the midst of the shifting traditions and misunderstandings swirling around me, I was brought back to the simpleness of life when one day earlier in my sophomore year, a new family, with laughter spilling from their moving truck and the excited energy of a fresh start, moved into the corner house across the street. Not just any family, this was a full-blown, real-life version of "Cheaper by the Dozen," except they had sixteen kids.

Sixteen! Their ages ranged from one to sixteen, with only one set of twins, which, frankly, felt like the universe showing restraint. Watching all those kids pile into their station wagon was like witnessing a clown car at the circus: faces pressed against every window, elbows and knees everywhere, and the vehicle groaning under the weight of so much youthful energy. If you listened closely, you could almost hear the car whisper, "Send help."

Their mother was a legend in her own right, a general commanding her troops with a voice that echoed through the neighborhood. On days when her patience wore thin (which, with sixteen kids, was probably every day ending in "y"), she'd bellow, "Go play on the freeway!" It was her way of saying, "I love you, but please, for the sake of my sanity, take your chaos elsewhere." You had to admire her stamina; running that household was like herding caffeinated cats.

The oldest son was a grade ahead of me and stood out for his athleticism and even temperament. He was much quicker on his feet than most of the other boys in the neighborhood, making him an excellent defensive back in football and a reliable outfielder in baseball. However, basketball was not his strong suit, and he wasn't very competitive when we played. Still, he was the kind of friend you wanted on your team, steady, humble, and always ready with a grin, even when he missed a layup by a mile.

During the winter months, a group of us regularly gathered at the local elementary school to play sandlot football. The weather rarely discouraged us; in fact, we welcomed the rain. The wetter the field became, the muddier it got, which only made the games more exciting and memorable. There's a special kind of thrill in sliding through the mud, chasing a football, and emerging looking like you lost a wrestling match with a swamp monster. We wore our mud stains like badges of honor.

Our matches weren't limited to just those from our immediate neighborhood. We often organized games against teams from other neighborhoods, bringing together enough players to compete in friendly but spirited contests. These inter-neighborhood games were the stuff of legend, epic showdowns where the only thing thicker than the mud was the sense of camaraderie. Win or lose, we'd shake hands, swap stories, and laugh about the time someone's shoe got stuck so deep in the muck it's probably still there.

During my teens, it wasn't just my own struggles for identity that weighed heavily on my parents. They were also carrying the immense burden of caring for my younger brother, Mike, whose needs were far more urgent than my own.

Mike had lived with hearing loss since birth, a hardship that shaped his world in ways I can only begin to understand. When medical advances finally allowed doctors to restore his hearing (plastic surgery), the joy that filled our home was indescribable. Witnessing Mike's happiness as he experienced sound like the rest of us for the first time was a moment of pure love and unity for our family. In that instant, hope blossomed amid the tension and uncertainty that had become our daily reality.

Yet, life's trials did not end there. Soon after Mike's hearing was restored, an unexpected and deeply unsettling new challenge emerged: he began suffering from grand mal epileptic seizures. The first episode struck without warning while he was on the playground in his fifth year of elementary school. The urgency and shock of that moment rippled through our family like a sudden storm. My sister Patty, Mike's twin, came running home, her face pale and eyes wide with fear, breathlessly delivering the news to Mom that Mike had collapsed at school.

The timing was as bewildering as it was heartbreaking. We had only just begun to celebrate the miracle of Mike's restored hearing, a hard-won victory after years of struggle and hope. Now, we were thrust into a new world of uncertainty and fear. None of us knew if the surgery that had given him back his hearing played any role in this new ordeal, but the seriousness of his condition was impossible to ignore.

The doctor prescribed a powerful barbiturate to help control the seizures, and I remember those early days vividly, Mike would sit for hours, his gaze distant, lost in a world none of us could reach. The medication, while necessary to manage his condition, seemed to wrap him in a heavy fog. It dulled his energy, slowed his movements, and left him disconnected from the lively, gentle brother I knew. Sometimes, it felt as if the medicine had taken away more than just the seizures, it had stolen a part of his spirit, leaving behind a quiet shell that was hard to recognize.

Watching Mike in that state was deeply upsetting. I felt helpless and frustrated, wishing there were something I could do to bring him back to us. It was heartbreaking to see someone so dear to me so changed, and it reminded us all of the fragility of health and the importance of patience and kindness. The experience left a lasting impression on me, teaching me not only about the challenges of illness but also about the quiet strength required to support a loved one through such difficult times.

I remember the humility that settled over our household in those days. There was no pretending to have answers, no bravado, just a raw, honest concern for Mike's well-being. Mom and Dad, already worn from years of caring for us, summoned a deep well of compassion and strength. They became tireless advocates for Mike, learning everything they could about epilepsy, comforting him through the confusion and fear that followed each seizure, and reassuring the rest of us that we would face this together.

From that point forward, our family became fiercely protective of Mike. We learned to recognize the subtle signs that a seizure was coming, watching over him with a tenderness born of love and humility. One afternoon in the garage, as I practiced jumping with ankle weights and dunking basketballs, I heard the familiar sound Mike made when trying to resist a seizure. Instinctively, I turned to him just as his eyes rolled back and he began to collapse. I caught him in my arms, gently lowering him to the floor, staying by his side until the episode passed and he was safe again. Mike would struggle with the incurable disease and the various medications required to help control it for the remainder of his life.

Back in school, it was clear my favorite subject was recess, and while I wasn't exactly unintelligent, I often found myself making choices that, in hindsight, danced on the edge between right and wrong. Early in my junior year of high school, I had an encounter that would test my understanding of justice, humility, and the unpredictable consequences of anger and fear.

It started in the central bathroom, where I was standing at a urinal, indulging in a rebellious cigarette, an act I knew was against the rules, but one that, at the time, felt like a harmless assertion of independence. Suddenly, the vice principal walked in and caught me red-handed. In that split second, fear surged through me, and I did what any self-preserving teenager might do: I tossed the cigarette into the urinal and braced myself for the inevitable reckoning.

As we began the silent march toward his office, a crowd of students gathered, eager for a glimpse of the latest schoolyard drama. On other occasions, students caught in similar situations would bolt, but I chose to walk beside the vice principal, determined to face the music with a shred of dignity. Perhaps I believed that accepting responsibility was the right thing to do, or maybe I was just too stunned to run.

But justice, as I learned, is rarely straightforward. Sensing my compliance, the vice principal suddenly grabbed my arm, maybe expecting me to make a break for it. In that instant, my reflexes, fueled by a cocktail of fear and anger, took over. Before I knew it, I had punched him in the face, knocking him to the ground. For a moment, time stood still. I was as shocked as he was, realizing that my actions had escalated a minor infraction into something far more serious. Fear overwhelmed me, and, ironically, I did exactly what he'd tried to prevent: I ran.

For the next few weeks, I did my best to avoid the vice principal, keeping my head down and moving through campus with the humility of someone who knew they'd crossed a line. Despite my efforts, our paths inevitably crossed again. One afternoon in printing shop class, I looked up to see him standing in the doorway, his finger curling in a silent summons that left no room for negotiation. The look in his eyes said it all: justice was about to be served, and there would be no escape this time.

As we walked in silence toward his office, he muttered, "If I would have caught you that day, I would have kicked your ass." The tension in his voice left no doubt about the seriousness of his intent. I met his gaze and replied, perhaps with more honesty than wisdom, that if he hadn't grabbed me, I would have gone peacefully. That brief exchange captured the animosity between us, but also a strange kind of mutual recognition: we were both caught in a moment where anger and fear had gotten the better of us, and now we had to face the consequences.

The vice principal wanted me out of the school for good, pushing for my transfer to the local continuation school. His sense of justice was clear, but so was his anger. It might have worked, too, if not for my Dad's timely intervention, a moment that would teach me about compassion, humility, and the complicated nature of right and wrong.

When my Dad was called in, he listened quietly as the vice principal recounted the events. Then he surprised me and turned to me and asked for my side of the story. I decided to be honest, admitting everything and explaining how things had unfolded. By then, Dad and I had already weathered our share of arguments, and I think he understood that if the vice principal hadn't grabbed me, we'd be sitting in that office much earlier, for a far lesser offense. No one condoned what I'd done, but Dad managed to persuade the vice principal that a week's suspension would be punishment enough, assuring him that nothing like this would happen again. And, true to his word, it didn't.

For the first time since the day my Dad used the belt on me for not admitting the truth about the oil sump, I began to see him not as my adversary, but as someone who stood in my corner, even when I didn't realize it. The events surrounding my suspension and my father's involvement helped me understand that justice isn't always about punishment; sometimes, it's about compassion, humility, and the willingness to see the humanity in each other.

I didn't immediately stop making poor decisions, old habits die hard, after all, but this experience marked the beginning of a shift in my thinking. I started to reflect more on my actions and their consequences, not just for myself, but for those around me. Gradually, I became more aware of the impact my choices could have, especially on my family. It was a turning point, laying the foundation for personal growth and a deeper appreciation for the support my father had always provided.

Looking back, I can't help but find a bit of humor in the whole ordeal. Life has a way of teaching us lessons in the most unexpected ways, sometimes with a punch, sometimes with a laugh, and always with a reminder that justice, right and wrong, humility, compassion, fear, anger, and humanity are all part of the same messy, beautiful story.

The one thing that brought me consistent enjoyment was playing basketball. It was more than just a game, it was my sanctuary, a place where I could exercise sound judgment. It was a place where I could truly be myself and find a sense of normalcy and control, no matter what challenges I faced elsewhere. On the court, mistakes from the outside world faded away, replaced by the rhythm of the game and the camaraderie of teammates. Whenever the chance arose, I would jump at the opportunity to play, eagerly joining any pickup game or organized match. The court was a place where worries dissolved, and the only thing that mattered was the next play.

Over time, my dedication and enthusiasm for the sport did not go unnoticed. I earned a reputation among my peers as a worthy opponent, not because I was the most talented, but because I played with heart, humility, and respect for everyone on the floor. Basketball was more than a pastime; it was a grounding force that helped shape my identity and provided much-needed balance during the turbulent years of adolescence. It taught me that winning wasn't everything, how you played, how you treated others, and how you handled both victory and defeat mattered just as much.

One of my regular basketball companions attended a Mormon church that featured a small indoor gym. The gym was especially appealing thanks to its wooden floors and quality backboards, providing an ideal setting for shooting hoops. Every Tuesday night, we had the privilege of using the gym and could play for hours, enjoying the freedom and camaraderie that came with access to such a great facility. Over time, I was invited to join their church basketball team, where I played point guard.

After one of our basketball games, the captain from the opposing team approached me. He suggested that I consider trying out for the junior varsity squad at our high school. It sounded good to me, and I soon found myself on their roster. At first, my skills were mediocre compared to some of the more experienced members of the team. However, thanks to the coach's guidance and support, I gradually earned more playing time, which allowed me to further refine my skills on the court.

This progression marked a significant turning point in my basketball journey, as I moved from being an ordinary player to becoming a reliable member of the team. As my abilities grew, so did my circle of friends. The experience of playing on the team and being part of a supportive group helped me become increasingly comfortable with who I was, allowing me to navigate the remainder of my high school years with a newfound sense of confidence and belonging.

The friend I played basketball with on the Mormon team was an only child, adopted by his parents at an early age. His father, a man well into his sixties, had seen much of the world and its conflicts, having fought in World War II and the Korean War, and had recently retired from a long career selling insurance. To me, his father was one of the coolest old men I'd ever met, always wearing a genuine smile and sharing fascinating stories from his past.

He was remarkably generous, often driving us all the way to Inglewood so we could attend professional Lakers games, then picking us up afterward and taking us home. He was always available to drop us off or pick us up from movies, or even give us a ride back from the beach, never asking what we did or where we went. Thanks to him, I was able to witness great players like Wilt Chamberlain, Jerry West, and Elgin Baylor dominate on the court.

Despite his father's kindness, my friend sometimes spoke disrespectfully about him in front of others. His words struck a nerve, and I felt compelled to confront him. I told him directly that I disagreed with his assessment and believed he was fortunate to have such a generous and supportive father.

My comment angered him, and in response, he hurled the basketball at me and tried to kick me. Instinctively, I caught his foot and shoved him to the ground. As he got up to continue the fight, I punched him in the face, effectively putting an end to the confrontation. Although the altercation was intense, it did not completely sever our friendship. We continued to be friends afterward, but there was a noticeable distance between us, shaped by the events of that day.

Through it all, the love of the game remained. It was the thread that tied us together, even when we disagreed. It taught me that humanity is found not just in how we play, but in how we treat each other, win or lose, right or wrong. And if you can't laugh at yourself after a missed shot or a heated moment, you're missing half the fun.

In the end, basketball gave me more than skills or trophies. It gave me a sense of belonging, a code of conduct, and a lifetime of stories, some funny, some humbling, all worth remembering. And for that, I am forever grateful.

I needed to get a car and therefore, make some money. My first taxable income came from washing dishes at a local steakhouse about a mile up the street from my high school. At $1.13 an hour, it wasn't exactly a king's ransom, but for a teenager in 1970, it felt like I'd struck gold. Within a week, I was promoted to busboy, a title that came with the added honor (and pressure) of earning tips from the waitresses. I quickly learned that tips weren't handed out just for showing up; they were earned through hustle, respect, and a genuine desire to make someone else's day a little brighter.

I took pride in keeping tables spotless, water glasses full, and always asking, "May I remove your plate?" with a smile. I realized early on that if the customer left happy, the waitress was happy. If the waitress was happy, she'd slip me a good tip. And if I was happy, well, that happiness rolled all the way down to my gas tank, school functions, and the occasional party with friends. It was a beautiful chain reaction of gratitude and goodwill, a lesson in humanity that's stuck with me ever since.

There was no expectation of tips just for going through the motions. I respected the work, and I respected the people I worked with. I understood that every dollar I earned reflected my effort and attitude. Looking back, I think that sense of humility and honor, knowing that nothing was owed to me, has been lost a bit over the years. But back then, it was a badge of pride.

By halfway through my senior year, I'd earned enough credits to leave school at eleven and report to my job. I worked the lunch shift five days a week and the dinner shift four nights a week, bringing home an average of $60 a week in tips alone. For a high school kid in 1970, that was a lot of green, enough to make me feel like a big shot, even if my "company car" was a hand-me-down gas guzzler that left a trail of smoke wherever I went.

I'm grateful for those early days, not just for the money, but for the lessons in respect, humility, and the simple joy of honest work. And if I ever got too full of myself, there was always a waitress ready to remind me, with a wink and a laugh, that the real secret to success was keeping your feet on the ground, your hands busy, and your sense of humor intact.

My first experience with owning a car was nothing short of a rite of passage. I scraped together $100, every penny hard-earned, and handed it over to my older brother for his old gas guzzler. Now, I couldn't tell you the make or model if my life depended on it, but I can tell you that car had character. It was a reliable junker, the kind of vehicle that left a trail of smoke wherever it went, as if it wanted to make sure everyone knew it had arrived. It wasn't much to look at, let's be honest, it was downright ugly, but it got me where I needed to go. In those early days behind the wheel, that car was my ticket to freedom, and I wore my ownership like a badge of honor.

Later, on my seventeenth birthday, my Dad and I decided to split the cost of a used 1962 Chevy Impala. We bought it from one of his friends and coworkers, and let me tell you, this car was a stunner. Completely original, meticulously cared for by its previous owner, and sporting a 283 engine, a small block for that model, but it felt like a rocket ship to me. The moment that Impala became mine, I couldn't resist putting my own stamp on it. I swapped out the wheels, lowered the suspension, changed the steering wheel, and installed plush carpeting throughout the interior. By the time I was done, it was the perfect cruiser, my pride and joy, and a rolling testament to teenage ambition and questionable taste.

I took ownership seriously, but not too seriously to miss the humor in it all. That Impala was more than just a car, it was my sanctuary, my escape pod, and, occasionally, my mobile smoke machine. I'd roll up to school with my friends, windows down, music up, like I was leading a parade. Sure, it wasn't the flashiest ride in the lot, but it was mine, and that made all the difference.

The second half of my senior year sparkled with a kind of magic I hadn't expected. It all began in mechanical drawing class, where I found myself utterly captivated by a girl whose talent was matched only by her radiant smile. She had a way of making even the most complicated assignments look effortless, and every time our teacher praised her work, I felt a mix of admiration and infatuation that made my heart race. I was new to dating, but something about her drew me in, maybe it was the way she tucked a strand of hair behind her ear when she was concentrating, or the easy laughter we shared over crooked lines and eraser smudges.

Summoning every ounce of courage (and rehearsing my invitation at least a dozen times in the mirror), I asked her out. To my delight, and slight disbelief, she said yes. I was determined to make our first date something special, not just the usual movie or dinner. After all, young infatuation deserves a little adventure. So, I hatched a plan: a double date to the Aquarius Theatre in Hollywood to see *Hair*, the hottest play in America at the time. I figured if the night went sideways, at least we'd have a wild story to tell.

The evening buzzed with excitement from the start. When I arrived to pick her up, I was greeted by a vision: her hair styled in soft curls that framed her face, white bell-bottom slacks that seemed to float as she walked, and a blue top that shimmered with every step. Around her neck, a blue ribbon with a shiny star caught the light, and, honestly, so did my heart. I did my best to play it cool, opening doors and offering my arm like I'd seen in old movies, but inside I was a bundle of nerves and giddy anticipation.

The drive to Hollywood was filled with laughter and playful banter, our friends egging us on, cracking jokes, and making sure there was never a dull moment. I remember glancing over at her, catching her eye, and feeling that electric spark of young love, the kind that makes you believe anything is possible.

At the theater, we found our seats and settled in, the air thick with the scent of popcorn and the buzz of the crowd. The play was a whirlwind of music, color, and energy, and I stole glances at her throughout, thrilled every time she laughed or leaned in to whisper a comment. There was a moment when our hands brushed, and I swear the world paused for just a second, long enough for me to realize I was completely smitten.

After the show, we all piled back into the car, still humming the tunes and joking about the wild costumes. I tried to keep the mood light, tossing in a few self-deprecating jokes about my dancing (or lack thereof) and making her laugh until tears sparkled in her eyes. The night ended all too soon, but as I walked her to her door, I felt a sense of gratitude and wonder. I'd managed to pull off a date that was fun, thoughtful, and just a little bit daring.

I continued to date her for the rest of the school year, creating memories filled with excitement, humor, and the sweet awkwardness of first love. Looking back, I realize it wasn't just the play or the fancy clothes that made that night unforgettable, it was the feeling of being young, infatuated, and brave enough to take a chance on something (and someone) wonderful.

The latter part of my senior year blindsided me with a lesson in humility I never saw coming. I failed my US Government class, a required course for graduation. The culprit? My own stubborn dislike for the teacher and the subject, which led me to skip class more often than a cat dodges bath time. By year's end, my chronic absenteeism and lack of engagement caught up with me, and the teacher, with a look that said, "I told you so," handed me a well-earned "F."

The realization hit like a cold shower: without passing US Government, I wouldn't graduate with my class. Fear and regret tangled in my gut. I was adamant, I did not want to repeat the year just to retake a single class. Swallowing my pride, I confessed everything to my parents. My dad, ever the practical psychologist, didn't scold or shame me. Instead, he offered a dose of compassion and a nudge toward honesty: "Go talk to your teacher. See if there's any way you can make it right."

So, on Friday during lunch, I mustered up the courage (and a healthy dose of fear) to approach my US Government teacher. I asked if he'd let me retake the final exam. He laughed, a sound that was equal parts amusement and suspicion, reminding me that I was notorious for skipping his class. "You earned that 'F,'" he said, his smile lingering with a hint of sarcasm. "And now you'll have to come back next year and sit through my class all over again. Now won't that be exciting?" His words dripped with wit, but the message was clear: actions have consequences, and sometimes a second chance isn't just handed out like extra credit.

But sometimes, honesty is the only card left to play. I surprised even myself when I blurted out, "Do you want to know why I ditched your class?" He nodded, curiosity piqued. I told him, straight up, it was because I didn't like him. I explained, perhaps too bluntly, that my dislike stemmed from the way the girls in class always crowded the front rows, vying for his attention, something he seemed to enjoy a little too much. I even joked, with a touch of suspicion and a raised eyebrow, that it wouldn't surprise me if he were involved with one of them. Then I finished, "There's no way I'm coming back next year to sit through your class again, even if it means not graduating."

The room went silent. The smile faded from his face, replaced by a look of genuine surprise, maybe even a flicker of respect for my honesty, or perhaps just shock at my audacity. For a moment, neither of us blinked. Then, after what felt like an eternity, he finally spoke: "I have an old test I could give you. But if you want a passing grade, you'll have to earn an 'A.' Come to my classroom during lunch on Monday, and you can take it."

That weekend, my Dad became my unlikely study partner. We crammed every detail from the study book into my brain, working intensely all weekend, with him showing more compassion and patience than I certainly deserved. Even as we reviewed for an hour before school Monday morning, I could sense his hope, and maybe a little fear, that I'd finally learned my lesson.

When I took the test, I felt confident I'd done well, though I doubted I'd actually achieved an "A." Still, I graduated with my class. Was the teacher guilty of favoritism, or perhaps bending the rules? Maybe, maybe not. I hope not. I prefer to think that, in a rare moment of humanity, he realized the best thing for someone like me was to offer a second opportunity, provided I could truly demonstrate my understanding by passing his final test.

Looking back, I see that episode as a crash course in humility, honesty, and the unpredictable psychology of second chances. It was a reminder that sometimes fear and compassion can coexist, suspicion can be met with wit, and humor can soften even the hardest truths. And if nothing else, it taught me that life's best lessons often come disguised as our biggest mistakes.

Chapter 6
Freedom Ride

During my senior year, I found myself in the company of a couple of good friends who, like me, were absolutely obsessed with motorcycles. It was the perfect symbiotic relationship: I had a motorcycle license but no bike, while my friends had bikes but no car. So we struck a deal, whenever they needed a car for a date, I'd toss them my keys, and when I wanted to impress my girlfriend with a ride on two wheels, they'd hand me the keys to their prized machines. It was the kind of arrangement that made you feel like you'd cracked the code to teenage freedom.

One particularly sunny day stands out in my memory, a day that felt like it was made for adventure. I picked up my girlfriend from her house, both of us buzzing with anticipation for the open road. For this ride, I was on a Harley with a six-inch front-end extension and a tall sissy bar in the back, complete with a diamond-shaped padded top for passengers to lean against. I mean, if you're going to make an entrance, you might as well do it in style. As we cruised along, I couldn't resist the urge to show off just a little. When we stopped at a red light, I revved the engine, making sure everyone within a three-block radius knew there was a Harley-Davidson in town. Subtlety was never my strong suit.

Then the light turned green, and that's when things got interesting. In my attempt to make a smooth, impressive start, I accidentally popped the clutch. Suddenly, the front wheel shot up, and there I was, performing a wheelie through the entire intersection. For a split second, time slowed down. I was Evel Knievel, king of the road, master of the universe... and also, internally, a guy thinking, Oh no, please don't let me drop this thing! Miraculously, I kept control and brought the front wheel back down with ease, continuing on our way as if I'd planned the whole stunt. My heart was pounding, my girlfriend was clinging to me, and I was doing my best to look cool while silently thanking every guardian angel in the vicinity.

I never confessed to my girlfriend that the wheelie was a complete accident, because, honestly, it looked so cool, and I suspected that if she knew the truth, she might never want to ride with me again. Sometimes, humility means knowing when to keep your mouth shut and just enjoy the ride. Looking back, I can't help but laugh at the sheer luck and ridiculousness of it all. Adventure, excitement, a dash of humility, and a whole lot of humor, that's what makes the best stories worth telling.

Before graduation, my friends and I hatched what can only be described as the ultimate teenage dream: a freedom ride that would stretch across an entire month, promising adventure, mischief, and a taste of independence we'd only seen in movies. Our plan was simple, grab some motorcycles, hit the open road, and let the wind (and maybe a little luck) decide where we'd end up. The only thing standing between us and the horizon? A few minor details, like the fact that we only had two motorcycles for three would-be road warriors, and one of our crew was still a year shy of graduation (and, more importantly, parental approval). But hey, what's an epic quest without a few obstacles to make the story worth telling?

Undeterred by planning or logic, we embraced the classic hippie spirit of the late '60s and early '70s. Back then, it was perfectly normal for a couple of long-haired teenagers to take turns "riding bitch", a term that, in retrospect, sounds a lot tougher than it felt when you were clinging to your buddy's back for dear life. To keep things fair (and to avoid any permanent bruises to our egos), we decided that every time we stopped for gas, we'd flip a coin to see who got to take the handlebars next. It was democracy at its finest, unless you lost the toss, in which case you just had to hold on and hope for the best.

Armed with $400 each (a fortune in our eyes), we packed our worldly possessions, basically a change of clothes and a sleeping bag, strapped everything to the bikes, and set off from Huntington

Beach, California, with nothing but youthful excitement and a vague sense of direction. Our destination: Portland, Oregon, and back, with plenty of detours for whatever trouble or adventure we could find along the way.

At just seventeen, we were technically underage for such a wild escapade, but our parents, perhaps fueled by a mix of hope, trust, and the desire for a little peace and quiet at home, supported our freedom ride. To keep the authorities at bay, they armed us with official-looking letters of approval, complete with emergency contact information. It was as if we'd been knighted by the parental council, sent forth to conquer the unknown with little more than optimism, a couple of motorcycles, and the kind of confidence that only comes from not knowing what you're getting yourself into.

Looking back, I can't help but laugh at our naïveté and marvel at the humility that comes from realizing just how little we knew. But that was the magic of it all: the open road didn't care about our plans, our age, or our lack of experience. It just asked that we show up, say yes to adventure, and be willing to laugh at ourselves when things inevitably went sideways. And trust me, they did, often in the most unexpected and hilarious ways.

Seven months before our legendary "freedom ride," I found myself in the front room with my family, all of us glued to the TV as the new draft lottery numbers were drawn. The tension was thick enough to cut with a butter knife. When my brother David's birth date was called as #49, the room went silent, except for the collective gasp. David had survived boot camp eight months earlier and was stationed at Fort Ord, clinging to the hope that fate wouldn't send him off to Vietnam. As much as I was itching for the open road and the thrill of our upcoming motorcycle adventure, nothing was more important than seeing my big brother before he shipped out to who-knows-where.

Fueled by a mix of excitement and nerves, we made the army base at Monterey Bay our first stop on the journey. Pulling up to the entrance, we half-expected to be turned away for looking like a couple of young hippies straight out of central casting. Instead, the guards at the gate surprised us with smiles and directions, proof that sometimes even the universe likes to keep you guessing.

Our first attempt to find David landed us in the officers' barracks, where we were politely redirected (with just a hint of "you boys are lost, aren't you?"). While waiting in the right spot, we killed time with a few games of ping-pong against some soldiers. I'd like to say we let them win out of respect for the military, but honestly, I think they just had better aim.

When David finally arrived, he greeted us with a grin and a warning: his commanding officer thought it best if we, the "long-haired visitors," made ourselves scarce before we accidentally started a peace rally in the mess hall. We left the base, but not before making plans to meet up for a couple of beers later. Of course, our timing was impeccable, it was payday on base, and nothing says "suspicious" like two hippies hanging around when everyone's pockets are full. We were eyed as if we might be smuggling in weed disguised as peace offerings. Still, despite the brief visit and the comic suspicion, we managed to reconnect with my brother and promised to swing by again on our way home.

The next day, we rolled into San Francisco, hearts pounding with anticipation and the kind of reckless optimism only youth and a full tank of gas can provide. Our first mission: secure the motorcycle. We found a spot so well hidden behind two towering pillars outside the YMCA downtown that even Sherlock Holmes would have needed a magnifying glass to find it. With our trusty steed locked up, we set out to conquer the city.

San Francisco was a sensory overload, a kaleidoscope of trolley bells, the aroma of Chinatown's sizzling woks, and the electric pulse of Haight-Ashbury, the legendary hippie haven. We rode the iconic cable cars, clinging on for dear life as they rattled up and down the hills, and wandered through Chinatown's bustling streets, where every corner promised a new adventure (and, if you weren't careful, a mysterious herbal remedy for ailments you didn't know you had). The city buzzed with life, and we were right in the thick of it, wide-eyed and grinning like kids at a carnival.

At one point, as we strolled through Chinatown, I noticed a camera pointed our way from a passing car. At the time, I shrugged it off, maybe they thought we were celebrities, or perhaps they just liked our hair. Later, I learned that San Francisco was a magnet for runaway teens, and sometimes people were paid to film possible underage kids. I guess we looked the part, two scruffy travelers with more enthusiasm than common sense. If only they'd known the only thing we were running from was a lack of adventure.

After a day packed with sightseeing, we returned to our motorcycle, rolled out our sleeping bags, and set up camp, one on each side of the bike, as if we were its loyal bodyguards. But sleep was elusive. From somewhere around the corner came a rhythmic thud, echoing through the night like a heartbeat. Curiosity got the better of me (as it often does), so I crept off to investigate, half-expecting to stumble upon a secret midnight bakery or a jazz band in full swing.

Instead, I found an old, boarded-up movie theater, and outside, a wild-looking man practicing his knife-throwing skills on the plywood-covered entrance. The knives hit the wood with a satisfying thunk, over and over, a sound that, under different circumstances, might have been comforting. I quickly decided that this was one San Francisco "show" I didn't need front-row seats for. With all the humility of someone who knows when they're out of their depth, I tiptoed back to our sleeping spot and whispered the news to my friend. We agreed to take turns sleeping in shifts, just in case the knife-thrower decided to audition for a new act.

The next morning, we set off again, crossing the iconic Golden Gate Bridge. The view was nothing short of breathtaking, mist swirling around the towers, the city fading behind us, and the promise of new adventures ahead. Our route wound through the majestic redwood forests, the highway a simple two-lane ribbon flanked by ancient giants that made us feel both tiny and invincible. We stopped occasionally to smoke a cigarette and stretch our legs, soaking in the serene atmosphere and marveling at the sheer scale of the trees. It was humbling to stand among such living legends, and I couldn't help but joke that if one of those redwoods ever decided to fall, we'd be nothing but a footnote in the forest's history.

As dusk settled over the rolling hills of Northern California, we rumbled into Santa Rosa, a town that, back then, felt like a hidden gem nestled fifty miles north of San Francisco. The town square was alive with the golden glow of streetlights and the easy laughter of young people. Suddenly, we spotted two cars cruising side by side, windows down, hands reaching across the gap to pass a joint between them. The carefree spirit of the era was contagious, and with a grin, we decided to join the parade. Revving our motorcycle, we slipped between the cars, and, like a scene out of a counterculture movie, someone handed us the joint mid-ride. Laughter erupted from all sides, the kind that instantly makes strangers into friends. For a moment, we were all just kids on the same wild ride, united by the thrill of the unexpected.

We all pulled over, introductions flowing as easily as the jokes. There was no pretense, just the warmth of new connections and the shared excitement of being young and free. When we asked about a safe place to crash for the night, our new friends didn't hesitate. They pointed us toward a campground up a nearby canyon, even gifting us another joint for the road, a small act of kindness that felt like a blessing to two travelers with nowhere to go.

The adventure didn't stop there. As we wound our way up the canyon, the headlights caught a Volkswagen "love van" parked on the roadside, looking as if it had just rolled out of a psychedelic dream. A woman stood at the back, draped in a flowing white dress, beads around her neck, and flowers woven into her hair. The van itself was a rolling canvas of peace signs and the slogan "MAKE LOVE NOT WAR." We stopped to offer help, and her boyfriend, grease-stained and grinning, emerged from beneath the van, announcing the fix was done. They were the kind of people you meet once and never forget: open, genuine, and radiating the easy kindness that defined the best of the hippie era.

They quickly noticed our road-worn look and the fact that we were living off our motorcycle. Instead of suspicion, they offered curiosity and compassion, asking about our journey and listening with real interest. After hearing our story, they revealed they lived just a mile further up the canyon, their home accessible by a small bridge over the creek. They were headed out to pick up her mother, a nurse at the local hospital, and they both worked there too. With plans for dinner and a movie, they expected to be home late, but, showing a level of trust and generosity that humbled us, they offered their front porch as a place to sleep until they returned. We gratefully accepted, marveling at the kindness of strangers who treated us like old friends.

We rode up the canyon, found their porch, and settled in. The night air was cool, the stars bright, and the world felt wide open. We smoked the joint we'd been given earlier, swapping stories and laughter until sleep crept in. Sometime in the early hours, our new friends returned. Instead of waking us with suspicion, they welcomed us inside, offering a comfortable spot on their living room floor. There was no judgment, only the quiet understanding that sometimes, the road brings people together in the most unexpected and beautiful ways.

That night, adventure and excitement mingled with humility and gratitude. We were reminded that the world is full of good people, those who open their homes, share a laugh, and offer a helping hand to travelers on life's winding road. And as we drifted off to sleep, we knew we'd carry the memory of their kindness with us, long after the journey continued.

The following morning greeted us with the irresistible aroma of freshly brewed coffee, a scent that promised new beginnings and the kind of comfort only found in the company of newfound friends. Our hosts, ever the embodiment of kindness and hospitality, prepared a light breakfast and welcomed us to join them outside for a bit of gardening. There was something quietly adventurous about helping tend to their little patch of earth, our hands in the soil, laughter mingling with the morning breeze. Even the simplest acts, passing a trowel, sharing a story, or just soaking in the sun, felt like a celebration of human connection.

After a while, as we warmed up the motorcycle, the anticipation of the open road began to bubble up inside us. The engine's rumble was a call to adventure, and our hearts beat a little faster with the promise of whatever surprises the day might bring. But before we could set off, our hosts gathered with us once more. We exchanged heartfelt goodbyes, each word laced with genuine gratitude for the compassion and generosity they had shown two wandering strangers. There was humility in their farewell, a sense that, for all their giving, they felt just as lucky to have shared a moment of their lives with us.

And then, with a wink and a smile, they extended an invitation that sparkled with excitement: "If you're passing through on your way back from Oregon, stop by again! We'll take you to a concert at the Fillmore West." The offer was delivered with such warmth and humor that we couldn't help but laugh, partly at the idea of two scruffy bikers rubbing elbows with San Francisco's music scene, and partly at the sheer unpredictability of life on the road.

As we rode away, the memory of their kindness lingered, a reminder that adventure isn't just about the places you go, but the people you meet and the compassion you share along the way. Sometimes, the greatest stories are born not from grand gestures, but from simple acts of humanity, a cup of coffee, a helping hand in the garden, and an open invitation to keep the adventure (and the music) going.

After days of exhilarating freedom on the open road, my friend and I rolled into Medford, Oregon, our spirits high and our hearts hungry for adventure. The night at my friend's uncle's house was a rare oasis, warm, welcoming, and filled with the laughter and comfort that only family can provide. We slept soundly, grateful for a roof over our heads and the sense of belonging that, for two young wanderers, felt almost magical.

But the next morning, the mood shifted. Eager to share our journey, we decided to visit another of my friend's uncles before leaving town. As we approached the house, the air seemed to thicken with tension. The front door creaked open, and there stood his uncle, eyes narrowed, jaw set, and a shotgun cradled in his arms. The sight sent a jolt of fear through my veins, the kind that makes your heart pound in your ears and your palms go cold.

He didn't mince words. "You boys aren't welcome here," he growled, his gaze fixed on my friend's long hair and our road-worn, hippie appearance. The barrel of the shotgun gleamed in the morning light, a stark reminder that we were far from the safety of last night's embrace. My friend's face flushed with embarrassment and pain, but neither of us dared argue. The agony of rejection stung, but the threat was real and immediate. We backed away, every step heavy with humiliation and the primal urge to survive.

We barely made it out of town before the next wave of trouble crashed over us. Red and blue lights flashed in the rearview mirror, a police car, siren silent but presence unmistakable. My pulse quickened as the officer approached, his hand resting casually on his holster. He questioned us about our purpose in town, his tone polite but edged with suspicion. The conversation was brief, but the message was clear: "You boys best move along." With a courteous but firm escort, he led us to the edge of Medford and watched as we disappeared down the highway, the town shrinking in the distance behind us.

As the city faded from view, a cocktail of emotions churned inside me, adrenaline from the close call, the sting of being unwelcome, and the lingering fear of what might have happened if we'd pushed our luck. The adventure had turned dangerous, the excitement laced with real peril. We rode on, the road ahead uncertain, but our resolve hardened by the ordeal. In that moment, we understood that the freedom of the open road comes with its own price, a lesson paid for in fear, agony, and the thrill of survival.

After those tense encounters, our journey north through Oregon became a rolling adventure, each mile a new chapter in our two-wheeled odyssey. The landscape unfurled before us, towering pines, misty hills, and the promise of the unknown around every bend. We were on a mission to visit the boyfriend of his cousin, a student at the University of Oregon in Eugene, and the road itself seemed to buzz with anticipation.

When we finally arrived, her boyfriend, an easygoing guy, greeted us with the kind of hospitality only college students can muster. He handed us the key to his dorm room, grinned, and said, "I've got plans tonight, but make yourselves at home. Just leave the key on the desk and lock up when you leave." It felt like we'd just been handed the keys to the kingdom.

Settling in, we decided to celebrate our good fortune in true road-trip fashion: we lit up a joint and soon found ourselves in fits of uncontrollable laughter, tears streaming down our faces, our eyes redder than a stop sign. The conversation turned philosophical, comparing the grumpy uncle who'd greeted us with a shotgun to the free-spirited, joint-sharing crew in Santa Rosa. The contrast was hilarious, and we couldn't help but marvel at the wild spectrum of humanity we'd encountered. Eventually, the munchies hit with a vengeance, so we set off on a late-night quest for food, wandering the campus, checking out quirky head shops, and finally grabbing some fast food before collapsing back in the dorm for the night.

The next morning, Oregon greeted us with its signature rain, but we were undeterred. We pressed on, riding through the drizzle all the way to Portland, where we spent a couple of days in laid-back bliss. Most of our time was spent atop a hill overlooking the Columbia River, hanging out with my friend's cousin and her crew, the air thick with the haze of weed and laughter. Honestly, the details of those days are a little fuzzy, let's just say the fog wasn't all from the weather.

After Portland, we decided to take the scenic (and slightly more adventurous) eastern route toward Crater Lake, passing through Bend. The trip stretched over a couple of nights, each one a new opportunity for mischief and discovery. The day we finally reached Crater Lake dawned with clear skies and crisp air, perfect riding weather. As we climbed higher, patches of snow began to appear, growing into impressive banks along the roadside. By sunset, the temperature had dropped so much that I could barely feel my fingers or toes. When I finally spotted a gas station, my body was so numb that I overshot it by thirty yards and had to double back, moving like a frozen robot.

That's when it hit me, if a moose, a bear, or even a squirrel had wandered onto the road, I'd have been a goner. We were in the middle of nowhere, with only a gas station and a tiny motel across the highway advertising "Hot Chili" in the window. That night, we splurged on a motel room, the only time on the whole trip we did so, and I swear, that bowl of chili tasted like pure salvation. We thawed out, grateful for warmth, shelter, and the kind of comfort only a roadside motel can provide after a day of freezing adventure.

The next morning was still chilly, but we were back on the bikes, determined to finish our ride around Crater Lake and continue south through Klamath Falls, eventually crossing back into California. We stopped in the small town of Tulelake for a pit stop at a modest gas station. That's when the universe decided to throw us a curveball.

After I finished at the urinal, I was washing my hands when I heard my friend yelping in pain. I turned to see him frantically punching himself in the groin, hopping around like he was auditioning for a slapstick comedy. Turns out, a bee had somehow flown up his pant leg and, after a slow and stealthy ascent, delivered a stinger right where it hurt most. The sight of my friend, pants unbuttoned, doing battle with an invisible enemy in a gas station bathroom was so unexpected and ridiculous that I burst out laughing. It was, without a doubt, one of the funniest moments I've ever witnessed, a perfect reminder that on the road, adventure and humor go hand in hand, and humility is never more than a bee sting away.

The next morning, with the spirit of adventure still buzzing in our veins, we set out for Santa Rosa to pay a visit to our hippie friends, not knowing that the coming days would be a whirlwind of surprises and unforgettable moments. The first day drifted by in a mellow haze, the anticipation of that night's concert at the legendary Fillmore West building with every passing hour. By 6:00 p.m., five of us, crammed into the back of their iconic love van, were already laughing, swapping stories, and passing around a bottle of wine and a couple of joints. By the time we rolled up to the Fillmore, we were feeling pretty "groovy," to say the least.

The marquee outside promised a night of electric blues with Fleetwood Mac, Buddy Miles, and Albert Collins. At the time, I didn't know Fleetwood Mac from a hole in the wall, and Albert Collins was just another name to me, but that didn't matter. The sheer thrill of being an underage kid, stoned and about to step into the legendary Fillmore West, was enough to make my heart race. Our hippie friends, ever resourceful, seemed to have connections everywhere. Someone greeted us at the door and whisked us straight to our seats, no waiting, no fuss, just a little Fillmore magic.

The concert itself was a blur of sound and color. I remember flashes of Buddy Miles' wild guitar, the crowd swaying in unison, and the feeling that I was part of something much bigger than myself. To be honest, I was so high that most of the night is a patchwork of fleeting memories, just the nostalgia of being inside that famous venue was enough to make it remarkable. The drive back to Santa Rosa was even hazier, filled with laughter and the kind of camaraderie that only comes from shared adventure. We tumbled into our friends' house and crashed, grateful for a safe landing after such an exhilarating night.

The next day, after a hearty breakfast and a few laughs about the previous night's escapades, our hosts suggested a country drive to visit some friends living in a nearby hippie commune. Always up for a new experience, we piled into the van and headed out. We parked beside a white wooden fence, climbed over it, and began hiking down a wooded trail, the air thick with the scent of pine and possibility.

Suddenly, out of the trees stepped a man, completely naked except for his long hair and scraggly beard, waving at us like we were long-lost family. Our lady friend called out, "Hey, Funkdog!" and he grinned, explaining that he was just gathering leaves to make himself a bed under the trees. His carefree spirit was contagious, and we couldn't help but laugh at the unexpected greeting.

A little further down the trail, it opened into a sunlit meadow where a large tree stood, a triangle ringer hanging from one of its limbs. Beneath the tree, a half-naked woman stirred a meal in an oversized iron pot suspended over a fire. Off to the side, a family-sized canvas tent beckoned. We were welcomed inside by a couple who greeted us with kindness and, true to commune hospitality, lit up a couple of joints to share. As we passed the joint and listened to the rules of the commune, I was struck by the genuine warmth and compassion of these strangers, who treated us like old friends.

We settled in the shade, someone strumming a guitar, laughter and music mingling in the air. When the dinner bell rang, a triangle's clear chime echoing through the meadow, I was amazed at how quickly the gathering grew. Dozens of people seemed to materialize from the woods, washing their hands before forming neat rows on the grass. Before serving the food, a communal prayer of thanks was offered. There were no tables, no plates, just bowls passed from hand to hand, each person scooping out a portion with their bare hands. The humility and simplicity of the meal, the communal prayer, and the shared gratitude for the food were deeply moving.

I'll admit, as the bowls came my way, I couldn't help but worry about catching something, hepatitis, maybe, or some other bug. So, with a sheepish grin and a polite nod, I passed the bowl along, choosing to go without dinner that night. My friends teased me, but I took it in stride, grateful for their good-natured ribbing and the lesson in humility.

After dinner, the festivities continued with more music, laughter, and the kind of fun that only comes from being surrounded by kind souls in a place where everyone is welcome. As dusk settled, we made our way back to our hosts' home, hearts full and spirits high.

The next morning, we said our goodbyes, thanking our friends for their generosity and kindness. Though I never saw my hippie friends again, the experience left an indelible mark on me, a firsthand glimpse into a lifestyle that most people only read about or see in documentaries. It was a wild, wonderful adventure, filled with excitement, surprises, and the kind of compassion and kindness that remind you how fun and unpredictable life can be when you open yourself to new experiences.

Our second attempt to visit my brother David at Fort Ord was already tinged with the thrill of the unknown. This time, luck, or perhaps the universe's sense of humor, was on our side, and we were waved onto the base with little more than a nod. The narrow streets bustled with soldiers, some marching in tight formation, others jogging in loose, laughing packs. The air was alive with energy, and as we cruised by, we received a mixed bag of greetings: peace signs from some, and the classic "bird" from others. It was as if the base itself was daring us to see the world through both the lens of camaraderie and the edge of irreverence.

But adventure, as always, had a twist in store. Upon reaching David's barracks, we learned that civilians weren't supposed to linger. No problem, rules are just suggestions on a freedom ride, right? We agreed to regroup later at a small market in nearby Seaside, where the real fun began.

That evening, over quick sandwiches and cold beers, David suggested we follow him back to his barracks, this time, in what is now Presidio Park. To my surprise (and a bit of nervous excitement), we ended up spending the night in his barracks, civilians among soldiers. The place was divided into two worlds: one side for those about to ship out to Vietnam, the other for those just returning. David, ever the guide, led us into the returning soldiers' section, cautioning us to keep it cool and quiet.

There, we sat, sipping beer and listening as the soldiers swapped stories from Vietnam. Some tales were wild, some somber, all of them laced with the kind of humor that only comes from surviving the unimaginable. It was a masterclass in humility, these men, who had faced the worst, now laughed at the absurdities of army life and the quirks of homecoming. Their compassion for each other was palpable, and their willingness to let a couple of long-haired civilians into their circle for a night was a lesson in unexpected kindness.

The army, it seemed, had figured out that the best way to help returning soldiers acclimate was to let them decompress among their own before sending them home. It was a system built on empathy, and we were lucky enough to witness it firsthand.

Early the next morning, before the sun had even considered rising, we said our goodbyes. We all left the base together, soldiers, civilians, brothers, each of us a little changed by the experience. Within two days, our freedom ride was complete, but the memories lingered: the laughter, the humility, the sense of being part of something bigger than ourselves.

And as for David? Four months later, he shipped out to Vietnam, where he served a full tour of duty. Our adventure had been a brief, shining moment of fun and connection before the world called him to a different kind of adventure, one that demanded all the courage, compassion, and humor he could muster.

Looking back, I couldn't help but smile at the wild ride we shared. Sometimes, the best stories are born from a willingness to say yes, to embrace the unknown, and to find joy, and a little mischief, wherever the road leads.

Chapter 7
Eighteen

Following my Freedom Ride, I landed back at my parents' house, only to be greeted by the cold, hard reality that "free room and board" came with a catch. My dad, a firm believer in the gospel of self-sufficiency, made it clear that anyone living under his roof had to contribute financially to the family, or else pack up and learn the fine art of independence the hard way. There were only a few exceptions to this rule: if you were attending college and working part-time, or if you were employed full-time. But even then, making a financial contribution to the household was as non-negotiable as his morning coffee. As for me, with pockets emptier than my gas tank, I suddenly felt a deep sense of responsibility, mostly because I was too broke to afford the alternative!

Reflecting on my older brother and several friends who had previously worked at old man George's gas station, I remembered how much they seemed to enjoy their time there. For them, the gas station was more than just a job, it was a social hub, a place where the evening shift often turned into a gathering of friends plotting their next afterwork adventure. I suppose you could say it was the original "networking event," just with more oil stains and fewer business cards.

One day, as I was driving past the local high school, I spotted a help wanted sign in the window of a nearby gas station. Driven by curiosity (and, let's be honest, the need for a paycheck), I stopped in to ask about the job. To my surprise, I was given an immediate interview and, before I knew it, I was hired on the spot. Sometimes, life doesn't wait for you to overthink it.

Starting the job, I quickly learned a wide range of car maintenance skills, pumping gas, changing oil, repairing brakes, belts, windshield wipers, tires, and water pumps. I became a jack-of-all-trades, though master of none, except perhaps for the fine art of getting grease on every article of clothing I owned. The pay was modest, let's just say I wasn't in danger of buying a yacht, but there was genuine satisfaction in helping people and picking up practical knowledge.

The best part was the camaraderie: friends would drop by for quick visits, and I'd even get the occasional tip from a grateful customer, especially the waitresses from the Mexican restaurant next door. I suspect they tipped me more for my effort than my expertise, but I took it as a win either way.

I noticed some amusing patterns in customer behavior. Women typically stayed in their cars, waiting for me to check the oil or top off the windshield wiper fluid, and they almost always refueled before their tanks hit the halfway mark. Men, on the other hand, seemed to treat the gas gauge as a test of courage, waiting until the needle was flirting with empty before pulling in. Some would get out and chat while the gas was pumping, following me around as I checked the air in their tires, especially eager to inspect the dipstick themselves, as if it held the secrets of the universe.

Then, one day, the owner blindsided me with an accusation: he said I was stealing from the cash register and fired me on the spot. I was completely innocent, and the accusation stung. I did everything I could to clear my name, but nothing I said made a difference. It was a humbling experience, one of those moments when you realize that sometimes, no matter how honest you are, life can still throw you under the bus (or, in this case, the gas pump).

Months later, the truth finally surfaced. The owner came to my house, looking more sheepish than I'd ever seen him. He explained that the thefts had continued after I left, and after setting a trap, he discovered the real culprit: his own brother-in-law, who also happened to be my direct supervisor.

I remembered this man well. He was the assistant manager and my direct supervisor, the kind of boss who could spot a crooked stack of windshield wipers from a mile away. He'd once mentioned that he used to work at LAX as an air traffic controller but lost his job due to a layoff. (I always wondered if he tried to direct planes the way he directed me: "Turn left at the squeegee, descend to the oil rack, and please don't forget to check the dipstick.")

When I worked the day shift, we often worked side by side. Occasionally, when I had the night shift, he'd show up during my hours, inspect the station, read the logbook, and even check the money at the pump islands. At the time, I thought nothing of it, he was my boss, after all, and I assumed he was just doing his job.

The owner offered me a formal apology and a thorough explanation, which finally cleared my name. He even offered me my job back, expressing his regret for the misunderstanding. I thanked him for his honesty and for setting the record straight, but I respectfully declined the offer to return. After all, once you've been accused of grand theft gas station, it's hard to go back to pumping regular with a straight face.

After my abrupt (and, let's be honest, rather humbling) exit from the gas station, fired for a crime I didn't commit, like a character in a low-budget detective novel, I found myself on the hunt for my next big adventure. That's how I landed at the Rickenbacker Guitars Factory in Santa Ana. The place was a wonderland for any music lover: the air buzzed with the scent of sawdust and lacquer, and the walls echoed with the twang of freshly strung guitars. It was both nostalgic and fascinating to see how legendary instruments were born, but, alas, the pay was about as thin as a guitar pick. I quickly realized that, unless I planned to live on a steady diet of guitar strings and dreams, I'd need something a bit more sustainable.

So, with the spirit of a treasure hunter, I kept searching. Soon, opportunity knocked in the form of a local entrepreneur who owned a chain of five takeout pizza shops. The real draw? Several of my close friends were already part of the pizza posse, and their stories of camaraderie and after-hours escapades made the job sound like a cross between "Cheers" and "Fast Times at Ridgemont High." When an opening popped up, I jumped in, eager to join the team and see if I could toss dough with the best of them.

Some friends worked part-time to bankroll their college adventures, but a few of us brave souls dove headfirst into full-time management roles. The pay? A whopping $152 per week, which, for an eighteen-year-old, felt like hitting the jackpot (or at least the quarter slots at a smoky casino). The owner sweetened the deal with an incentive program: stick around for five years, and you could open your own store. It was like the pizza version of "Survivor", outwit, outlast, and out-bake, and you might just become the boss.

The schedule was a test of endurance and appetite: five or six days a week, eight to ten hours a shift, and you absolutely had to work Thursday through Sunday, the pizza world's equivalent of the Super Bowl. But despite the long hours and the occasional flour fight, I genuinely enjoyed the job. Closing time wasn't the end of the day; it was the start of the real fun. We'd gather for poker games, hit the bowling alley, or, on special nights, sneak into the high school gym (thanks to my brother-in-law, the world's friendliest security guard) for some late-night basketball. When the weather was right, I'd dash to the beach, body surf like a wannabe champion, soak up the sun, and then race home for a quick shower before heading back to the pizza trenches.

Looking back, those days were a whirlwind of adventure, excitement, and a fair share of humility, because nothing keeps you grounded like dropping a pizza face-down in front of your boss. But above all, it was fun: a time of laughter, learning, and the kind of lighthearted mischief that makes for the best stories later in life.

My girlfriend completed her senior year of high school in June, yet she was already ambitious, juggling her regular classes with additional coursework at the local junior college. Our schedules were a whirlwind, her notebooks always seemed to be filled with assignments, while my hands were usually dusted with flour from the pizza shop. Still, we cherished every moment we could carve out together. Whether we escaped to the beach, spreading out a blanket for a simple picnic, or found ourselves bowling gutter balls and laughing at our lack of skill, each date was a small adventure.

Sometimes, we'd opt for dinner or late night at the drive-in, sharing popcorn and inside jokes, talking about everything and nothing at all.

Looking back, those were carefree days, filled with the optimism and intensity of young love. We didn't have much, but we had each other, and that felt like enough. There was a gentle compassion in the way we supported one another through the stress of exams and the exhaustion of late-night shifts. We learned early on that understanding meant more than just listening; it meant showing up, even when we were tired, and finding humor in the little mishaps that life tossed our way.

Our love story wasn't perfect, whose ever is?, but it was real, and it was ours. We navigated the ups and downs with a mix of patience, forgiveness, and the kind of lighthearted teasing that only two people truly comfortable with each other can share. Through it all, we discovered that love isn't just about grand gestures or dramatic declarations; sometimes, it's about holding hands during a sunset, sharing a smile after a long day, or simply being present for each other, come what may. So, at least that's what we thought!

Chapter 8
Young Marriage

When we first discovered the pregnancy, the world seemed to tilt on its axis. The seriousness of the moment hit us both, hard. There was a hush, a shared look, and then a thousand questions racing through our minds. Were we ready? Could we do this? The answer, if we were honest, was a resounding "probably not." But beneath the concern and uncertainty, there was also a spark of excitement, a sense that, ready or not, we were about to embark on the greatest adventure of our lives.

We tried to steady ourselves with the belief that love would see us through. Sure, we were young, a little reckless, and our bank accounts were more "empty pizza box" than "nest egg," but we convinced ourselves that together we could build a life for our growing family. If nothing else, we had each other, and a stubborn optimism that sometimes bordered on delusion.

Of course, the universe wasn't about to let us off easy. Financially, we were barely scraping by: she was working at a department store, and I was earning my keep by tossing pizzas. Our combined income could just about cover rent, groceries, and the occasional splurge on a second-hand baby book. The real wild card, though, was her parents. From the start, they made it clear that their expectations for their daughter soared somewhere above my current pay grade. Their feelings toward me were, let's say, "room temperature", not quite frosty, but definitely not warm and fuzzy. Behind closed doors, they lobbied for an early end to our relationship, hoping their daughter would come to her senses.

This persistent lack of approval weighed heavily on her. She was so anxious about how her parents would react to the news that she insisted we keep the pregnancy a secret for as long as possible. I understood her fear, after all, if we couldn't tell her parents, it hardly seemed fair to spring the news on mine. But we both knew that secrets, like babies, have a way of making themselves known eventually.

Just when things felt most uncertain, adventure knocked, disguised as family. Earlier that summer, my Aunt Mary and Uncle Phil visited from Kentucky. Uncle Phil, a true jack of all trades, offered me a chance to come work with him and learn a couple of honest trades. He ran a carpet shop, a sheet metal business, and even kept a few cows and horses on the side. If there was a job to be done, Uncle Phil was your man. The offer was tempting: a fresh start, a little distance from parental scrutiny, and the promise of learning skills that didn't involve pizza dough.

After talking it over, we agreed that Kentucky might be just the adventure we needed. I called Uncle Phil, told him I was getting married, and asked if his offer still stood. He said yes, and just like that, our next chapter began to take shape, equal parts daunting and exhilarating, with a dash of "what could possibly go wrong?"

We began the next step in our journey by nervously meeting with my girlfriend's parents to formally request their permission to marry. The air was thick with concern, ours and theirs. As expected, her parents didn't exactly leap for joy at our announcement. Their disapproval was clear, and for a moment, I wondered if we'd accidentally asked for her hand in marriage or for the keys to their car. Still, we listened with humility and respect as they voiced their worries, each word a reminder of how much they cared for their daughter's future.

Determined to show them that our decision wasn't just a product of youthful recklessness (though there was plenty of that, too), we laid out our plan for building a life together, complete with hopes, dreams, and a budget that could barely stretch to cover pizza on a Friday night. Despite their lingering reservations, love and a bit of stubborn optimism won the day, and they ultimately gave us their blessing, though I suspect it was delivered with a side of crossed fingers and whispered prayers.

That same evening, we set off on another adventure: seeking my own parents' approval. We walked into the house to find my father asleep on the sofa, snoring so loudly I briefly considered checking for a hidden chainsaw. My mother, ever the gracious host, paused her favorite TV show and welcomed us in. As I tried to wake Dad, he mumbled, "I can't hear you, there's something wrong with my hearing." Only after a moment did he realize his little finger was stuck in his ear. With a sheepish grin, he pulled it out and announced, "Oh, it was my finger, I can hear you just fine now." The room erupted in laughter, instantly melting any tension that had followed us in.

With the mood lightened, we shared our plans to marry. My parents, who had once been young and impulsive themselves, gave us their approval. I suspect their willingness was a mix of empathy for our excitement and a secret hope that, with three kids down and two to go, they were inching closer to a little peace and quiet.

Of all the possible dates to tie the knot, we boldly chose Friday the 13th, August 13, 1971. Thankfully, it wasn't a full moon, though I'm sure some of our relatives checked the calendar twice just in case. Our wedding unfolded in a small, charming chapel, the kind of place where you half expect Elvis to make a cameo. Only our closest friends and family attended, making it an intimate gathering that perfectly matched our circumstances, and our budget. The reception was held at her parents' home, a modest but fitting venue that let us celebrate without breaking the bank. The atmosphere was lighthearted, fueled by a few drinks and some heartfelt, if slightly slurred, speeches. We cut the cake, opened gifts, and did our best to thank everyone for joining us.

As the evening wound down, we made our escape like a pair of newlywed bandits, quietly slipping away to begin our new life together, and allowing my newlywedded wife to unleash the constraints of her belt. Our honeymoon was less "jet-set adventure" and more "budget road trip," but we embraced it with the same spirit. We drove to Palm Springs and checked into the most affordable motel we could find, "no frills, but at least the air conditioner worked." After one night, we set out for Kentucky, embarking on a cross-country trek that was equal parts adventure and test of marital patience. Several days and countless fast food joints later, we arrived at my aunt and uncle's home. They generously offered us a room for six weeks, giving us time to save up for a place of our own and to start building our future, one humble, hopeful step at a time.

Life swept me up quickly and early, each day beginning before the sun had even stretched its golden arms across the sky. Aunt Mary, with her gentle warmth and boundless energy, would prepare a quick breakfast for us while the old truck rumbled to life outside. There was a quiet joy in those mornings, a sense of togetherness and purpose as we shared a meal, exchanged smiles, and readied ourselves for the day's adventure.

Uncle Phil, a steadfast and determined country boy, became both mentor and companion on this journey. He taught me not just how to lay out and install carpet or hang HVAC ducting beneath floors, but also how to approach each task with pride and resilience. Along the way, I picked up a variety of new skills, each one a small victory, broadening my sense of what I could accomplish. The work was demanding, long hours that stretched from the first blush of dawn to the quiet hush after sunset, five days a week, and sometimes even Saturdays. Yet, there was a camaraderie in our shared effort, a sense of adventure in tackling each new challenge side by side.

Sundays, however, were sacred, a day reserved for rest, reflection, and the embrace of family. We would gather together for church in the morning, our voices rising in song and gratitude, well, at least Aunt Mary and Uncle Phil's voices chimed in, and then return home for an early dinner. These moments were filled with laughter, stories, and the simple pleasure of being together, reinforcing the bonds that held us close.

Aunt Mary was remarkable in every way. Her beauty radiated from within, shining through her intelligence, humor, and unwavering devotion to her family and community. She was the heart of our home, nurturing us with compassion and guiding us with gentle strength. Uncle Phil, the son of a preacher, carried a determined sense of purpose and an unbreakable spirit. Together, they created an environment where love, support, and adventure flourished, a place where I learned not only the value of hard work but also the importance of kindness, fun, and the enduring power of family.

I'll be the first to admit, when it came to cows and horses, I was about as green as the grass they grazed on. The idea that a cow could leap a fence seemed as likely as pigs sprouting wings, until one of Uncle Phil's cows did exactly that, vanishing into the wild unknown of the nearby creek. Suddenly, our quiet country life turned into a full-blown cattle caper.

Determined to reclaim his runaway bovine (and perhaps his pride), Uncle Phil sprang into action with the kind of gusto usually reserved for rodeo stars. He saddled up two horses and loaded them into the back of his pickup truck. The sight of us, a pair of would-be cowboys, bouncing down the road with horses in tow, must have been enough to make the neighbors reach for their popcorn.

Once we reached the creek, the real adventure began. We unloaded the horses and set off, riding up and down the creek bed like a couple of explorers on a quest for the Holy Grail, except our grail was a cow with a taste for freedom. We searched every nook, cranny, and suspicious-looking bush, calling out for our four-legged fugitive. After hours of fruitless searching, we finally admitted defeat and headed home.

In the months that followed, Uncle Phil kept getting calls from neighbors claiming to have spotted the elusive cow somewhere in the area. Personally, I suspected they just enjoyed the spectacle of Uncle Phil saddling up and riding through the creek beds like a scene out of an old Western. As for the cow, well, I like to think she's out there somewhere, living her best life, but odds are, she ended up at the slaughterhouse, her legend living on in local lore and every family story told around the dinner table.

One day, while I was working in the carpet shop, my Aunt Mary gently pulled me aside to share a heartfelt observation about my wife's behavior during our stay in her home. With genuine concern and a motherly touch, she explained that whenever I was away, my wife would quietly retreat to the bedroom, only emerging briefly to eat or use the restroom before returning to her solitude.

Aunt Mary admitted that this pattern felt unusual and, to her, a bit hurtful, especially since my wife never offered to help with even the simplest household tasks, like doing the dishes. She worried that this distance might be a sign of discomfort or even disrespect, and her words were spoken not in judgment but out of a deep desire for harmony and connection within the family.

Listening to Aunt Mary, I felt a wave of empathy for both women. I knew my wife's actions were not meant to offend but rather reflected her own vulnerability and uncertainty in a new and unfamiliar environment. With honesty and affection, I shared the truth with Aunt Mary: my wife was already four months pregnant, and the weight of that secret, combined with her anxiety about how others might perceive her, made her feel exposed and out of place.

I had brought her halfway across the country, asking her to live with people she barely knew, even if they were family. The culture of the Baptist Bible Belt, with its churches on every corner and the ever-present visits from ministers eager to share the gospel, was a world apart from what she'd known. Even attending Mass with her grandmother had been a rare experience for her, and now she found herself surrounded by customs and expectations that felt overwhelming. Aunt Mary embraced me warmly, assuring me of her love and support. She told me not to worry and that she would always have my back.

Sometimes, even the most heartfelt intentions of those who love us can't shield us from life's difficult realities. About three months after I started working for my uncle, I learned that he had offered me the job out of kindness and a genuine desire to help, but the financial strain was simply too much for him to bear. Despite paying me $5 per hour, a generous wage for the area, he was already supporting his brother-in-law full-time, and keeping both of us on the payroll was making it hard for him to make ends meet. When he sat me down to explain the situation, I could sense his concern and the weight of responsibility he felt, not just as an employer but as family. There was an unspoken wish to protect me from hardship, even as he faced his own.

Recognizing the reality of our circumstances, we talked openly about our options. Uncle Phil's support didn't end with that difficult conversation. Instead, he took it upon himself to help me find new work, determined to ensure I wouldn't be left adrift. He introduced me to a friend in Paducah who owned a carpet shop and managed installations. The interview went well, and I felt understood and encouraged. Although the owner couldn't hire me until the fall, he outlined a training program and promised that within a year, I'd have my own truck and steady work, an assurance that brought a sense of hope and relief for the future.

Afterward, Uncle Phil introduced me to another friend who was a supervisor at Murray State University, about twenty miles away. After a brief interview, I was offered a position as a groundskeeper. Although the job didn't pay much, it provided steady income and, importantly, health insurance for my growing family. With this new opportunity, we moved to the Shady Oaks Trailer Park just outside of Murray, rented a one-bedroom trailer, and settled into our new home.

With a profound sense of relief, I embraced the exhilarating freedom and independence that came with finally being 100% on our own. Starting my job as a groundskeeper at Murray State University was more than just employment, it was the beginning of a new adventure. Each day brought fresh challenges and opportunities to prove myself, not only to others but to myself as well.

I found myself working alongside a small group of retired farmers, all in their sixties. As a young man with long, blondish hair, a stark contrast to their weathered faces and traditional ways, I stood out immediately. Their initial teasing, calling me "Custer" in reference to General Custer, was their way of testing the newcomer, a rite of passage that I accepted with humility and a smile.

Our responsibilities were as varied as the changing seasons: transplanting small trees and shrubs to keep the campus vibrant, driving the trash truck to collect refuse from office buildings and dormitories, and, come fall, operating the leaf bailer to gather and haul away the mountains of fallen leaves. In the colder months, we sharpened axes and cleared dead growth along the stream beds, braving the elements together. Every task, no matter how menial or demanding, became a lesson in perseverance and respect, for the land, for the work, and for each other.

Despite our differences, I gradually earned my place among these seasoned men. I admired their grit and the quiet pride they took in their work, even as age pressed against their limits. Whenever I finished my own assignments, I would jump in to help each man complete his, moving from one task to the next until all the jobs were done. There was a deep satisfaction in this shared effort, a camaraderie forged through sweat, laughter, and mutual respect.

I sensed that, over time, these men came to appreciate the young "hippie" kid from California who was always willing to lend a hand, not out of obligation, but out of genuine humility and a desire to belong. In their acceptance, I found not only respect but also a deeper understanding of what it means to face life's challenges with an open heart and an adventurous spirit.

From the moment I can remember, animals have always held a special place in my heart, and, as fate would have it, in my home. My longtime dream of owning a Saint Bernard finally came true after a bit of searching: we spotted an ad in the local newspaper and set off on a journey deep into the countryside, winding through backroads and farmland for over an hour. When we arrived at the farm, I was greeted by a litter of rollicking Saint Bernard puppies, each one more adorable than the last. But as soon as I locked eyes with one particular pup, I knew he was the one. I named him Harley on the spot, because, let's be honest, a dog that size deserves a name with a little horsepower behind it.

While I was busy falling in love with Harley, my wife was equally smitten by a litter of kittens tumbling around nearby. She chose a tiny female tabby and named her Precious. Little did we know, these two would become the dynamic duo of our household. Harley and Precious quickly formed an unlikely but heartwarming bond. They shared meals from the same dish (Harley, ever the gentleman, never complained about the portion sizes), and at night, Precious would curl up in the crook of Harley's massive paws, purring contentedly as if she'd found her own personal bodyguard. Harley, for his part, had a quirky habit of drinking from the toilet, always freshly cleaned, of course. Precious, meanwhile, seemed to have discovered the secret to eternal youth, remaining kitten-sized for as long as she was with us. I sometimes wondered if she was sneaking my wife's anti-aging cream from the bathroom cabinet.

We let both Harley and Precious roam freely around the neighborhood, and it wasn't long before Harley became a local celebrity. The trailer park residents adored him, especially the owner, who claimed Harley was better at making friends than most people. Precious, on the other hand, was a bit more cautious. Whenever the other neighborhood dogs came sniffing around, she would dart under the trailer faster than you could say "catnap."

One day, though, adventure took a dramatic turn. Two of the local dogs managed to corner Precious, grabbing her in a canine tug-of-war, one on her head, the other on her tail. It was a scene straight out of a slapstick cartoon, except the stakes were real. Harley, ever the hero, sprang into action. With a burst of Saint Bernard bravado, he charged over, broke up the scuffle, and gently scooped Precious up in his jaws (with all the delicacy of a giant cradling a teacup). He carried her back to the trailer, setting her down so she could scurry to safety beneath it. I like to think Harley gave the other dogs a look that said, "Mess with my family, and you'll answer to me."

I had always considered myself a dreamer, often experiencing vivid and memorable dreams. But one night, a dream unsettled me in a way I had never known before. In it, I was back inside my parents' house, standing next to my brother David, who had just recently returned from Vietnam. The overwhelming relief and joy I felt at seeing him home safe and sound was so intense that I rushed to give him a heartfelt hug, clinging to him as if to reassure myself that he was truly there and unharmed. Yet, as dreams do, the scene shifted abruptly, and suddenly we were together in the living room.

David handed me a drink and suggested we sit down. There was a heaviness in the air, a sense of foreboding that made my heart pound with anxiety. Then, with an air of seriousness that sent a chill through me, he looked at me and said, "I'm blind," delivering the news with a bluntness that left me frozen in fear. The shock of that moment jolted me awake, tears streaming down my face. I was gripped by a deep, gnawing worry for my brother's safety, unable to shake the vividness of the dream.

My emotional reaction startled my wife awake, and through my tears, I recounted the dream to her, my voice trembling with concern and helplessness. The fear and uncertainty lingered with me for two full weeks, casting a shadow over my days. I found myself haunted by the possibility that something terrible had happened to David. The worry was so consuming that I eventually called home, desperate for any news about him, but there was none at the time. I was left with nothing but my own humility in the face of how little control I had over the fate of someone I cared about so deeply.

A couple of months later, David did return from Vietnam. After spending some time with family and friends, he flew out to visit us and stayed for a few weeks. Seeing him in person and knowing he was safe and unharmed, I dismissed the dream as simply a bad nightmare, chalk it up to an overactive imagination and maybe a little too much weed. But, as life often does, it had one more twist in store for us.

One evening, the three of us went out to see a movie and later stopped for pizza at a local parlor. My wife, ever the curious soul, asked if I had ever told David about my dream. Her question piqued his curiosity, so I shared the story, half-expecting a laugh or a playful jab about my "psychic" abilities. But as I finished, David's expression changed; he turned pale and pulled down his lower eyelids, showing us what he said was scar tissue in his eyes. He explained that the scars resulted from flash burns during a firefight in Vietnam, which had caused him to be temporarily blind for two weeks.

When we compared the timing, we realized his period of blindness coincided exactly with the time I had the dream. The coincidence was uncanny and left a lasting impression on me. I couldn't help but feel a little humbled, and, truth be told, a bit spooked, by the realization that sometimes the universe has a way of connecting dots we didn't even know existed. In the end, we all shared a laugh, grateful that the only thing permanently damaged was my reputation as the family skeptic.

Harley, our ever-curious Saint Bernard, had developed a rather persistent fascination with the chain-link fence surrounding the small pond where the white geese resided. Each day, he'd make valiant attempts to wriggle under the fence, only to be foiled by the geese's uncanny ability to spot him and make a hasty, honking retreat to the far side of the pond. It became a bit of a neighborhood spectacle, Harley, the would-be goose wrangler, outsmarted by a flock of feathered escape artists. I sometimes wondered if the geese secretly enjoyed the daily chase as much as Harley did.

Then winter arrived, bringing with it a blanket of snow and a new twist to our ongoing animal drama. As the temperatures dropped, the pond froze over, transforming the geese's watery sanctuary into a slippery stage. On one particularly dark and chilly morning, I let Harley outside before heading to work, trusting that my wife or brother would bring him in later, as was our routine. Little did I know the day was about to take an unexpected turn.

That morning, my brother David woke up early for a cigarette and to check on Harley. What he discovered was the kind of scene that makes your heart sink: a trail of feathers stretching from the pond all the way to our trailer, a very deceased goose, and Harley himself looking as guilty as a dog can possibly look, face smeared with evidence, eyes wide with the canine equivalent of "I can explain!" It was clear that Harley's goose-chasing days had finally caught up with him, and he'd crossed a line from playful pursuit to actual mischief.

David, to his credit, handled the aftermath with remarkable care and compassion. He cleaned up the mess thoroughly before anyone else could discover what had happened, ensuring Harley's involvement remained our little secret. The owner of the trailer park was understandably upset about the loss of one of his prized geese and launched a full-scale investigation to find the culprit. Meanwhile, Harley did his best to look innocent, thanks to David, the truth never came out, and Harley was spared from being labeled the neighborhood's most wanted dog.

One sunny day, my wife and I decided it was high time to give my brother David a taste of country life, after all, what's the point of having relatives with land if you can't show it off every now and then? Uncle Phil, never one to miss an opportunity to play tour guide, led us down a gravel road that seemed to stretch on forever, dust swirling behind us like we were in a low-budget Western. At the end of the trail, we arrived at his latest pride and joy: thirteen acres of open land, complete with three horses, each with more personality than some people I've met at family reunions.

There was the Tennessee Walker, tall and elegant, looking like he'd just stepped out of a horse fashion magazine; a retired Quarter Horse with the kind of wise, world-weary eyes that said, "Kid, I've seen things;" and a small painted pony who, frankly, seemed to be plotting mischief from the moment we arrived.

David, fresh home from war and still getting used to civilian life, was instantly smitten with the Tennessee Walker. He mounted up, looking every bit the cowboy hero, if you ignored the slightly nervous grip on the reins, and set off along the fence line, his silhouette framed against the endless sky. It was a scene so picturesque, I half-expected a movie director to yell, "Cut!"

But then adventure called, and I, never one to let a good opportunity for excitement pass me by, answered with gusto. Overcome with a wave of gratitude and a sudden urge to show off, I leapt onto the Quarter Horse, let out a country-boy yell that probably startled birds three counties over, and dug my heels in. The Quarter Horse, clearly a fan of drama, took off like a shot, hooves thundering across the field as we chased after David. For a moment, I felt like I'd become one with the horse, a regular centaur, minus the mythical abs and flowing mane.

We tore along the fence line, wind whipping past, the world blurring into a rush of green and gold. I caught up to David just before the next corner, and together we rode side by side, laughing like kids who'd just gotten away with sneaking cookies before dinner. The joy and freedom of that ride were palpable, two brothers, reunited and racing across open land, leaving worries and war behind for a few precious moments.

When we finally pulled up and dismounted, I glanced over at Uncle Phil and Aunt Mary. To my surprise, their eyes were glistening with tears, not from the dust, but from the emotion of the moment. Uncle Phil, usually as stoic as a fence post, was genuinely moved. "I've never seen anything like that," he said, shaking his head in disbelief. "A long-haired beach boy riding like he was born in the saddle. You belong in the country, son." I grinned, feeling both humbled and a little bit like I'd just won the blue ribbon at the county fair for "Most Unexpected Cowboy."

That day left a lasting impression on all of us. It was a reminder that adventure can find you in the most unexpected places, that laughter and humility go hand in hand, and that sometimes the best way to show you care is to saddle up, let loose, and race your brother across a field, just to see who gets to the corner first. And if you happen to surprise a few relatives (and maybe yourself) along the way? Well, that's just the icing on the country cake.

Shortly before our precious son Jeremy was born, life seemed to pause in anticipation, and our family's love and concern gathered around us like a warm embrace. My brother David returned to California, making space for Mom, who traveled all that way just to be by our side. Her presence was a blessing, she arrived not only with her suitcase but with a heart full of devotion, ready to lend a hand and offer comfort during those uncertain, hope-filled days.

Early one cold winter morning in late January 1972, just past four, the world shifted for us. My wife's water broke, and in that instant, excitement and worry mingled in our hearts. We hurried to the hospital, each moment heavy with both concern for her well-being and the overwhelming love we already felt for the child about to enter our lives. I remember feeling helpless and humbled by the hospital's rules, being told I could not be by her side during labor felt like a small heartbreak. Yet I was grateful that my mother was allowed in, her gentle strength a source of reassurance for us both.

Labor was long and arduous, and in those ten hours, my wife endured pain with a courage that filled me with awe. There were no epidurals then, only the raw, unfiltered experience of childbirth. According to my mom, my name was not far from my wife's lips, though not always in praise!, as she damned my name through each contraction. I felt a mix of humility and pride, knowing that the journey to bring our son into the world was as much hers as it was mine, and that I could only stand by, waiting with hope through every moment.

When Jeremy finally arrived, he was more than just our son, he was a living testament to our hopes, our love, and the sacrifices made by those who came before us. My mother stayed with us for several weeks after his birth, her hands and heart steady as she helped us navigate those first fragile days. She cared for us all, allowing my wife the time and space to regain her strength and giving me the chance to marvel at the tiny miracle we had brought into the world.

After three months of wrangling weeds and wrestling with Kentucky's stubborn grass as a university groundskeeper, it became clear that my modest paycheck was no match for the growing needs of a young family of three. Adventure, it seemed, was calling us westward once again. My wife, ever the intrepid soul, had grown weary of Kentucky's rolling hills and was gently (and sometimes not-so-gently) campaigning for a return to the sunny promise of California. As much as I cherished the country lifestyle, where the biggest traffic jam was a herd of cows crossing the road, I knew that true contentment meant seeing my family happy, even if it meant trading bluegrass for ocean breezes.

Once Jeremy hit the three-month milestone and was robust enough to handle the journey, we knew it was time to pack up and head for Southern California. Our little car, which had bravely carried us this far, was now bursting at the seams with baby gear and dreams for the future. So, in a move that felt both practical and a little bit legendary, we traded it in for a used Ford Econoline Van. This wasn't just any van, it had once served as a local telephone company vehicle, which meant it came with a bit of character and plenty of space.

As moving day approached, we faced a dilemma that tugged at our hearts: there simply wasn't enough room for Harley, our beloved Saint Bernard, who had become something of a local celebrity (and, unbeknownst to most, a goose's worst nightmare). Thankfully, the trailer park owner, who had grown quite fond of Harley's gentle ways, offered to adopt him. The owner never knew about Harley's secret life as a goose wrangler, and we decided it was best to let sleeping dogs (and geese) lie.

At least we could leave knowing Harley would be loved and spoiled in familiar territory. As for Precious, our eternally kitten-sized cat, the details of her new home were a bit fuzzy, much like she was, but I'm confident we found her a safe and caring place to land. After all, ensuring our pets' well-being was just as important as packing the baby bottles and the last box of memories.

Just as we were tying up the last loose ends, the universe decided to test my resolve with a final twist: a long-awaited call from Paducah came through, offering me a job laying carpet, exactly one week before our planned departure. The offer was tempting, like a golden ticket dangled just out of reach. But I'd already given my word to my wife that we'd return to California. With a deep breath and a dash of humility, I turned down the opportunity, choosing to honor my promise and embrace the next chapter of our adventure together. Sometimes, the greatest journeys are the ones where you keep your word, even when the road ahead is uncertain, and maybe, just maybe, a little exciting.

Fortunately, in July 1972, my father, who was employed in the petroleum industry for a major oil consortium in Long Beach, played a crucial role in helping me launch a new career. With his support and guidance, I secured my first position in the industry as a roustabout. I was hired by the construction and maintenance subcontractor that worked for my father's company, marking the beginning of my journey in the oil patch.

We faced genuine hardship, living with the constant strain of making ends meet. Our financial situation meant we had little choice but to rent the most affordable apartment we could find, an older complex nestled close to our families, where many other young families were also struggling to get by. The sense of community was both a comfort and a reminder that we were not alone in our challenges.

Despite our best efforts to adapt and support one another, the weight of our circumstances sometimes crept into our relationship. We did our utmost to cope with the daily pressures, but inevitably, the stress would surface in the form of uncomfortable disagreements. In those early days, these conflicts were usually brief, but they left us both feeling vulnerable and uncertain. Through it all, we tried to meet each other with patience and understanding, even when we fell short.

The demanding nature of life in the oil patch placed profound constraints not only on my own life but also on the lives of my family members. The relentless schedules, unpredictable hours, and ever-present risks of the job meant that time at home was often scarce and precious. The oil patch demanded a kind of honor and resilience, not just from those who worked in it, but from the families who waited and worried at home.

I could never have anticipated just how profoundly the demands of the oil patch would shape not only my own life, but the very foundation of my marriage and family. At the time, the oilfield wasn't just a job, it was my only real shot at building a future, a path I clung to out of necessity and hope. Yet, the long hours, unpredictable shifts, and constant pressure slowly began to erode the connection between my wife and me. What started as small cracks, missed dinners, forgotten anniversaries, exhaustion that left me numb, grew into a widening gulf. It didn't happen all at once, but looking back, the decline felt both sudden and inevitable.

The truth is, neither of us was prepared for how much we would change, or how the weight of unspoken expectations would pull us apart. We each grew in different directions, shaped by stress, fatigue, and the silent disappointments that come from unmet needs. There were moments when I saw a side of myself, and of my partner, that I'd never seen before: frustration, resentment, and a longing for understanding that neither of us could fully express. We were both searching for something more, but neither was willing, or perhaps able, to bridge the distance that had begun to form between us.

There were nights when I lay awake, torn between the ache of wanting to provide for my family and the guilt of knowing my absence was carving out a hollow space in our home. I felt genuine concern for my wife, who bore the brunt of my absence, and confusion over how something that began with so much hope and caring could unravel into hurt and misunderstanding. I saw her struggle with loneliness and the burden of running the household while I was away, and yet I often felt powerless to change the circumstances. My own independence, once a source of pride, began to feel like selfishness, as if my drive to succeed was coming at the expense of the very people I loved most.

Looking back, I recognize that the strain of this life was not just physical, but emotional and psychological as well. My own immaturity and lack of perspective at the time made it harder to appreciate the depth of my wife's patience and the weight of her concerns. She bore her own burdens, often feeling isolated and unsupported, and she'd begun to blame me for holding back the hands of time, anxious to move forward with the future.

For my part, I truly struggled to balance the demands of work, family, and the ever-present pull of maintaining a social life. I often felt caught in a whirlwind, working hard to provide, yet never quite sure if my efforts were seen or appreciated. There was a persistent ache inside me, a sense that no matter how much I gave, it might never be enough. This uncertainty sometimes left me feeling invisible and misunderstood, and in my confusion and frustration, I found myself blaming my wife for the distance growing between us.

We both clung to our independence, fiercely protecting our own needs and hurts, and in doing so, we built walls instead of bridges. There were times when forgiveness seemed out of reach, when old wounds festered and neither of us could find the words to heal them. Despite our differences, we both genuinely wanted our marriage to succeed. Yet, we hesitated to seek professional counseling. Perhaps it was pride, or perhaps a quiet fear that counseling might not save us but instead hasten the end we were both trying to avoid.

I loved my family with all I had, and the situation at home weighed heavily on me, far more than anyone ever realized. I wasn't the type to reach out for help, not to my parents, not to hers. I kept our troubles private, somehow believing things would work themselves out in time. But the truth is, sometimes love alone isn't enough to mend what's been broken by concern, confusion, hurt, and the stubbornness of two people who cared deeply but didn't know how to forgive or let go. Still, even in the darkest moments, I held onto hope, that somehow, we might find our way back to each other, or at the very least, to a place of understanding and peace.

Even as my marriage was weathering its most difficult storms, the news that my wife was pregnant with our second child brought a surge of genuine concern and cautious hope. The anticipation of a new life entering our family became a fragile thread that helped us set aside our differences, if only for a while. We clung to the possibility that this new beginning might help us rediscover the love and unity we once shared.

Regina was born just before Valentine's Day, a date forever etched in my memory, not only for its symbolism but for the whirlwind of emotions that surrounded her arrival. On the day she was born, my wife had a routine doctor's appointment. Because I was working the day shift, I asked my younger brother Mike to drive her to the doctor's office, trusting him to be there for her when I could not.

When the doctor examined her, he discovered she was already in labor, dilated and unaware. The urgency of the moment was unmistakable. The doctor instructed Mike to take her straight to the hospital, telling him not to hesitate for anything, even to run red lights if needed to get her there safely and in time. Mike called me as soon as they reached the hospital, his voice carrying both excitement and worry.

By the time I caught the next boat to shore and rushed to the hospital, my wife was already on the brink of delivery. The moment I entered the room where she was being monitored, she looked up at me with a mixture of relief and exhaustion and declared that the baby was coming right then. My heart pounded with concern and awe, I quickly stepped into the hallway and called out for a nurse.

The medical team responded with remarkable compassion and efficiency, tossing me a gown as we hurriedly rolled her across the hall to the delivery room. Within five minutes of arriving at the hospital, Regina made her dramatic entrance into the world, and the moment she was safely in her mother's arms was unforgettable and deeply moving.

The first year that followed brought a welcome calm to our marriage, with only the occasional disagreement interrupting what felt like a return to routine. Yet, as we moved into the second year, old patterns began to quietly resurface. The arguments and constant bickering returned, creating an environment that was not only unhealthy for us but especially difficult for our children, who found themselves caught in the crossfire of mounting tension and uncertainty.

It became heartbreakingly clear that the persistent issues between us were not going to resolve on their own. Despite our best intentions and the love we still felt for our family, we both realized that without professional help, we were unable to break free from the cycle of conflict and resentment. However, professional counseling was outside our compromise. We both wanted what was best for our children, and one night, during a particularly heated argument, I made the painful decision for the both of us to separate, for the good of all.

The months that followed were filled with uncertainty and sorrow, but also with a sense of relief that perhaps, in time, healing could begin. We made one last attempt to reconcile, driven by hope and a desire to mend what had been broken. Unfortunately, the core issues that had divided us remained unaddressed, and our efforts, though sincere, were not enough. The reconciliation lasted only a short while before we both accepted that our differences were irreconcilable. In December 1977, our marriage officially ended.

The dissolution of a marriage, especially one involving children, is one of the most difficult experiences a parent can endure. Despite how things may have appeared to others, my greatest concern was always for my kids. I did not want them to grow up in a home overshadowed by conflict and negativity. After much soul-searching, I came to realize that the most loving thing I could do was to step aside, hoping to protect them from the ongoing turmoil and give them a chance at a happier, more peaceful life.

Relationships are shaped by numerous factors, many of which are at times difficult to identify or fully comprehend. This ambiguity often leads to confusion and the development of self-justifications for things said and done, words and actions that, in hindsight, everyone wishes could be taken back. The emotional toll of living through the highs and lows of a love-hate relationship tested me in ways I never anticipated.

As time quickly passed, I observed that their mother moved on and soon remarried. My hope was that her new partner would bring harmony and stability into their lives. My upbringing instilled in me the belief that children should remain with their mother unless she was deemed unfit, and in this situation, there was no question about her fitness as a parent.

I make no excuses for my actions or, at times, my lack thereof. I will not pretend to be proud of any aspect of my failures as a husband and father. The choices I made and the mistakes I committed left lasting impacts on those I care about most. Rather than justifying my behavior or seeking to shift blame, I accept responsibility for the consequences of my actions, acknowledging the pain and disappointment that resulted from my shortcomings in these crucial roles.

Chapter 9
The Oil Patch

No one ever truly forgets their first day stepping into a career that will potentially shape the rest of their life, and I was no exception. My adventure began with a set of instructions that sounded simple enough: catch a crew boat bound for an oil and gas facility in the bustling harbor of Long Beach. As the boat cut through the morning mist, my heart pounded with a cocktail of excitement and nerves. Was I about to embark on a grand adventure, or had I just signed up for a lesson in humility?

Upon arrival, I made my way to the field office, where I was told to wait in an adjacent room until someone came to collect me. There I stood, a rookie in borrowed boots, peering out the window at the organized chaos of the oil patch. Every clang of metal and shout from the yard seemed to echo the question in my mind: "What have I gotten myself into?"

My anxious thoughts were interrupted by the quiet entrance of an elderly gentleman, who closed the door behind him with the kind of stealth that only comes from decades of sneaking up on unsuspecting newcomers.

"First day on the job, son?" he asked, his hands clasped behind his back and a gentle smile on his face. There was a twinkle in his eye that suggested he'd seen more first days than I'd had hot breakfasts. He began to share stories from his own forty-year odyssey in the oil patch, tales of building facilities around the world, from the dusty fields of the Middle East to the wilds of Texas. He spoke with a humility that only comes from a lifetime of hard work, assuring me that, despite the grime and the grit, I'd never find a finer group of people than those in the petroleum industry. I listened with respect, hoping some of his wisdom would rub off on me, preferably before the oil did.

Suddenly, the door burst open with the subtlety of a freight train. In stomped a man who looked like he'd been carved out of a whiskey barrel, 250 pounds of pure intimidation, complete with a beer belly that could have had its own ZIP code. He fixed me with a stare that could curdle milk and barked, "Are you Hayes?" My nerves nearly leapt out the window, but I managed a meek, "Yes sir, I am."

Without missing a beat, he growled, "Come with me."

As I followed him out to his battered old work truck, I couldn't help but wonder if I'd just signed up for an adventure or a disaster. If I didn't have mouths to feed and bills to pay, I might have taken the next boat back to shore and called it a day.

But as soon as we climbed into his truck, the man's demeanor shifted. The gruff exterior melted away, replaced by a sly grin. He introduced himself and confessed that the tough act was just for the benefit of the old man, who, as it turned out, was the company's site construction supervisor. I let out a breath I didn't know I was holding, realizing that in the oil patch, sometimes the scariest monsters are just old hands with a sense of humor and a soft spot for rookies.

And so began my journey, equal parts anxiousness, humility, and the kind of excitement that comes from not knowing whether you're about to strike oil or just get stuck in the mud.

My grand adventure in the oil patch began at the very bottom rung, as the so-called "cellar rat." This was the job reserved for the greenest rookie, and let me tell you, it was a humbling initiation. My daily mission? Scrub every wellhead, pipe, and gadget that managed to get itself slathered in oil, which, as luck would have it, was pretty much everything. By the end of each shift, I looked less like a worker and more like a walking oil slick, a living testament to the phrase "getting your hands dirty."

Cleanliness became a distant dream, and my nightly ritual involved scrubbing myself down with diesel fuel (nobody told us about carcinogens back then) and then attacking the grime with a bar of lava soap. At nineteen, I didn't know much about workplace hazards, but I did know that when the boss barked an order, you jumped, no questions asked, even if you had no clue what you were about to get into.

After months of hard-earned grit and a few close calls with permanent oil stains, I finally graduated from cellar rat to more respectable duties. Suddenly, I was learning the ropes from welders, training as a pipe fitter, and even getting my hands on heavy machinery, skip loaders, cherry pickers, and forklifts. My eagerness to learn didn't go unnoticed. Before long, the crew started calling me a "hand", their way of saying, "You're one of us now." I wore that title with pride, knowing it was earned through sweat, persistence, and a willingness to laugh at myself when things went sideways (which, in the oil patch, was often).

My first taste of overtime came on a Friday evening, a rite of passage for any aspiring oilman. I was put in charge of a skip loader, mixing sand with contaminated drilling fines and loading the whole mess into trailer bins. As dusk settled, a group of seasoned production hands approached, forming a loose half-circle around me. One of them produced a bottle of whiskey and handed it over with a single word: "Drink."

This wasn't a suggestion; it was a commandment. I tried to explain that hard liquor wasn't really my thing, but my protest was met with stone faces. The message was clear: if you wanted to be part of the crew, you had to drink with the crew. Their logic was simple, if you joined in, you were one of them, and you couldn't badmouth anyone without implicating yourself. It was a lesson in camaraderie, commitment, and the peculiar honesty of oilfield brotherhood.

After a moment of tense silence, the group burst out laughing, revealing the unwritten rule: "If you're going to work with us, you're going to drink with us, or you're not going to work here at all." Faced with the reality of bills to pay and mouths to feed, I took the drink. From that moment on, I was in. The work was still tough, the hours still long, but now I was part of the tribe, a little wiser, a little humbler, and a lot more appreciative of the strange, wonderful adventure I'd stumbled into.

And if I ever forgot to laugh at myself, there was always someone nearby to remind me, with a wink, a joke, or a bottle of whiskey passed around at the end of a long, greasy day.

Throughout my time on the job, I made it my mission to pay close attention to every detail, sometimes to the point where my coworkers wondered if I was secretly auditioning for a role as "Inspector Gadget." I dove into learning every aspect of the work, volunteering for overtime whenever it popped up, partly out of ambition and partly because, let's face it, I hadn't yet discovered the joys of a weekend off. Each extra shift was a new adventure, and I was determined to prove myself, even if it meant scrubbing oil stains off my hands that would make a mechanic weep.

About a year in, just as I was starting to think I might finally have figured out which end of the wrench to use, the site construction supervisor, the same wise, soft-spoken gentleman who'd given me a pep talk on day one, pulled me aside. He told me he'd been watching my progress. (No pressure, right?) He said he saw real potential in me, which was both flattering and a little terrifying. The company, he explained, was forming a new team of roustabouts who'd get the chance to train as operators. Then he asked if I was interested.

Was I interested? I nearly tripped over my own boots saying yes, I might have even saluted.

That Monday, I reported to the company's main office at 8:00 a.m. sharp, feeling like I was about to embark on the journey of a lifetime. By midday, I was back at the offshore facility, but this time, everything felt different. Gone was my battered green hard hat, which had seen more diesel fuel than a truck stop restroom. In its place was a shiny new blue company hard hat, a symbol that I'd graduated from "contractor" to "company man." I strutted around like I'd just been knighted, grinning so wide my face hurt. Sure, I was still at the bottom of the company food chain, but now I had a steady paycheck, benefits, and two whole weeks of paid vacation, and I felt like I'd won the lottery.

Of course, I knew I wasn't the most academically gifted guy in the room. If there was a quiz on pipe fittings, I'd probably need a lifeline. But I also knew that hard work and a willingness to learn could take you places. That realization fueled my determination to work twice as hard as anyone else and to keep my sense of humor intact.

The roustabout gang was a motley crew: one foreman and about fifteen roustabouts, each with their own quirks and stories. Our daily tasks ranged from cleaning up minor messes to organizing stacks of casing, drill pipe, and production tubing on the pipe racks. But the real adventure was knowing that, at any moment, we could be called up to fill in as utility or process operators, whenever someone went on vacation, got sick, or decided they'd had enough of the oil patch for one lifetime. It was a wild ride, and I was just grateful to be along for it, learning, laughing, and occasionally wondering if I'd ever get all the oil out of the pores of my skin.

During my time with the company, I had the good fortune to meet a colorful cast of characters on the operations team. Fast-pitch softball games after work weren't just about winning, they were about forging friendships, swapping stories, and, occasionally, discovering who could slide into third base without tearing their pants. Among these folks, the daylight operator, known to all as Sweetpea, stood out as the undisputed guru of the facility's processes. If knowledge were oil, Sweetpea would have been a gusher.

I was hungry to learn, and I knew that if I wanted to climb the ladder from roustabout to permanent operator, I'd need more than just elbow grease, I'd need hands-on experience and a mentor willing to show me the ropes. So, with a mix of humility and a dash of adventure, I approached Sweetpea with a proposal that was equal parts honest and audacious: "If you can keep me off the roustabout gang and teach me your job, I'll gladly do your duties every day of the week." It was a win-win opportunity, he got a break, and I got a crash course in operations. Sweetpea, never one to pass up a good deal (or a good laugh), agreed on the spot.

From then on, Sweetpea would stroll up to my foreman each morning, requesting my help with a grin that said, "Trust me, this is for everyone's benefit." At first, the foreman didn't bat an eye. But as the days rolled by and Sweetpea kept picking me out of the roustabout lineup like a favorite tool from the box, the foreman's eyebrows started to rise. Suspicion brewed, was this favoritism or just a clever workaround? Either way, it was starting to look like I'd found the secret passage in the game of career advancement.

The foreman, to his credit, tried to keep things fair. He encouraged Sweetpea to rotate helpers, hoping to give everyone a shot at learning. But Sweetpea, ever the straight shooter, kept requesting me. This led to a bit of grumbling and a few side-eyes from the crew. The foreman, feeling the heat, took his complaints up the chain of command, but the supervisors shrugged it off, leaving him to sort it out. Sometimes, the adventure of the workplace isn't just in the work, it's in the politics.

Eventually, the foreman filed a formal complaint with the construction superintendent, the very person who'd hired me. One Friday, just before lunch (because, of course, these things always happen before lunch), Sweetpea delivered a message: I was wanted at the main office. My heart pounded with a mix of excitement and dread. Was this the end of my grand experiment, or just another plot twist?

At the office, the superintendent greeted me with a handshake and a smile that hinted he already knew the punchline. He explained the complaints but quickly added that the operations department had nothing but praise for my work. After chatting with Sweetpea, he'd uncovered my little scheme, and, to my relief, he admired it. "I wish I had fifteen roustabouts with your drive and work ethic," he said, grinning. Then, in a move that felt like winning the workplace lottery, he gave me the rest of the day off, with pay.

Before I left, he offered a final bit of wisdom: "On Monday, share the learning with the other roustabouts, everyone deserves a shot." He assured me not to worry about the complaints, he'd handle it. That day, I learned that honesty, integrity, and a willingness to take calculated risks can open doors you never knew existed. Sometimes, the best adventures at work come from thinking outside the box, owning your choices, and keeping your sense of humor, even when the stakes feel high.

Looking back, I couldn't help but smile at the whole episode. It was a little bit of mischief, a lot of initiative, and a reminder that the path to growth is rarely a straight line. Sometimes, you just have to pitch your idea, swing for the fences, and trust that, with a little humility and a lot of heart, you'll land on your feet, maybe even with a day off to celebrate.

Four months after embracing this bold new approach, I was rewarded with my first promotion to Utility Operator within the operations department. This wasn't just a title, it was a testament to the honesty and integrity I brought to my work, and to the trust I'd earned from my supervisors and peers. Reporting directly to the production supervisor and working a rotating shift schedule, I dove into my new responsibilities with humility and a sense of adventure. Managing the mixing and inventory of the mud plant, overseeing the transfer of drilling and production rig fluids, and coordinating the movement of equipment in and out of the rigs, all of these tasks offered hands-on experience that deepened my understanding of the operational heartbeat of the site. Each day was a new challenge, and I approached every one with passion and excitement, eager to learn and contribute.

Six months later, driven by a relentless desire to grow and fueled by the excitement of mastering new skills, I advanced to the role of Production Operator. Like the Utility Operator, this position reported to a production supervisor and required me to adapt to the ever-changing rhythm of a rotating shift environment. The primary responsibility, ensuring that all production processes at the site were conducted in the most optimal and efficient manner, was both daunting and exhilarating. Although both roles offered the same wage and demanded teamwork and mutual support, I found the Production Operator position far more fulfilling. Here, I could directly influence process optimization and operational efficiency, making a tangible impact that resonated with my professional passions and personal values.

Yet working a rotating shift was not without its sacrifices. The unpredictable hours and constant changes in schedule tested not only my resilience but also the patience and adaptability of my family and friends. It was a humbling reminder that the pursuit of adventure and professional growth often comes with real costs. Medical professionals have long warned that those who work rotating shifts may face a shorter life expectancy, by as much as seven years, and are more likely to develop various health conditions as a result of this demanding work pattern. Still, I faced these hardships with honesty and steadfast commitment, never shying away from the truth of what was required.

No matter the occasion, birthdays, anniversaries, weddings, or holidays, if duty called, I showed up. Integrity meant honoring my commitments, even when it meant missing out on life's milestones. If the person scheduled to relieve me failed to appear, I shouldered the responsibility, working an additional eight-hour shift without complaint. The need for extra income was always present, and whenever an opportunity for overtime arose, I seized it, driven by both necessity and the excitement of rising to the challenge.

The rotational schedule itself was a rigorous test of endurance and adaptability: seven consecutive eight-hour day shifts, followed by two days off; then seven straight eight-hour swing shifts, another two days off; and finally, seven eight-hour graveyard shifts, capped by three days off before the cycle began anew. This relentless rotation demanded not just physical stamina, but humility and mental fortitude from everyone involved. Through it all, I remained passionate about my work, honest about its challenges, and grateful for the adventure that each new day brought.

I worked alongside a remarkable group of men who, despite their rough and untamed nature, took immense pride in their craft. Their commitment to the job was unwavering; every day, they put in hard work and dedicated themselves to getting the job done well. Yet, for all their grit and skill, there was an undercurrent of something darker, a tendency to push themselves past the edge, as if proving their toughness required not just endurance on the job, but a willingness to court self-destruction after hours. I saw it in myself, too, though I rarely admitted it at the time.

Their intensity on the job was matched by their enthusiasm for letting loose once the workday was over. After a long and demanding shift, the party would begin the moment we set foot in the parking lot. Bottles of whiskey were passed around, marking the transition from a day of labor to an evening of reckless celebration. Once the bottles ran dry, the group would move on to a local watering hole to keep the festivities going well into the night.

There were occasions when the drive home felt like a wild roller coaster ride, especially with the influence of the party still lingering. At times, the mix included not just alcohol but also marijuana and speed, which some used to maintain their stamina. I wasn't immune to these temptations. While I enjoyed the celebratory atmosphere that followed a hard day's work, more often than not, I found myself leaving the party early and heading home rather than lingering with the group, at least during my initial days on the job. But as time wore on, the line between discipline and indulgence blurred.

The men I worked with were a rugged and resilient bunch, yet beneath their rough exteriors was a genuine concern for one another. Regardless of how someone felt, whether they were sick, suffering from a hangover, or physically exhausted from putting in sixteen-hour shifts day after day, the expectation was simple: you showed up to work.

Attendance was a non-negotiable part of the culture, and being present meant that you could rely on your coworkers to support you through whatever challenges you faced. This sense of mutual responsibility was an unspoken rule, and it fostered a strong bond among the crew. But it also meant that no one talked about the toll our lifestyle was taking on us, or the ways we were quietly unraveling.

The oil patch lifestyle demanded resilience, sacrifice, and a commitment to both the job and the team, and these values shaped the way we worked and lived every day. Yet, looking back, I can see how easily those same values became excuses for ignoring our own well-being, for masking pain with bravado, and for letting self-destruction masquerade as strength.

During my time in the oil patch, I forged many strong relationships with my coworkers, each of whom had their own unique personality and background. Some of the men I worked with found enjoyment in outdoor sports, while others had grown up frequently getting into and out of trouble, a quality that, in some ways, made it easier for them to fit in with the more rough-around-the-edges, redneck side of oilfield life.

I admired their resilience, but I also recognized a familiar restlessness in them, a hunger for escape that mirrored my own. The diversity of personalities and life experiences among my colleagues created a dynamic and lively work environment. Those who enjoyed outdoor sports often brought stories of their latest fishing or hunting trip to share during breaks, their enthusiasm for the outdoors providing a welcome distraction from the rigors of the job.

On the other hand, coworkers who had a history of getting into trouble seemed to adapt naturally to the unrefined, sometimes chaotic atmosphere that characterized our daily routines. Their resilience and street smarts helped them navigate the unpredictable nature of oilfield work, and their knack for handling difficult situations made them valuable members of the team. But for all our differences, we shared a common vulnerability, a tendency to hide our struggles behind humor, hard work, and the next round of drinks.

To give a sense of the type of characters I'm trying to describe, I recall one particular night that stands out in my memory. After finishing a swing shift, four of us decided to stop at a well-known combination café and bar in the Harbor of Long Beach. This place was famous for attracting both longshoremen and oilfield workers, a mix that was known to be combustible at times.

We took our seats at the end of the bar and ordered beers. The bar itself had a unique shape, and as it turned a corner, there sat a group of four longshoremen. These men were loudly boasting about their toughness and the rugged nature of their work, speaking with such bravado that it was clear their remarks were meant for our ears.

Sitting next to one of the longshoremen was my friend Bob. Bob had a reputation that could have earned him the nickname "Rocky", he was big and solid, strong as an ox, yet surprisingly agile. He became noticeably quiet, which was a sign that he was deep in thought, a state that was rarely a good omen.

Bob turned to the man beside him and said, "You boys think because you're longshoremen, you're pretty tough." The longshoreman responded without hesitation, "Tough enough to kick your ass."

In a flash, and while still seated, Bob doubled his fist and delivered a punch so forceful that it knocked the man off his stool. As the longshoreman struggled to regain his footing, his back hit the wall a couple of feet behind him. Bob, being swift on his feet, was already landing bone-crunching punches to his midsection as he drove that man to the ground. It was clear the man was badly hurt, as he lay in a puddle of his own stomach fluids and piss.

Then Bob quickly reeled around to the other three men and said, "Who's next?" The three men replied, "Hey, mister, we don't want any trouble with you," to which Bob said, "Then get your buddy and yourselves out of our bar and don't come back." They immediately grabbed their friend and left. It all happened so quickly that not one of the three of us had time to get off of our own chairs, just in case we were needed.

I left the bar that night with a sense of unease, knowing that the line between camaraderie and chaos was thinner than any of us cared to admit. As I drove home, the echoes of bravado faded, replaced by the quiet realization that, for all our strength, we were still vulnerable to the choices we made, and the damage we sometimes did to ourselves along the way.

In the middle of after-work follies and my advancing career, I also experienced an unfortunate setback in life called divorce, which deeply soured an internal part of me. I was unprepared for the reality of fighting for my rights as a father. Ultimately, I was granted visitation only twice a month. Scheduling proved to be a constant challenge, as my work allowed me just one weekend off each month.

If my free weekend didn't align with my designated visitation, my ex-wife was unwilling to trade weekends, resulting in long stretches, sometimes months, when I was unable to see my children at all. Each missed visit felt like a fresh humiliation, a reminder of how powerless I was to protect my place in their lives. Sadly, the dysfunction that had plagued our marriage continued into our lives as divorcees. Our relationship remained strained and uncooperative, as challenging and chaotic as it had been during our marriage.

During this turbulent period, I allowed myself to spiral into self-destructive habits. The pain and disappointment stemming from the end of my marriage and the growing distance from my children weighed heavily on me, and instead of confronting these emotions directly, I numbed myself in every way I could. I drank too much, stayed out too late, and surrounded myself with people who were just as lost as I was, misery loves company.

There were nights I'd close down the bar, stumbling home in a fog, only to wake up the next morning with a pounding head and a heart full of regret. I refused to let anyone in my life help, convinced that I deserved the loneliness I felt. The humiliation of knowing I had failed as a husband didn't hurt half as much as knowing I was on a fast track to failure as a father. It was a constant ache, one I tried to drown with every reckless choice.

I purchased a used Harley, and that bike became more than just a means of transportation, it was my escape. I rode it everywhere, regardless of the weather, sometimes pushing through rain or cold simply because the open road felt like the only place I could breathe. Each mile was a way to outrun the gnawing sense of failure I carried in my personal life.

The long, grueling hours in the oil patch had begun to harden me, awakening a rugged, redneck side that seemed to blend seamlessly with my lingering, biker-friendly, hippie disposition.

I became someone I barely recognized, tougher, yes, but also more closed off, less willing to let anyone see the cracks beneath the surface. I never sought out conflict, but I was no longer the type to back down from it either. Time blurred; days melted into weeks, weeks into months, and sometimes it felt as if the years themselves were slipping away, lost in a haze of routine and regret.

When I wasn't working, I drifted through my free time in a fog of self-destruction. Most nights, I was either high, drunk, or both, using whatever I could to dull the ache that gnawed at me from the inside out. The biker bars became my sanctuary away from work, places where I could shoot pool and blend in with others who were also running from their own pain.

There was an unspoken humility in those rooms, a silent agreement that no one would ask questions, no one would judge. We were all just trying to survive in our own way, each of us quietly nursing wounds we didn't have the words or the courage to share.

On the rare occasions I found myself in a nightclub, I became a master of disguise, adept at navigating the subtle games of deception that played out in those dimly lit corners. I learned to blend in, to keep up appearances, to engage with others as skillfully as anyone else. But beneath the surface, I was hollowed out by my own choices.

I made a conscious decision not to seek out or pursue any deep or meaningful connections. I was steadfast in my resolve that I would never let myself be vulnerable again, never risk the pain of caring too much. The failures of my past had left me convinced that I was better off alone, and I wore that isolation like a badge of honor, a bitter kind of humility that came from knowing just how much I had lost.

During that period, I was surrounded by people who had easy access to every kind of drug imaginable. Many of these connections were through friends-of-friends, most of whom are likely no longer alive. Back then, it seemed as if the supply was endless, marijuana, cocaine, speed, whatever you wanted, you could find it.

If I ever wanted anything, it was never a problem. Yet I also knew people who desperately wanted to get their hands on these drugs but couldn't. The contrast was stark, and it only deepened my sense of detachment from the world around me. I was both an insider and an outsider, drifting through a scene that was as destructive as it was seductive.

Some memories from those years remain vivid, etched into my mind as cautionary tales. I remember one night, sitting at a table, staring at a tray with a massive ball of high-quality Peruvian flake cocaine, easily the size of a softball. On another occasion, I visited a house where fifty kilos of top-grade marijuana were stacked behind the couch, an almost surreal sight. There were acquaintances who claimed they had direct connections to sources for uncut speed, underscoring just how prevalent and accessible these substances had become in that chapter of my life.

Looking back, I see now how lost I was, how humility, in those days, meant recognizing the depths to which I had sunk, and how far I still had to go to find my way back. But I still had one ace up my sleeve, known as work.

Despite the darkness my personal life experienced, work had also become my sanctuary, a place where, amid personal turmoil, I could anchor myself in the dignity of honest effort. Each day, I approached my responsibilities with humility, recognizing that mastery was not a destination but a journey. I took on every assignment offered, not out of ambition alone, but from a growing sense of self-respect.

I slowly began to pick myself up off the floor and dust my britches off. I began to clean myself up, stopped doing drugs (except on occasion), and proved to myself that I was worthwhile, that I could be counted on, no matter the challenge. My willingness to fill in for supervisors, to step up when needed, was not just about reliability, it was about discovering my own capacity for growth and resilience.

By 1980, my dedication was rewarded with a promotion to production supervisor, the youngest in the company to hold that title. It was a moment of pride, but also of humility. I understood that leadership was not about wielding authority, but about serving others with integrity and respect. The generous benefits and vacation time were symbols of success, yet I soon realized that true fulfillment could not be measured by titles or paychecks alone.

The relentless demands of the rotating shift schedule continued to exact a personal cost. I missed moments with my children, birthdays, milestones, the quiet joys of family life. Despite outward achievements, I felt an ache inside, a sense that I was sacrificing what mattered most for the sake of professional validation. This realization humbled me, forcing me to confront the gap between the life I was living and the life I thought I wanted.

After fourteen years, as I reached my early thirties, the workplace itself began to change. The energy that once made each day an adventure faded, replaced by routine and obligation. I found myself drifting, the excitement of new challenges replaced by the monotony of repetition. For someone who thrived on purpose and discovery, this was a wake-up call. I began to reflect deeply on my path, questioning whether I was living up to my own potential or simply coasting on past accomplishments.

In this period of introspection, I forced myself to look honestly at my future. I imagined myself decades later, overweight, balding, sitting behind the same desk, performing the same tasks. The vision was sobering. I realized that security, while comforting, could also become a cage. I yearned for freedom, for the chance to test myself in new ways, to rediscover the sense of adventure that had once defined me. My self-respect began to rise, not as arrogance, but as a quiet confidence that I could shape my own destiny if I had the courage to try.

When the oil and gas industry slumped in 1986, my company offered a "golden handshake", an early retirement package meant for those at the end of their careers. Though I was young, I met the requirements. The offer was both a risk and an opportunity: a chance to step away from the familiar and leap into the unknown. The decision was not easy. My employer, friends, and family urged caution, warning me not to throw away a secure future. Their concern was rooted in love, but I knew in my heart that regret would haunt me more than failure ever could.

With humility, I listened to their advice but ultimately chose to trust my instincts. My decision came not as an escape, but as an act of self-discovery, a commitment to honor my own journey, to seek out new challenges, and to grow beyond the boundaries I had once accepted. It was a leap of faith, fueled by the dignity of knowing that life's greatest adventures often begin when we dare to step through an open door. In July 1986, I accepted the golden handshake and said goodbye to the company, determined to set out in search of a new and exciting beginning.

Chapter 10
Strange Tales

The issues and impact of my first failing marriage, combined with my experiences working in the oil patch, along with alcohol and drugs, spilled over into every part of my life. As these challenges mounted, I began to notice strange occurrences unfolding around me, a reflection of just how deeply these struggles affected my entire world. In sharing these memoirs, I have had to reach deep into my soul and confront the demons I wrestled with, acknowledging the turmoil I contributed to during those years.

Yet, as I look back, what stands out most is the profound sense of humility that emerged from these hardships. Each setback, each moment of pain, stripped away layers of pride and forced me to recognize my own limitations and vulnerabilities. I came to understand that I was not immune to failure, nor was I above making mistakes that hurt those I cared about. This realization was both sobering and transformative. It taught me to approach my life, and the stories I share, not from a place of self-justification, but from a place of honest reflection and acceptance.

Humility became the lens through which I could finally see the truth of my journey: that growth often comes not from our triumphs, but from our willingness to admit our faults, learn from our missteps, and seek forgiveness, from others and from ourselves. In writing these words, I do so with a spirit of humility, hoping that by exposing my own struggles and shortcomings, I might offer understanding, connection, and perhaps even a measure of comfort to others who find themselves facing similar battles.

The following stories are all true, and I have done my best to interpret them with humility and a little lighthearted humor.

The Night I Outran Trouble: A Road Rage Tale

Some stories in life sneak up on you, like a pothole you don't see until it's too late. This one started on a warm summer night, when I left work in a hurry, eager to get home and put my feet up. The city air was thick with the scent of cut grass and distant barbecue, and I was feeling that familiar mix of exhaustion and impatience that comes after working a double shift.

As I pulled up behind a couple of cars at a stoplight, I was already rehearsing my late evening plans in my head, until the light turned green and the car in front of me, a gleaming 1956 Chevy, decided to take the world's slowest right turn. I mean, this guy was moving so cautiously, I half-expected him to get out and check the crosswalk for snails. My own frustration started to bubble up, but I kept my cool, at least outwardly.

When the turn was finally complete, I saw my chance and zipped around him, only to catch a glimpse of the driver: a mountain of a man, so tall he had to tilt his head to avoid the Chevy's roof. He looked like he could bench-press my car, and he was glaring at me with a fury that could melt chrome. To my surprise, he started waving his middle finger with the kind of gusto usually reserved for auctioneers. I'll admit, I'd rolled up a little fast at the light, but I'd left plenty of space, no harm, no foul, right?

Apparently not. His anger was dialed up to eleven, and I could feel my own irritation rising to meet his. In a moment of honest (and, in hindsight, ill-advised) provocation, I rolled down my window and gave him a look that said, "Really?" Maybe I even smirked. That was all the invitation he needed. He sped up, pulled alongside me, and started gesturing for me to pull over, mouthing threats that would make a sailor blush. My frustration turned to a mix of caution and surprise, this was escalating fast.

We raced down the boulevard, two grown men acting like teenagers in a Fast & Furious audition. When we hit the red light at Cherry Beach, I stopped, heart pounding. He pulled up next to me, still seething, and began wrestling with his door. It took him a moment, apparently, even rage can't defeat a stubborn Chevy door, but he finally managed to force it open and step out. He was even bigger standing up, towering over his car like a linebacker on a mission, glaring at me with the clear intent to rearrange my face.

I watched as he started running around his car, never taking an eye off me, and when he turned the corner between our two vehicles, humility (and a healthy dose of self-preservation) kicked in. I realized that whatever point I thought I was making, it wasn't worth a trip to the ER. So, with a burst of lighthearted humor only visible in hindsight, I floored it, ran the red light, and sped away at nearly 100 mph, leaving the angry giant standing in the middle of the street, shaking his middle finger and probably wondering what just happened.

I never saw him again, but I like to think he tells the story of the night he almost taught a lesson to a guy in a hurry, only to be left in a cloud of dust and a punchline about the one that got away. Sometimes, the best way to win a fight is to know when to drive off and live to laugh about it later.

A Mystical Morning: An Encounter with Fate and Compassion

My wife's love for antiques was more than a hobby, it was a gentle ritual that brought us together, weekend after weekend, as we wandered through the antique shops of Orange. Each outing was a small adventure, a shared search for treasures that carried the weight of other people's stories. Sometimes we'd find a glass door handle, sometimes a clock or a table, but always, we found a moment of connection, something to remind us that beauty often hides in the overlooked corners of the world.

One early Saturday, I took our four-year-old son, Jeremy, with me on one of these treasure hunts. I was searching for a birthday gift for my wife, hoping to find something that would light up her eyes and remind her of the joy we found in these simple journeys together.

On the drive home, the day took an unexpected turn. A sharp thump echoed beneath us, a nail in the tire. I pulled off the road, only to discover the car's jack was missing. Stranded, I felt a wave of frustration, but also a strange calm. Across the street, a small strip mall beckoned. I took Jeremy's hand, and together we walked over to find a pay phone. My first call home was met with silence, a reminder that even in family, there are days when words are hard to find. I called a friend, who promised to come help, but it would be forty minutes before he arrived.

With time to fill and a restless child, I bought Jeremy a soft drink in a small food joint. When we stepped outside, the air was suddenly charged, a commotion at the far end of the parking lot drew my attention. Raised voices, a crowd, and the unmistakable tension of something gone wrong.

Curiosity and concern pulled me closer. I saw an old man pressing a younger man against a truck, a knife at the young man's throat. The crowd watched, frozen by fear and uncertainty. In that moment, something extraordinary happened. A surge of energy coursed through me, from the crown of my head to the soles of my feet. The world seemed to glow with a blinding brightness, yet my vision was clearer than ever. I felt as if I could see into the hearts of everyone present, as if some unseen force had awakened a deeper awareness within me.

With humility and a sense of awe, I led Jeremy to a sturdy pillar and knelt beside him. "Stay here," I whispered. "I'll be right back." Guided by something beyond myself, I walked into the center of the parking lot, placing myself between the old man and his would-be victim. Without thinking, my voice erupted, loud, commanding, yet filled with compassion. I spoke not just to the old man, but to everyone: "Whatever happened, it's not worth taking a life."

The words were short, but the effect was immediate. The crowd fell silent. The old man's grip loosened, and the young man slid to the ground, hands clasped in gratitude, as if in prayer. Relief and humility washed over me as he thanked me for intervening. In that moment, I felt the invisible threads that bind us all, fear, hope, the longing for peace, woven together in a tapestry of shared humanity.

Then, as quickly as it had come, the energy surged from my body. My legs trembled, and I felt utterly drained, as if the spirit that had moved through me had returned to wherever it came from. I gathered Jeremy, who looked up at me with wide, trusting eyes, and we walked back to the car. The crowd watched us go, their faces a mix of wonder and disbelief. My friend arrived soon after, jack in hand, and helped me fix the tire. As we drove home, I felt a quiet gratitude, for the safety of my son, for the kindness of a friend, and for the mysterious grace that had allowed me to be present, truly present, in a moment that could have ended so differently.

I am humbled by the experience. I do not claim to understand what moved through me that day, whether it was fate, faith, or simply the deep well of compassion that lives in all of us, waiting for the right moment to rise. What I do know is that we are all capable of extraordinary acts when we let go of fear and open ourselves to the needs of others. Sometimes, the most mystical moments are those that call us to act with honesty, humility, and love, even when we least expect it.

A Surreal Evening and Out of Body Experience

One evening, after finishing my swing shift, I found myself sitting in the parking lot, the weight of my dysfunctional marriage pressing down on me like a heavy fog. My friend and I, trying to shake off the day's burdens, shared a doobie and let music fill the silence between us. Yet beneath the surface, anxiety simmered, a gnawing sense of despair that no amount of laughter or smoke could truly dispel. As the music faded and my friend left, I felt an urgent need for solitude, to untangle the worries that had become knotted in my mind.

Instead of heading home by my usual route, I chose the long way, as if fate itself were nudging me toward something unknown. The streets of Belmont Shores slipped by, familiar yet distant, and

I soon found myself on Westminster, and finally on the lonely stretch past the bunkers at Los Alamitos Naval Shipyard. It was here that the world shifted: a dense, almost mystical fog rolled in, swallowing the road and reducing visibility to less than thirty feet. The surreal quality of the night mirrored my inner turmoil, each mile a slow crawl through both literal and figurative haze.

As I drove, my thoughts spiraled. Worry and despair mingled with a sense of wonder at how life could become so tangled, so uncertain. The fog pressed in, and with it, my foot unconsciously pressed harder on the gas pedal. Soon, I was barreling down the highway at nearly 120 miles per hour, utterly blind to what lay ahead. The only thing visible was a blurred white line at the edge of my left headlight, a thin tether to reality. In that moment, anxiety gave way to a strange surrender. The risk didn't seem to matter; the combination of emotional chaos and the night's surreal atmosphere propelled me forward, faster and faster, into the unknown.

Then, as if time itself bent to the moment, everything slowed. The world moved in slow motion, and amid the chaos, a voice, calm, reassuring, almost mystical, echoed in my mind: "Don't worry. Everything will be alright." The despair that had gripped me was suddenly replaced by a profound sense of tranquility, as if fate had intervened. Instinctively, my foot eased off the accelerator, and the car slowed to a safe speed. The fog began to lift, and clarity returned, both on the road and within myself. I finished the drive home in a state of quiet awe, reflecting on how close I had come to disaster and how, by some mysterious force, I had been guided safely through.

When I finally arrived home, the house was dark and silent, a stark contrast to the storm of emotions inside me. I moved through the motions: a simple meal, a long, hot shower, each act an attempt to wash away the residue of anxiety and despair. Yet, as I lay in bed, staring at the ceiling, the night's events replayed in my mind with vivid intensity. The fog, the speed, the voice, the sense of fate and the mystical, each detail shimmered with meaning, begging for reflection.

Then, something extraordinary happened. A subtle tingling began in my feet, like an electric current, and quickly surged upward, enveloping my entire body. In an instant, I was no longer in my body, I was floating above the bed, gazing down at myself and my wife. The scene was both unsettling and strangely peaceful, as if I had crossed into a realm where the boundaries between mind and body, between the real and the surreal, no longer applied. I was filled with wonder and a sense of mystical possibility, yet also a deep worry: what if I could not return?

As I hovered near the ceiling, I realized that this part of me was unbound, able to travel anywhere with just a thought, while my physical body lay rigid and anxious below. It was a surreal tug-of-war between freedom and restraint, between the desire to escape and the longing to be whole again. Despair threatened to creep in, but so did a sense of awe at the strangeness of the experience.

Desperately, I focused all my energy on returning to myself, willing even the smallest movement or sound to bridge the gap. Suddenly, as the struggle reached its peak, I felt my voice erupt in a scream, a sound that, to my wife, was just a squeak, but to me, was the roar of consciousness snapping back into place. She rolled over, concern etched on her face, and asked if I was all right. I nodded, still shaken, the memory of the out-of-body experience lingering like a dream that refuses to fade.

In the days and years that followed, I reflected deeply on what had happened. Was it fate, a mystical intervention, or simply the mind's way of coping with overwhelming anxiety and despair? The experience left me with more questions than answers, but also with a renewed sense of wonder at the mysteries of existence. I became more committed than ever to caring for my physical and mental well-being, finding solace in yoga stretches, running along the perimeter of the park, and the simple rituals that grounded me in the present. The night of the fog became a turning point, a moment when anxiety, despair, and worry gave way to wonder, reflection, and the enduring belief that even in our darkest hours, something greater may be guiding us through.

The Swiss Alps to Paris and a Dash of Magic

Despite the chaos that often surrounded my life, there was another side of my personality that stood in sharp contrast. I have always firmly believed in the strong connection between physical health and mental well-being. This conviction led me to make regular exercise and self-care a top priority. At home, I dedicated time to yoga stretches, which not only improved my flexibility but also provided a sense of calm and relaxation. Occasionally, I would go jogging, sometimes around the perimeter of the park, other times along the beach, covering anywhere from a mile to three miles. These runs offered both a physical challenge and a peaceful escape, allowing me to enjoy the outdoors while supporting my overall well-being.

To maintain a consistent approach to my health and well-being, I made a firm commitment to my fitness routine by joining a gym. I set a goal to attend every other day, and over time, this routine became almost second nature, something I followed with near-religious dedication. My workouts were structured and efficient, each session lasting exactly sixty minutes. This discipline not only helped me build and maintain a toned physique, but also instilled a sense of accomplishment and routine in my daily life.

Beyond the gym, I discovered a deep sense of peace and renewal through snow skiing during the winter months. There was something uniquely calming about gliding silently over fresh snow, surrounded by the quiet beauty of winter landscapes. Skiing became more than just a physical activity; it was a form of meditation that helped me restore balance and reinforced my belief that caring for the body is essential to nurturing the mind.

A few years into this journey, some colleagues from work invited me to join them on a ski trip to Switzerland. Although the cost was more than I could afford at the time, I recognized the value of the experience and decided to seize the opportunity. To make it possible, I took out a small loan, viewing it as an investment in both adventure and personal growth. The trip turned out to be unforgettable, offering not only the thrill of skiing in the Swiss Alps but also the chance to deepen friendships and create lasting memories.

Our adventure began with a flight to Geneva, but the real magic started when we boarded a bus bound for Zermatt, a town so snug beneath the mighty Matterhorn that it felt like we'd stumbled into a snow globe. Our home for the next four days was a charming little chalet, the kind of place where you half expect to find a yodeling goat in the lobby. Zermatt, in its quirky wisdom, had banished cars and buses from its streets, so the only way to get around was by foot, ski, or the town's silent electric carts that zipped luggage from the edge of town to the hotels. The result? A peaceful, invigorating atmosphere where the only traffic jam was a flock of skiers crossing the street, and the only honking came from the occasional overexcited tourist.

We spent our days carving up the legendary Gornegrat slopes, laughing at our own wipeouts, and soaking in the kind of alpine beauty that makes you believe in fairy tales. Evenings were for wandering the picturesque streets, where the air was crisp, the fondue was hot, and the sense of camaraderie among travelers was as warm as the chalet's fireplace.

Although it wasn't more than a young man's dream, I secretly hoped that I would meet a "Swiss Miss" on the slopes or perhaps in one of those cozy mountain pubs over a steaming mug of glühwein. The Swiss Alps, with their crisp air and postcard-perfect scenery, seemed to promise adventure at every turn. One beautiful day, as I was carving my way down the powdery slopes, feeling like a cross between James Bond and a slightly less coordinated St. Bernard, I suddenly found myself entangled with another skier. In a flurry of skis, poles, and laughter, we tumbled together, twisting and turning until we finally rolled to a stop in a heap of snow.

As I brushed the snow from my face, I looked up and found myself staring into the eyes of the most attractive woman I'd ever seen, her smile as bright as the Alpine sun. Just as I was about to muster my best "international man of mystery" introduction, she beat me to it, speaking up in the clearest, unmistakable American English: "We're going to have to stop meeting like this." For a split second, I was caught between the thrill of the moment and the comic realization that, of all the people to crash into in Switzerland, I'd managed to find another American. So much for my dreams of a Swiss romance!

Still, there was something wonderfully human and humbling about the encounter. Here we were, two strangers from the same country, colliding halfway across the world, sharing a laugh in the snow. I helped her up, found her skis, and apologized with as much dignity as a man can muster when he's just been bested by gravity and fate. As I skied away, I couldn't help but chuckle at the irony. Of all the women to run into in Switzerland, it had to be an American. I didn't even invite her for an apology drink, though in hindsight, maybe I should have. But that's the thing about adventure: sometimes it's not about finding what you're looking for, but about embracing the unexpected, laughing at yourself, and collecting stories that remind you how delightfully unpredictable life can be.

But the adventure didn't end in Switzerland. When our ski escapade wrapped up, a couple of friends proposed we keep the fun rolling by hopping a "milk train" to Paris, with stops in Monte Carlo and Nice for good measure. Who could say no to that? We were off, chasing the horizon with the kind of reckless optimism only travel can inspire.

Paris greeted us with its usual flair, a city of lights, history, and the ever-present possibility of the unexpected. We checked into a budget-friendly hotel (the kind where the elevator is smaller than your suitcase and you have to decide whether to send your luggage up first or yourself), then set out to conquer the city's greatest hits: the Louvre, the Eiffel Tower, Sacré-Coeur, Notre-Dame, and the Arc de Triomphe. We crammed centuries of art, architecture, and culture into two whirlwind days, our feet sore but our spirits soaring.

On a cold, overcast Parisian day, as we strolled toward the Eiffel Tower, the story took a turn for the mystic. Amid the bustle of window shoppers and street performers, I noticed a little old man, dressed in rags, crouched against a building. He wasn't begging or causing a scene, just quietly existing on the margins, as if he were part of the city's ancient stonework. Our eyes met, and in that instant, he sprang up with surprising agility. He reached into his pocket, pulled out something I couldn't see, and approached me, speaking rapid-fire French and offering a handshake.

Instinctively, I clutched my camera case, unsure if I was about to be blessed, bamboozled, or perhaps recruited into a secret society of Parisian street magicians. But the old man wasn't after my camera or my wallet. Seeing my hesitation, he revealed a coin, a French Franc. He pressed it into my hand, insisting, "It's for you, it's for you," according to my friend who spoke a bit of French. I tried to refuse, feeling awkward about taking money from someone who looked like he needed it far more than I did. But before I could protest, he placed the coin on my camera case and vanished, no alleys, no side streets, just gone, as if he'd stepped through a hidden door in the Parisian mist.

My friends and I stood there, bemused and a little mystified, wondering if we'd just been touched by a bit of Parisian magic. Was he a guardian angel in disguise, a philosopher with a flair for dramatic exits, or simply a man who found joy in surprising strangers? I tucked the coin into my wallet as a token of good luck, a reminder that sometimes the universe sends you gifts in the most unexpected ways, often wrapped in humility, humanity, and a dash of mystery. And if you ever find yourself in Paris, keep your eyes open. You never know when a little old man might appear, ready to remind you that kindness, and a sense of humor, can be the greatest souvenirs of all.

Our journey continued to Monte Carlo, where the famed Royal Casino beckoned. Lady Luck, perhaps still smiling from that

Parisian encounter, was on my side: I won $400 at the tables, enough to keep the adventure rolling and to add a little swagger to our step as we made our way to Nice and, eventually, home.

Looking back, it wasn't just the places we visited or the sights we saw that made the trip unforgettable. It was the laughter shared on snowy slopes, the kindness of strangers, the humility of accepting a gift you don't understand, and the sense that, just maybe, there's a little magic waiting for all of us, if we're willing to look up from our maps and meet the world with open eyes and an open heart.

The Swiss Franc and Mystic Fortune Teller

A couple of weeks after I returned home, I was in the kitchen when the wall phone rang. In that instant, my sister Kaye's face flashed before my eyes and disappeared just as quickly. Somehow, I instinctively knew it was her calling. We hadn't spoken in months, so I had no logical reason to expect her call, unless, of course, you count sibling telepathy as a valid explanation. Nevertheless, when I picked up the phone, I greeted her immediately: "Hello, Kaye, how are you?"

There was a moment of dead silence on the other end until she stuttered in surprise, "How did you know it was me?" I explained, as honestly as I could, that I'd seen a glimpse of her face flash before me as the phone rang and simply knew she was reaching out. Sometimes, life gives you a nudge from the universe, or maybe it's just a trick of the mind, but either way, it keeps things interesting.

During our conversation, I shared stories about my recent trip to Switzerland and the unusual encounter with the old man in Paris. From that moment onward, Kaye became determined to persuade me to visit her Palm Reader. Now, in principle, I've always been a bit skeptical of people who make a living reading palms, tea leaves, or the occasional unlucky chicken bone. But Kaye was relentless. She lobbied harder than a politician before election day, and after much persistence (and perhaps a little sibling guilt),

I eventually gave in and agreed to set a date for the following Saturday.

When Saturday finally arrived, Kaye and I set out together to visit her Palm Reader. I was surprised to discover that her chosen psychic was located on Beach Boulevard, not far from the railroad tracks and within shouting distance of Knott's Berry Farm. We found a parking spot, made our way to the entrance, and rang the bell. It wasn't long before a woman answered, asking about the reason for our visit.

We explained that we were interested in getting a reading. The woman invited us inside, leading us into a spacious room furnished with several comfortable chairs arranged beneath a large altar. She directed us to take a seat and assured us she would return shortly. After a few minutes, she reappeared, now dressed in a colorful outfit that lent a sense of ceremony to the occasion. Taking her place at the altar, she began the session by asking what type of reading we were seeking, setting the stage for what would become a memorable and unusual experience.

Curious about the significance of the coin I had received in Paris, I produced it during our session and asked whether her psychic abilities could reveal anything special about it. She descended from her altar, carefully holding the coin up to the light for examination. After a moment of study, she identified it as a French Franc. I found her response amusing and acknowledged that we already knew its denomination, but pressed her to share any deeper insights she might detect. After all, if you're going to consult a psychic, you might as well get your money's worth, or at least a good story.

This prompted the reading to take an intriguing turn. The psychic asked me to recount how I had come into possession of the coin, so I shared the story of the mysterious encounter with the old man in Paris. Listening intently, she then revealed an extraordinary interpretation: according to her, the French man was a spiritualist who had recognized a dark cloud surrounding my aura. The coin, she explained, had been given to me as a token of good luck, meant to help lift that darkness and guide me toward my true path in life, a path, she said, destined to lead me to become a great spiritual leader. (At this point, I was beginning to wonder if I should start practicing my "wise sage" look in the mirror.)

However, she cautioned that the coin alone would not be sufficient to dispel the dark cloud. Making a bold pronouncement, she declared, "God sent you to me!" She claimed to be the only one capable of removing the dark cloud that was blocking my true destiny. To accomplish this, she said she would need to perform an ancient ceremony at a particular church, using special candles and prayers. When I inquired about the cost of such a ceremony, she quoted $400, explaining that the money was not for her but would be used to purchase the special candles and as a donation to the church itself.

She emphasized that her services were free, insisting that God had brought me to her because the world was waiting for a new spiritual leader. I smiled at my sister Kaye, expressed my gratitude to the psychic for her reading, and told her I would consider the offer before making any decision. After paying for the session, I quickly ushered my sister out to the car, with no intention of ever returning. (If destiny were calling, I figured it could leave a message after the beep.)

I kept the coin in my wallet for another fifteen years before eventually passing it on to someone I felt was the right recipient. To this day, I sometimes wonder whether that person ever fulfilled the destiny the psychic had described. Maybe the coin is still out there, quietly working its magic, or maybe it's just buying someone a cup of coffee in Paris. Either way, the adventure, and the mystery, live on.

A Psychic Adventure in Los Angeles

When my sister Kaye set her heart on visiting a world-famous psychic in Los Angeles, I'll admit I was skeptical. The city's psychic scene was legendary, this particular psychic's reputation stretched from Hollywood actors to presidents, and her warehouse was a veritable carnival of mystics, each stationed at their own table, ready to peer into the unknown. The place was so vast it could have hosted a high school basketball tournament and a séance at the same time.

Kaye, ever the adventurer, was determined to have her fortune told. Despite my best efforts to steer her toward a less supernatural afternoon (maybe a Dodgers game or a trip to the beach?), her resolve was unshakable. So, with a mix of curiosity and brotherly duty, I joined her on this quest for cosmic insight.

Inside, the atmosphere buzzed with excitement and a touch of the mystical. We wandered the rows, Kaye scrutinizing each psychic as if she were picking a champion racehorse. Finally, she settled on a tarot reader whose wall was plastered with descriptions of psychic phenomena, telepathy, clairvoyance, and, my personal favorite, "telekinetic spoon-bending." I couldn't help but chuckle, wondering if anyone had ever bent a fork by accident.

As Kaye shuffled her tarot cards, I found myself drawn to the wall, reading about the various psychic arts. Suddenly, the psychic fixed her gaze on me and declared, "You're an actor." I couldn't resist a little Shakespeare: "Life is a stage, and we're all actors." Honesty compelled me to admit I wasn't a thespian, unless you count my dramatic exits from awkward family gatherings. She smiled, undeterred, and continued with Kaye's reading.

But the psychic wasn't finished with me. After the first reading, she handed the cards back to Kaye and, once again, turned her attention my way. "You're a musician." I laughed and confessed that while I owned a guitar, my playing was more "campfire chaos" than Carnegie Hall. Still, she smiled, as if she knew something I didn't.

On the third shuffle, things took a turn for the truly mystical. As I tried to finish reading the wall, one word, "telekinetic", seemed to pulse and shimmer in my mind's eye. Before I could process this, the psychic announced, "You're a disc jockey." At this point, I had to laugh. "Not a DJ either," I replied, "though I've spun a few records at parties, mostly to clear the dance floor." I teased, "That's your third strike; you're out." She grinned, unfazed, and wrapped up Kaye's reading.

As we prepared to leave, my curiosity got the better of me. I asked the psychic if she specialized in any particular phenomenon. She replied that she did. Emboldened by the adventure, I asked if her specialty was "telekinetic", the very word that had flashed in my mind. Her eyes widened in surprise. "Yes, it is, and I am humbled. Clearly, we are both sitting on the wrong sides of this table." For a moment, the line between skeptic and believer blurred, and I felt a genuine sense of connection, a reminder that sometimes honesty and openness can reveal unexpected truths.

As Kaye and I made our way to the exit, I glanced back to see the psychic conferring with the warehouse's owner and two others, all glancing our way. Whether they were discussing my latent psychic abilities or just my questionable sense of humor, I'll never know. Feeling a mix of excitement and humility, I hurried Kaye out the door, both of us laughing at the surreal adventure we'd just shared.

This story, at its heart, is about more than just tarot cards and psychic predictions. It's about the honesty of admitting what we are (and aren't), the humility to laugh at ourselves, the humanity in connecting with strangers, and the excitement of stepping into the unknown, even if it's just for an afternoon in a Los Angeles warehouse. And who knows? Maybe there's a little mystic in all of us, waiting for the right moment to pulse to the surface.

A Night of Spirits, Shadows, and a Spooked Shepherd

Every so often, I'd find myself swept up in the lively orbit of Kaye and her friends, where the conversation was as unpredictable as a magician's hat, one moment about the best barbecue in town, the next about the wildest psychic encounters we'd ever had. On one particularly spirited evening, Kaye, with a mischievous twinkle in her eye, announced to the group that I was psychic. Instantly, the room buzzed with excitement. Suddenly, everyone wanted to hold a séance. Despite my best efforts to steer them toward less ghostly pursuits (like charades or maybe a nice board game), their enthusiasm was relentless. Eventually, against my better judgment, and perhaps lured by the promise of a good story, I agreed to lead the séance.

The stage was set: four brave souls, a single candle flickering in the center of Kaye's dining table, and the rest of the house plunged into darkness. We joined hands, forming a circle around the candle's glow, each of us half-expecting a ghostly hand to join in at any moment. I guided everyone through deep breaths and gentle suggestions, encouraging them to relax and open their senses to the mysteries of the night. The air was thick with anticipation, and maybe a little bit of nervous laughter.

Just as I was about to channel my inner medium and speak, the silence shattered. One of the girls let out a scream that could have woken the dead (if they weren't already invited). The sudden burst of terror sent us all scrambling for the light switch, our séance circle dissolving into a flurry of startled limbs. When the lights came on, she sheepishly explained she'd seen something lurking in the darkness. Of course, there was nothing there, except our collective relief and a round of laughter at how easily we'd all been spooked. The spirits, it seemed, had a sense of humor.

After the excitement died down, I excused myself for the night, feeling both amused and a little relieved to escape any further ghostly mischief. At the time, I was renting a room from a Harley-riding friend, whose large white German Shepherd was more guardian than greeter. When I got home, I followed my usual routine: let the dog out, poured a glass of water, turned out the lights, and headed to bed, ready for a well-earned rest.

But the night had other plans. Just as I was drifting off, a thunderous bang echoed through the wall behind my head, like someone had hurled a softball at the house. My heart leapt into my throat. I sat up, ears straining in the darkness. Then came the unmistakable sounds of cupboards and drawers opening and closing in the kitchen. My mind raced: burglar, poltergeist, or maybe just the world's nosiest raccoon? With no gun for protection, I grabbed my trusty baseball bat (because nothing says "I'm ready for adventure" like facing the unknown in your underwear with a Louisville Slugger).

Creeping down the hallway, I flipped on the dining room lights, half-expecting to find an intruder, or at least a very guilty-looking ghost. But the room was empty, save for a few slightly ajar cupboards. Both the front and garage doors were locked tight. The only thing out of place was the eerie silence.

Then, as I approached the sliding glass door, I saw something that made my hair stand on end. Pressed against the glass, cowering and shaking like a leaf in a hurricane, was the German Shepherd. I'd never seen the dog so terrified; it looked as if it had just seen the ghost we'd been joking about earlier. I quickly let the poor creature inside, locked the door, and decided that tonight, the dining room light would stay on. The dog slept in my room, glued to my side, both of us seeking comfort after a night that had gone from playful mysticism to a real-life ghost story.

Looking back on that night, I can't help but marvel at how easily the line between playful curiosity and genuine fear can blur. What began as a lighthearted attempt to entertain friends with a séance quickly turned into an experience that left both me and a tough old German Shepherd seeking comfort in the glow of a nightlight. It's funny how, even as adults, we're not immune to the power of suggestion, or to the mysteries that sometimes seem to linger just out of sight.

But perhaps the real lesson is this: whether the bumps in the night are caused by restless spirits, creaky pipes, or our own overactive imaginations, it's our response that matters most. That night, laughter and camaraderie proved to be the best antidote to fear. And when the shadows grew a little too long, it was the simple act of letting a frightened dog sleep by my side that brought the greatest peace.

Mysteries and Mushrooms

During a particularly vivid chapter of my life, the boundaries between the ordinary and the extraordinary seemed to blur. My journey into the world of psychic experiences was already unfolding in unexpected ways, but it was during this period that things truly took a turn for the surreal. Alongside these uncanny moments, I occasionally dabbled in the realm of psilocybin mushrooms, nature's own invitation to adventure and introspection.

One memorable day, a group of friends and I concocted a potent brew of magic mushrooms, honey, and orange juice before heading out for a round of frisbee golf. The day was already humming with excitement, our spirits high and laughter echoing across the field. We were still under the spell of the mushrooms when we returned to the apartments, tossing the frisbee with the carefree abandon of children who had forgotten the world's worries.

But as the sun climbed higher, so did the temperature. Without realizing it, I began to feel the heat pressing in, my vision shifting until everything was bathed in a deep, almost otherworldly shade of red. Recognizing that I might have pushed my limits, I excused myself from the group and sought refuge in the shade beside the building. Leaning back against the cool wall, a wave of anxiety washed over me, a sudden, humbling reminder of my own vulnerability. Was I on the verge of a heart attack? A stroke? The mind can be a trickster, especially when adventure edges into the unknown.

As I gazed up at the sky, the clouds above began to morph and swirl, taking on the forms of four Native American forefathers. In that moment, a voice, gentle, reassuring, and utterly unexpected, drifted down from the heavens: "Don't worry, you're going to be just fine." Instantly, the red tint vanished from my vision, replaced by a sense of calm and renewal. It was as if the universe itself had reached out with a compassionate hand, reminding me that sometimes, even in our wildest moments, we are watched over by something greater than ourselves.

With my energy restored and my worries set aside, I rejoined my friends and finished the frisbee game. Looking back, it remains one of the most vivid hallucinations I have ever experienced, a strange, beautiful adventure that left me with a sense of humility and gratitude. Sometimes, the most profound truths arrive when we least expect them, wrapped in the guise of a psychedelic afternoon.

On another occasion, emboldened by our previous escapade, we repeated the ritual, this time heading to the beach, frisbees in hand and spirits high. As we made our way along the sand, I noticed an attractive woman sitting alone against the cliffs, quietly observing the surfers and beachgoers. Never one to pass up a chance for a new connection, I struck up a conversation. She was friendly and pretty, and we chatted for about ten minutes, sharing lighthearted banter and the easy camaraderie that comes when two strangers meet under the sun. I learned her boyfriend was out surfing, and after a while, I politely excused myself to rejoin my friends.

That's when the universe decided to add a dash of humor to the day. One of my friends, notorious for his impulsive antics, accidentally hurled the frisbee straight into a surfboard being carried by a man just a few feet away. I couldn't help but laugh, telling my friend he should apologize to the surfer, who was clearly less than amused. Then, without thinking, I remarked, "Besides, that's that girl's boyfriend." My friends, and the surfer, looked at me as if I'd just claimed to be psychic. As the surfer continued up the beach, I told my friends to watch: he was going to walk through the sand and join the very woman with whom I'd just been speaking. They laughed at my prediction, but sure enough, the surfer did exactly that, confirming my uncanny intuition.

Reflecting on these moments, I'm struck by the wild tapestry of adventure, excitement, and humanity that life can weave when we let go of our expectations. There's humility in recognizing our limits, compassion in the gentle reassurances we receive (from friends or from the clouds), and a lighthearted humor in the way the universe sometimes winks at us, as if to say, "You're not alone in this grand, unpredictable journey."

Turning Point and Reflection

Over the years, I became close friends with an old neighbor who worked in real estate. He was divorced, though he maintained an amicable relationship with his ex-wife, and together they had two children. His girlfriend also lived with him, and she possessed a real talent in the kitchen. Lucky for me, every time I visited, no matter the hour, they were just about to eat and would always invite me to join their meal.

Our visits were lively; we spent many evenings indulging ourselves with smoking weed and playing countless board games, especially Dungeons and Dragons. It was during one of these game nights that I experienced the wrong kind of psychic phenomena, one that would forever change my direction away from the psychic world.

It was a warm summer night, the kind where the air hums with possibility and the world feels just a little more alive. Around 9 p.m., after a night of laughter and games, I decided it was time to leave. My friends lived in an upstairs apartment in the city of Orange, not far from the famed Crystal Cathedral. The moment I stepped through their door, a chill ran up and down my spine, a sensation so sudden and intense that it felt as if the universe itself was whispering a warning. The air, moments before thick with the scent of food and the echo of laughter, now seemed to pulse with an otherworldly energy. Every sense sharpened: the distant hum of traffic, the faint rustle of leaves, even the rhythm of my own heartbeat seemed amplified, as if my body were tuning in to a frequency just beyond the ordinary.

As I descended the stairs, the air grew noticeably colder, and the hair on my arms stood up in response. Each step felt heavier, as if I were wading through invisible currents. The path to the parking garage at the edge of the apartment complex stretched before me, shadows pooling in the corners. With each step, the chill deepened, and I was certain that something was imminent.

Still, I pressed on, deliberately staying in the center of the driveway between the garages, constantly glancing behind and to the sides. My mind raced with primal calculations, fight or flight, logic or instinct. I figured this would give me at least a few steps to react if anything were to jump out, but nothing did. The silence was thick, almost sentient, and I felt as if I were being watched by eyes I could not see.

Eventually, I reached the gate at the front entrance. Before opening it, I checked to see my truck parked just ahead in the first spot by the curb, and I scanned the area for any sign of movement outside. My heart was pounding, and the hair on the back of my neck was standing on end as I opened the gate and stepped through. The gate closed behind me, and immediately to my left, I saw it.

Standing before me on the other side of the driveway entrance was an extremely tall, dark silhouette of a man that wasn't a man, a spirit cloaked in a full hooded robe. The figure appeared to be about eight feet tall and kept its gaze fixed downward. I noticed a deep red emblem hanging from a chain around its neck, and in its right hand, it gripped a long staff.

Frozen in place, I stared in disbelief, overcome by fear and shaking so violently that it felt as if my legs might give out, leaving me to collapse helplessly. The world seemed to narrow to a single point: me and the spirit, suspended in a moment that felt both eternal and fleeting. As I struggled to process what I was seeing, the spirit ever so slowly lifted its hooded head until our eyes met. I can't describe its face, but the eyes conveyed a clear warning. Though it never spoke aloud, it conveyed its message: I was headed down the wrong path in life, and if I did not change soon, something far worse than I could ever imagine would happen to me.

In that instant, fear became a living thing, an electric current that surged through my body, igniting every nerve ending. My senses were on fire: the cold night air, the roughness of the keys in my hand, the distant sound of a car passing on the street. Every detail was etched into my memory with crystalline clarity. In a flash, I bolted to my car, jumped inside, and sped away from the spirit, glancing repeatedly in my rearview mirror to see if it was following.

Then it struck me how pointless that was, realizing the spirit could appear anywhere it wished, even right next to me in the car. The adventure had turned into a flight for my very soul, and humility washed over me as I realized how small and vulnerable I truly was in the face of forces I could not comprehend.

After this chilling encounter, I consciously decided to block all psychic phenomena that I had previously been open to. The last thing I wanted was another confrontation with that spirit, and I took its warning to heart. More than forty years have passed since that night, and I remain committed to keeping it that way. The memory lingers, not as a source of pride, but as a humbling reminder of the thin veil between the seen and unseen, and the consequences of wandering too close to the edge.

In the days and weeks that followed, I found myself reflecting deeply on the choices I had made, the parties, the late nights, the reckless abandon. I came to the realization that my lifestyle choices were leading me down a dangerous path and that there were things in life I truly cared about. As a result, I decided to step back from the constant partying and mainly focused my energy on work and going home at the end of the day. I still went to bars and continued to date from time to time, but I was careful not to allow myself to become deeply involved.

It was during this period of self-reflection and change that I met someone through my family connections, my sister's boyfriend's adopted daughter from a previous marriage. Despite the convoluted family ties, she quickly made an impression on me. She was warm, approachable, and had a vivacious personality, as well as an open-minded outlook on life. We connected easily and began dating, gradually developing a committed relationship.

Looking back, that night stands as a turning point, a moment when fear, adventure, and the elevated senses of psychic realism collided, forcing me to confront my own humility and the need for change. It is a story I carry with me, a reminder that sometimes the most profound lessons come not from triumph, but from the shadows we dare to face and the courage it takes to walk a different path.

Chapter 11
Time To Fly

Despite not having a clear plan for the future, I felt an undeniable certainty deep within me: it was time for a change. The life I had known, the routines and relationships I had built, all seemed to point toward a crossroads, a moment when staying put was no longer an option. There was a necessity, almost urgent, to step beyond the familiar and embrace the unknown, even if it meant leaving behind much of what I cared for most.

The woman I had been dating sensed this shift as well. Her spirit for adventure matched my own, but she brought a humility to the journey that grounded us both. She didn't want to simply follow along as a companion; she wanted to stand beside me as my wife, to face whatever lay ahead together, with equal commitment and courage. Recognizing the sincerity and excitement in her desire, I didn't hesitate. We made the decision with clarity and mutual respect, choosing to marry in a small chapel in Las Vegas, a leap of faith that felt both exhilarating and necessary.

Our wedding was not just a ceremony but the beginning of an adventure that would define us. With humility and hope, we set out on an extended honeymoon, crossing America by car, camping beneath the stars in national parks, and creating memories that would become the foundation of our new life. Each day brought new challenges and unexpected joys, reminding us that the best journeys are those taken with open hearts and a willingness to embrace both the excitement and uncertainty of the road ahead.

After leaving Orange County, California, our adventure began with the kind of optimism only a road trip can inspire. We pointed our car north on I-15, hearts full of excitement and the trunk packed with camping gear, snacks, and just enough common sense to keep things interesting.

Our first stops were Bryce Canyon and Zion National Parks, where we camped under a sky so full of stars it looked like someone had spilled glitter across black velvet. We hiked, we laughed, and we marveled at the red rock formations, each one more dramatic than the last. Nature's grandeur had us feeling both humble and exhilarated, as if we were tiny explorers in a land built for giants.

But every great adventure needs a plot twist. Ours came in the form of a rest area just outside Salt Lake City. After a quick pit stop, we were back on the road, until, twenty minutes later, my wife's eyes widened in horror. "My wallet!" she gasped. Cue the dramatic U-turn and the frantic dash back, only to find the wallet had vanished, presumably off on its own adventure. We reported the loss to the state troopers, who, with a sympathetic smile, assured us that wallets have a way of turning up, eventually. We called the credit card companies, chalked it up to the universe's sense of humor, and pressed on, determined not to let a little setback dampen our spirits.

Next stop: Jackson Hole, Wyoming, gateway to Yellowstone National Park. We camped for four days, exploring geysers that erupted with the punctuality of a Swiss watch and marveling at landscapes so surreal they seemed painted by imagination itself. We watched bison graze, listened to the bubbling mud pots, and tried (with mixed results) to outwit the local squirrels who had clearly mastered the art of snack theft.

From Yellowstone, we headed east to Michigan, crossing into Canada at Sault Ste. Marie. On Drummond Island, we stayed with friends of my wife whose hospitality was as warm as the summer sun. The party started with a morning doobie and breakfast, because nothing says "good morning" like a little herbal encouragement and eggs. Then it was off for a little fun on the water skiing, where my main goal was to stay upright after jumping the wakes behind the boat. Mid-afternoons were ripe for the BBQ, with enough food to make the folks back home jealous. And after dinner, forget Netflix; in Drummond Island, the real entertainment is watching bears go dumpster diving. It's like "Survivor: Bear Edition," only with more fur and fewer immunity challenges.

After a few days of laughter and storytelling, we drove along the Canadian border and boarded a car ferry into Ontario. Our journey took us to Niagara Falls, where we stood in awe of the roaring water, getting just close enough to feel the mist and contemplate whether we'd packed enough dry socks. From there, we made our way to Boston, where we dined at the legendary "Cheers" restaurant. I half-expected everyone to shout our names when we walked in, but we settled for a hearty meal and a few laughs about our growing collection of travel mishaps.

From Boston, we cruised down I-95 through New York City, making a point to see the Statue of Liberty. There's something humbling about standing before such an iconic symbol of hope and freedom, especially when you're running on gas station coffee and the last of your clean T-shirts.

As we journeyed down the East Coast, we managed to dodge a hurricane that was making mischief along the North Carolina coastline. (Pro tip: nothing bonds a couple like outrunning a storm with only a prayer.) Eventually, we reached Jacksonville, Florida, my wife's old stomping grounds. She was eager to reconnect with friends, and I was eager to see if Floridians really do put oranges in everything. We spent a few days socializing, celebrating, and swapping stories of the road.

After our time in Florida, we completed our cross-country adventure by driving back to California via I-10. As the miles rolled by, we reflected on the incredible experiences and memories we'd created, some planned, many unexpected, all unforgettable.

With our journey behind us, we found ourselves at a crossroads. Where to next? Maui, Hawaii, quickly became a top contender. Neither of us had ever been, so we booked a four-day scouting trip. The moment we stepped off the plane, the island's beauty and charm swept us off our feet. We fell in love with Maui's laid-back vibe, lush landscapes, and the promise of new beginnings.

The local newspaper even offered a glimmer of hope: construction jobs for me, waitress positions for my wife. It seemed the universe was giving us a wink and a nudge, adventure wasn't over yet.

In the end, our journey was more than a road trip, it was a masterclass in adventure, humility, and the joy of embracing the unknown. We learned that sometimes you lose a wallet, sometimes you dodge a hurricane, and sometimes you find yourself on a tropical island, ready to start the next chapter. And through it all, we laughed, a lot, because every great adventure deserves a little lighthearted humor.

Once back in California, we wasted no time putting our plan into motion. My truck was shipped on the first available barge to Maui, and, after it arrived, we sent my wife's car over as well. With our vehicles en route, we booked a one-way flight and set off for the island, hearts pounding with anticipation and a dash of "what could possibly go wrong?", ready to begin this exciting chapter of our lives together.

Upon our arrival on Maui, we landed at Napili Shores on the northern tip of the island. Within just a couple of days, and several celebratory Mai Tais, we each secured employment. I dove into construction, wielding a hammer with the confidence of someone who'd never actually built anything on a tropical island before. My wife, ever the quick study, found a job as a waitress, which she jokingly referred to as "slinging hash." Our downtime was a blur of island adventures: driving upcountry to explore the volcano, snorkeling at beaches so beautiful they made you forget about your sunburn, and, yes, indulging in a little pokalolo, "Maui Wowi", with the help of a local legend we called "Old Smoke." Every time we passed him in Lahaina, he'd whisper "smoke" like a secret agent, and we'd exchange a knowing nod. He became our regular source and, in a way, our unofficial tour guide to the island's more "relaxed" side of life.

But paradise, as it turns out, isn't all rainbows and pineapples. One day at work, I strained my lower back, apparently, my body wasn't as enthusiastic about construction as my spirit was. Forced to leave my job to recover, I quickly learned that living in paradise comes with a price tag. The cost of living on Maui was no joke, and I needed to find new employment before I ended up trading my truck for a surfboard and a spot in the local hippie commune.

One afternoon, while strolling down the boardwalk in Lahaina, I spotted a "Help Wanted" sign in a jewelry store window. Never one to pass up an opportunity (or a challenge), I marched in and asked about the job. The owner, a man who owned three stores on Maui, two on O'ahu, and a manufacturing facility in Los Angeles, happened to be there. He asked if I had any experience selling jewelry. I admitted I didn't, but, channeling my inner adventurer, I proposed a ten-minute challenge: let me prove myself. He agreed, probably thinking he'd get a good laugh.

I stepped outside and went full carnival barker, chatting up tourists, spinning tales, and inviting them into the store. In ten minutes, I'd wrangled a dozen curious customers inside, where the sales staff eagerly pounced. The owner, impressed by my people skills (and maybe a little worried I'd start auctioning off the display cases), hired me on the spot.

Victory! Or so I thought. Over the next several weeks, I worked shifts at each of his Maui locations. Drawing people into the store was easy, selling them jewelry, not so much. In fact, I soon realized I was buying more jewelry than I was selling. My wife started to wonder if I was running a secret black market in seashell necklaces. But instead of firing me, the owner recognized my strengths and promoted me to manager, putting me in charge of all three Maui stores while he jetted between islands and LA. It was a win, but also a lesson in humility: sometimes, the real treasure isn't what you sell, but what you learn along the way.

Living on Maui for an extended period reveals subtle but unforgettable details about the island and its visitors. The volcanic landscapes, lush greenery, and sandy beaches meeting the deep blue sea are just the beginning. Every day brought new wonders: double rainbows arching over the mountains, the air thick with the scent of fresh pineapples from trucks heading to market, and the kind of sunsets that make you believe in magic.

And then there were the people. Retirees, having spent a lifetime dreaming of Hawaii, would arrive and be struck by what I called "Hawaiian Euphoria." Suddenly, folks who hadn't jogged since the Nixon administration were running along the highways in ninety-five °F heat and 80% humidity, determined to squeeze every drop out of their vacation. I often worried one of these enthusiastic joggers might collapse just as I drove by, leaving me to perform mouth-to-mouth resuscitation in the middle of paradise. The thought became so persistent that I started averting my gaze whenever I passed a vacationing exerciser, just in case my luck ran out.

But as time passed, the challenges of island life became clear. The high cost of living meant that a few unlucky souls, after burning through their savings, found themselves stranded, forced to sell their trucks and tools or join the local commune just to get by. I was determined not to end up in the same boat (or on the same surfboard).

At the same time, my wife began bringing up the idea of starting a family. She wanted to discuss having a child, but I wasn't ready. I was still wrestling with unresolved feelings about my two other children, whom I missed, and the thought of complicating things further was daunting. I also knew it wouldn't be fair to deny my wife the chance to have a family. If she became pregnant, planned or not, continuing our Maui adventure would be nearly impossible.

After much thought (and more than a few late-night conversations under the stars), I suggested we move back to the mainland, reestablish our lives, and revisit the idea of starting a family when the time was right. It was a bittersweet decision, a small defeat, perhaps, but also a victory in choosing what was best for both of us.

Living on Maui was a truly memorable chapter, filled with adventure, excitement, fun, and a healthy dose of humility. There were victories and defeats, moments of lighthearted humor, and plenty of reminders that paradise is as much about the people you meet and the lessons you learn as it is about the scenery. In the end, I left Maui with a heart full of gratitude, a few extra pieces of jewelry, and a lifetime of stories, proof that, for people like me, the best adventures are the ones that surprise you, humble you, and make you laugh along the way.

After spending nearly a year on Maui, we decided to trade in our flip-flops for hiking boots and relocate to the storied gold country of Grass Valley, California. The move itself felt like an adventure, leaving behind the island's endless summer for the crisp mountain air and the promise of new beginnings. We rolled into town with high hopes, a truck full of dreams and tools, and just enough optimism to overlook the fact that our "moving budget" was mostly loose change and leftover beach sand.

Once settled, I dove headfirst into construction work, this time focusing on installing home insulation. Let me tell you, there's nothing quite like crawling through attics and squeezing into crawlspaces to make you appreciate the simple joys of a Hawaiian breeze. My pay was determined by the number of bags I installed and the houses I completed. If I managed to insulate one full house each day for five days a week, the earnings were actually pretty decent. Of course, some days the only thing I insulated was my own patience, especially when I found myself face-to-face with a family of startled raccoons.

Living in the heart of California's gold mining country was a rush in itself, every back highway seemed to whisper tales of fortune and folly, and my work took me up and down a ninety-mile radius of winding roads, each one promising a new story (and occasionally, a flat tire). My wife, ever the go-getter, quickly landed a job as a waitress in Nevada City, just a couple of miles away. She became a local favorite, charming the regulars with her quick wit and uncanny ability to remember everyone's coffee order.

When we weren't working, we made it our mission to explore every tavern and hiking trail the region had to offer. Some weekends, we'd stumble into a saloon that looked straight out of a Western, half-expecting to see a poker game in progress and a bartender polishing glasses with a suspicious eye. Other times, we'd lace up our boots and set off on a trail, only to get lost and end up debating whether we were blazing a new path or just hopelessly turned around. Either way, we always found our way back, eventually, usually guided by the scent of fresh-baked pie from a roadside diner.

But as winter crept in, the pace of construction slowed to a crawl. The mountain air turned brisk, and with fewer projects available, making ends meet became a real challenge. Our finances began to dwindle faster than the daylight hours, and we found ourselves counting pennies and rationing hot chocolate. Still, we cherished the experience of living in the mountains, the quiet mornings, the star-filled nights, and the sense of camaraderie that comes from weathering a little adversity together.

Recognizing the mounting challenges, we both agreed it was in our best interest to move back to Southern California, where I had originally started out. It wasn't an easy decision, but sometimes the greatest adventures are the ones that teach you when to hold on and when to let go.

Once the excitement and novelty of our mountain journey had faded, we took the time to reflect on our lives together. One evening, over a couple of mugs of strong coffee (and maybe a slice of that legendary pie), we shared a good laugh and came to the mutual realization that we were actually better friends than we were spouses. There was no drama, no hard feelings, just two people who'd shared a wild ride and decided to take the next fork in the road as friends. Acting on this understanding, we amicably pursued a divorce, but continued to maintain our friendship for several years afterward.

My Beloved Mother

A few years earlier, Mom and Dad suffered a terrible separation that took everyone in the family by surprise. The emotional shockwaves were profound and far-reaching, reverberating through each of our lives in ways we could not have anticipated. My mother was left grappling with deep feelings of hurt, anger, and despair, yet she faced each day with a quiet dignity that spoke to her enduring strength. Each of us siblings, in our own ways, struggled to process the pain and disappointment, often finding it difficult to express, or even fully understand, the depth of our emotions. The sense of loss and upheaval touched every aspect of our lives, making it a truly challenging and sorrowful time for the entire family. Looking back, all I can say is that the experience left lasting marks on each of our hearts, and it was a period none of us will ever forget.

As Mom approached the final chapter of her life, she did so with remarkable grace. She'd endured a lifetime of health challenges, each one chipping away at her independence but never her spirit. The most serious of these was poor circulation, likely the legacy of years spent smoking, a habit that, in the end, led to a series of amputations and, ultimately, the loss of her leg just above the knee. For many years, Mom relied on a prosthetic leg, determined to maintain her mobility and sense of self despite her disability. Her resilience was a quiet lesson in courage, teaching us all that dignity is not defined by circumstance but by the way we choose to meet it.

During these discerning times, my older sister Kaye and her husband moved Mom into their house and cared for her with unwavering devotion. They took her on adventures to places like Egypt, seeking to enhance her golden years as gracefully as possible.

As time passed, Mom's health became more fragile, and the complications multiplied. Kaye and David's dedication during this time was nothing short of remarkable. They shouldered the burden of care with grace and humility, their actions a testament to the strength of family bonds, a reminder that, in moments of greatest need, it is often those closest to us who rise to the occasion. They became her advocates, her comforters, and her daily companions, ensuring she was surrounded by love and dignity even as her strength faded. Their selflessness was a living example of what it means to honor one's family, not just in words, but in the quiet, everyday acts of care that define true devotion. Their compassion and sacrifice deserve not only acknowledgment but heartfelt gratitude and commendation.

When the time came to move Mom into a convalescent hospital, it was a decision made with heavy hearts but clear purpose: to ensure she would spend her final months in comfort, dignity, and peace. During this time, we all visited Mom as often as our schedules allowed, and my younger sister Patty often comforted Mom by providing personal care, clipping her nails, washing and brushing her hair, and, in general, giving Mom additional loving touches that she greatly appreciated. These tender gestures were expressions of love that transcended words, weaving a tapestry of comfort and connection in the face of loss.

As Mom's illness progressed, the doctors began to discuss the difficult realities we faced. They urged us to consider whether to continue the blood transfusions, explaining that stopping them would allow her to pass peacefully. Despite her declining health, Mom's spirit remained undiminished. During my visits, she made it clear that she was not yet ready to let go, her wish was to continue treatment for as long as possible. Her determination was both humbling and inspiring, a final act of agency in a life defined by quiet strength.

My siblings, more closely aligned with the doctors' perspective, felt it was time to follow medical advice. Ultimately, we had to accept the inevitable and allow her to pass peacefully, honoring both her wishes and the reality of her condition. Mom ultimately passed gently into the hands of the Lord, her journey marked by the love that had always surrounded her.

Looking back, I am filled with gratitude for the love my mother gave so freely and the lessons she imparted through her example. Her love for each of us was deep and unconditional, leaving us with a lifetime of cherished memories. Many of my own recollections of her kindness and devotion remain treasured, and I am proud to share them in these memoirs. In her final days, our family was reminded that true humanity is found in the way we care for one another, that humility is accepting help when we need it, and that endearment is expressed not just in grand gestures but in the gentle, everyday acts of love that bind us together.

Chapter 12
An Unexpected Opportunity

Sometimes, just when it feels like every option has been exhausted, life presents an unexpected opportunity, a door to a new beginning. After resettling in Southern California, I reached out to an ex-coworker, hoping for an employment lead. During our conversation, she mentioned a small refinery located in Santa Fe Springs. The refinery had a reputation for safe operations and was known for its reliability, despite its age. Learning that the facility had openings for two operator positions, I saw a chance to leverage my years of experience in the oil industry and felt I might have an advantage over other applicants.

Encouraged, I decided to apply for one of the positions. However, I soon discovered the competition was intense; there were already around fifteen hundred applicants vying for the same roles. The refinery's hiring process was rigorous, beginning with a series of written aptitude tests designed to assess each candidate's suitability. After completing these exams, successful applicants moved on to participate in several rounds of interviews. As the selection process progressed, the number of candidates steadily decreased. Eventually, the pool of applicants was narrowed down to just five finalists, and I was among them.

Reaching this stage was both humbling and affirming. I felt a deep sense of gratitude, not only for making it so far but also for the journey that had brought me to this point. I recognized that every candidate had their own story, their own struggles and hopes, and I respected the effort and determination it took for each of us to persevere.

The final stage of the hiring process was an interview with the refinery manager, a pleasant and personable man in his sixties, well respected in the industry. Upon entering his office, he introduced himself, we shook hands, and he invited me to take a seat. He expressed his interest in my background, noting that by the age of thirty-three, I had already reached a significant supervisory role with a major oil company and had retired with excellent recommendations. Although he did not ask for details about my retirement, he continued by outlining the refinery's requirements for employment.

He explained that every new operator begins at the "C" level and must pass the mandatory training program. The progression from "C" operator to "B" operator required passing the training program within eighteen months, and advancing to "A" operator demanded another eighteen months of demonstrated proficiency. Failure to meet these milestones would result in permanent dismissal from the company. He also informed me that operators below the supervisory level were required to join a workers' union. Seniority played a key role in career advancement, and it could take several years before a supervisory position became available, should one open at all. The manager's explanations almost felt as though he were attempting to persuade me to reconsider joining the company.

I listened with humility, appreciating his candor and the respect he showed for the realities of the job. His honesty about the challenges ahead made me reflect on my own motivations and the importance of approaching this opportunity with both open eyes and an open heart.

He then posed a single, important question: "If I hire you and, after investing the time and cost for you to become an 'A' operator, and someone offers you a supervisory position with another company, what would you do?" I found the question straightforward and replied with honesty and respect. I explained that I was grateful for the employment opportunity, but, like anyone else, if a substantial opportunity arose that could significantly improve my family's standard of living, I would have to seriously consider it. I responded to the manager's question with complete honesty, expressing my genuine intentions and values.

To my surprise, this approach proved to be the right one. A sincere smile spread across his face. He informed me that my answer had earned me the privilege of having first choice among the two available job openings at the refinery. In that moment, I felt a profound sense of recognition, not just for my experience but for my willingness to be honest and transparent, even when it might have been easier to say what I thought he wanted to hear.

The manager explained that one position was in the Crude Distillation Unit as a process operator, while the other was in the Tank Farm as a gauger. I conveyed my eagerness to learn all aspects of refinery operations, emphasizing that the Crude Unit seemed to be the best place to start for someone wanting a comprehensive understanding of the facility's processes. Ultimately, I chose the process operator role in the Crude Unit, and three days later, I began my first day at the refinery.

Stepping into the Crude Unit for the first time felt less like starting a new job and more like embarking on an epic quest. This wasn't just any corner of the refinery, it was a sprawling, intricate world of pipes, towers, and mysterious machinery, each with its own secrets and challenges. The Crude Unit was the initial step in refining, pulsing with integrated processes: Crude, Vacuum, and Visbreaker Distillation, Amine and Regeneration, Merox Treating, Sulfur Recovery, Tail Gas Treating, Sour Water Treating, and the ever-essential Cooling Water Tower. If you could master this labyrinth, you could survive anywhere.

Training here wasn't for the faint of heart. It was a rigorous, hands-on boot camp that combined chemistry, engineering, and a healthy dose of humility. Forget about fancy computer systems or digital diagrams, this refinery was old school. Operators were expected to memorize every twist and turn of the process, relying on pneumatic air controls and strip charts that looked like they belonged in a museum. The only "cloud" in sight was the one coming out of the steam stack on a foggy morning.

Each crew was led by a head operator, a wise, battle-hardened veteran who ran the unit with the precision of a ship's captain and the patience of a saint. My head operator was legendary for setting high standards and expecting nothing less than excellence. He believed that learning the process meant getting your boots dirty: walking every inch of the unit, sketching every valve and vessel, and, above all, never being afraid to ask questions (even if you risked a good-natured ribbing from the crew).

Now, here's where the adventure, and a bit of comedy, really began. Most trainees would grab a blank sheet of paper and start freehand drawing their process diagrams. The results? Well, let's just say some of those sketches looked like treasure maps drawn by pirates after a long night at sea. Determined to stand out (and maybe avoid getting lost in my own drawing), I decided to try something different. I bought 3D graph paper and, in the evenings, practiced plotting the process flows at home. My goal: a diagram so clean and organized, even the janitor could follow it.

After countless attempts (and a few eraser casualties), I could recreate the entire process from memory, every detail in its place. When the first written and process sketch test rolled around, I nervously asked the trainer if I could use my graph paper. He eyed my book suspiciously, probably wondering if I'd hidden the answers in the margins. But after I handed in my drawing, he stared at it in disbelief and blurted out, "You've got to be kidding me." For a split second, I thought I'd drawn the whole thing upside down. But then he grinned and admitted he'd never seen a trainee submit such a professional-looking diagram in all his years.

That moment was a turning point. With a mix of excitement and humility, I realized that hard work, and a willingness to do things differently, could pay off. I completed the three-year training program in just twelve months, leapfrogging nearly everyone who started before me. I mastered every aspect of the unit, from the grunt work to the control panel, and earned the respect of my peers and supervisors alike.

Four years later, my commitment was rewarded when I was chosen as one of only eight operators to train on the refinery's first distributed control system (DCS). It was a milestone for the plant and for me, a chance to step into the future, armed with the lessons (and laughs) from my days in the trenches.

Looking back, the Crude Unit was more than a workplace, it was a proving ground, a classroom, and, at times, a comedy club. It taught me the value of respect for those who came before, the importance of humility when facing the unknown, and the power of a little creativity (and a lot of graph paper). And if you ever find yourself lost in a refinery, just remember: every adventure starts with a single step, and maybe a really good map.

It was during this time of my life that my children's lives had become a whirlwind of activities, ambitions, and the ever-present hum of adolescent independence. They were busy carving out their own paths, each day seemed to bring a new adventure for them, and for me, a new opportunity to try and stay connected. Despite their packed schedules and growing social circles, I made it a point to reach out, especially to my daughter, Regina. Our visits, though occasional, became little islands of joy in the sea of teenage busyness.

One afternoon, during one of our cherished get-togethers, Regina confided that she wasn't able to invite her friends over to her mother's house. This revelation sparked a wave of concern in me, a cocktail of parental curiosity and protective instinct. I found myself wondering: Did her mother know who her friends were? What kind of adventures were they getting up to? My mind raced with possibilities, some realistic, others bordering on the plotlines of teen sitcoms. With gentle compassion, I expressed my interest in knowing more about the people she spent time with, hoping to strike that delicate balance between caring parent and not-so-embarrassing dad.

To my delight, this conversation opened a new chapter in our relationship. Regina began calling me nearly every week. Each call was a little adventure in itself, her voice bubbling with excitement as she recounted stories of trips to Disneyland, spontaneous escapades to Knott's Berry Farm, and the ever-changing cast of friends she met along the way. I listened with genuine interest, sometimes marveling at how much the world of teenage girls had changed since my own youth, and sometimes just trying to keep up with the latest slang. While her tales sounded innocent enough, I couldn't help but worry a little, after all, it's a parent's job to imagine every possible scenario, from the mundane to the melodramatic. Still, I chose to keep most of my concerns to myself, focusing instead on being a good listener and maintaining a presence in her life.

One evening, Regina asked if she could bring a couple of friends to a fire pit gathering at the beach. I agreed, feeling a surge of hope that this might be a chance to meet the mysterious characters from her stories. She arrived with a girlfriend, and later, two boys joined the group. As they all decided to take a walk together, I seized the moment to greet one of the boys with a firm handshake, just firm enough to communicate, "If you ever mistreat my daughter, you'll have to answer to me." I must have gotten the message across, because for whatever reason, I never saw that boy again. Sometimes, a handshake is worth a thousand words, and possibly a thousand awkward future encounters.

My interactions with my son during this period were even less frequent, which made the rare moments we shared all the more precious. On one memorable occasion, there was a knock at my door, and there he stood, a beautiful girl by his side. For a split second, I wondered if he was about to announce an engagement, my mind leaping ahead to wedding speeches and father-son dances. Instead, we spent a couple of hours enjoying a pleasant visit, sharing snacks, and even strumming a little guitar together. The visit was brief but filled with warmth, laughter, and the quiet joy that comes from simply being together, even if only for a short while.

Looking back, these short flashes of memory, fleeting as they were, filled me with a deep sense of joy and gratitude. There was adventure in every conversation, compassion in every concern, and hope in every handshake and phone call. Everything I felt fell in line with the things I had heard. Parenting teenagers is a bit like trying to catch fireflies on a summer night: you chase after the light, sometimes missing, sometimes catching a brief, beautiful glow.

And if you're lucky, you get to share a laugh or two along the way, like the time I realized my "dad handshake" might just be the most effective boy-repellent ever invented.

Through it all, I learned and understood that staying connected with your children, especially as they grow into their own, is an adventure in itself, one filled with surprises, challenges, and the kind of love that keeps you hoping, listening, and showing up, no matter how busy life gets. Sometimes, easier said than done.

In 1992, after five years of hard work and study, the refinery where I'd built my recent career was shuttered and mothballed. I found myself standing at a new crossroad, one of those moments when life seems to nudge you out of your comfort zone and whispers, "Adventure awaits, if you're brave enough to answer." The shutdown was bittersweet: a chapter closing, friendships scattering, and the familiar rhythm of daily work replaced by uncertainty. Yet, in the midst of this upheaval, opportunity came knocking in the most unexpected way.

The refinery manager, a person I'd come to respect for both candor and knowledge, pulled me aside. With a twinkle in his eye and a tone that suggested he was about to share a secret recipe, he told me about a company in Houston, Texas. They'd just acquired a refinery in Aruba, yes, the Caribbean, where the only thing hotter than the weather is the local hot sauce. They were looking for thirteen head operators for two-year contracts. "If I were in your shoes," he said, "I'd go for it." His words were more than advice, they were a vote of confidence, a reminder that sometimes the best way to honor your past is to step boldly into your future.

With honesty and a healthy dose of nerves, I signed up for the interview. I'll admit, my heart was pounding like a jackhammer as I walked into that room. But I decided to lead with integrity, no embellishments, no bravado, just the truth about what I could offer and what I hoped to learn. The interviewer seemed to appreciate my candor, and as I left, he said, "I think we'll be seeing you." Of course, in the world of job hunting, nothing is official until it's in writing, so I kept my excitement in check, at least until I was out of earshot.

Back in the control room, my colleagues, many of them seasoned veterans, were curious about how it went. I shared my experience, trying to balance hope with humility. The more experienced operators just chuckled, their laughter a mix of encouragement and the kind of wisdom that comes from having seen a few too many "sure things" fall through. Still, I couldn't help but feel a spark of excitement. Maybe, just maybe, this was the start of something new.

A week later, the phone rang. The supervisor called me into the office, and on the other end was a representative from the Caribbean refinery. "We'd like to offer you the position," they said. I was officially hired. When I returned to the control room, the atmosphere was thick with anticipation, you could have heard a pin drop. Nearly every operator was still searching for a job, and as I shared my news, I saw a mix of relief, envy, and some deeper emotions in the eyes of a few.

Suddenly, the room erupted into a flurry of activity. Seasoned head operators scrambled to contact the company, hoping to snag a last-minute interview. But the window had closed; the final selections were made. The company advised them to submit resumes for future consideration, but for now, the ship had sailed, literally, in my case, toward Aruba.

One of those left behind was my head operator, the very person who had trained me. Curious, I asked why he hadn't thrown his hat in the ring. With characteristic honesty, he explained that as a head operator, he'd be expected to lead a team in a facility he'd never seen. "It doesn't make sense to direct a crew when you're the one who needs to be taught," he said. His humility and integrity struck me, sometimes, the bravest thing you can do is admit what you don't know.

That conversation highlighted a fundamental truth: some people are held back by the fear of failure, while others are willing to take a leap when there's nothing left to lose. For me, this was a chance to move forward, to embrace the unknown with a spirit of adventure. If it didn't work out, I could always try again. But if it did, well, who knew what possibilities might await?

As I prepared to leave, I found myself reflecting on my very first day in the oil patch and the advice given to me by a seasoned construction supervisor: "Keep your eyes open, your hands busy, and your sense of humor intact." With the benefit of hindsight, I realized just how wise those words were. Before I left, I sought out the refinery manager to thank him for his support. He shook my hand, smiled warmly, and said, "You've earned your place through hard work and dedication. The international sector will open up a world of possibilities for someone willing to embrace new challenges. Good luck, and don't forget to send us a postcard if you find a beach with a decent bar."

I walked away from that conversation feeling incredibly fortunate, not just for the job, but for the relationships, mentorship, and camaraderie that had shaped my journey. I carried with me a deep appreciation for the people who had helped me along the way, and a renewed respect for the power of honesty, integrity, and a little lighthearted humor to turn even the most uncertain moments into the start of a great adventure.

Chapter 13
An Expat Life

When I first set foot at the Aruba refinery in February 1992, I felt like an explorer landing on a new continent, except instead of jungles and wild beasts, I was greeted by a sprawling maze of pipes, tanks, and the ever-present aroma of crude oil. The facility was chugging along at 38,000 barrels per day, which, to my rookie eyes, already seemed like enough black gold to fill a small ocean. Little did I know, we were just getting started on this wild ride.

It was here that I had my first encounter with the mysterious Piping and Instrumentation Diagrams (P&IDs). These weren't your average treasure maps, no "X marks the spot" here. Instead, they were intricate blueprints that looked like the secret plans for a moon landing, and deciphering them felt like cracking the *Da Vinci Code*. I half-expected a hidden message to pop out if I stared long enough.

But the real showstopper was the refinery's old-school way of firing up the process heaters: burning pitch, a thick, tarry fuel oil that had long since been banished from the U.S. for being an environmental villain. Every day, the heaters belched out a dramatic, brown plume of smoke that stretched across the sky like a giant's cigar. The wind would sweep it out to sea, painting a streak across the horizon that was impossible to miss. It was so consistent, you could probably set your watch by it, "Ah, yes, it's 3:00 PM, time for the daily smoke signal to Venezuela!"

Naturally, my curiosity got the better of me. I asked the local operators, "Doesn't anyone worry about all this smoke?" They just shrugged and said, "It's going to Venezuela." I couldn't help but laugh, apparently, the prevailing winds were their environmental policy. It was a masterclass in island pragmatism: out of sight, out of mind, and definitely out of Aruba.

But the real adventure was just beginning. Over the next two years, our team became a band of refinery pirates, determined to push the limits. Through a mix of coordinated effort, operational wizardry, and a dash of stubborn optimism, we cranked up the refinery's throughput from a modest 38,000 barrels per day to a jaw-dropping 160,000 barrels per day. That's right, nearly four times the original capacity! If the refinery had a speedometer, we would've broken the needle.

Looking back, it was a journey full of surprises, laughter, and the kind of camaraderie you only find when you're elbow-deep in crude oil and chasing big dreams. We didn't just process oil, we processed memories, turning every challenge into a story worth retelling. And if you ever find yourself in Aruba, just look for the faint outline of a brown plume on the horizon. That's the mark of a refinery team that knew how to turn work into an adventure.

When I wasn't wrangling refinery valves or deciphering piping diagrams, I dove headfirst into the island's endless parade of adventure and beauty. The beaches, oh, the beaches!, were like something out of a travel magazine: powdery sand, turquoise water, and secret coves that felt like they'd been designed for pirates or poets. My free time became a quest for the perfect spot to unwind, whether I was basking in the sun, exploring lively restaurants, or sampling the nightlife (which, on this island, was as energetic as a conga line at Carnival).

One cove in particular became my personal oasis. Picture this: a tiny, postcard-perfect beach, with a humble shack perched just above the tide line. The menu was simple, hamburgers, hot dogs, cold beer, and sodas, but the view was five-star. The shack's proprietor was a character straight out of a Jimmy Buffett song, always ready with a story and a smile. We became fast friends, swapping tales as the sun dipped low and the waves whispered secrets to the shore.

But paradise, as it turns out, isn't always safe from bureaucracy. My friend confided that the island authorities were plotting to shut down his beloved shack, hoping to pave the way for something more "commercial." (Because what every idyllic cove needs is a parking lot and a souvenir stand, right?) I couldn't let that happen. Channeling my inner activist (and maybe a bit of Don Quixote), I suggested he put out some trash barrels and take charge of keeping the beach pristine, a win for the environment and a clever way to show the authorities he was a force for good.

Not stopping there, I drafted a petition, rallying tourists and locals alike. "A happy tourist means a happy island!" became our unofficial motto. A month later, my friend was back in business, license in hand and smile even wider. As a thank-you, he'd slip me a free beer and a sandwich, proof that good deeds really do come with tasty rewards.

The island itself was a kaleidoscope of excitement. Tourists flocked in from the Netherlands, Brazil, Venezuela, Colombia, and the U.S., turning every week into a festival. I'll admit, I got swept up in the fun, maybe a few too many parties, but hey, when in paradise! Somewhere along the way, I found myself in a whirlwind romance with a vivacious Colombian woman. The relationship didn't last (island flings rarely do), but I walked away with a new skill: conversational Spanish. Now, I could order a beer, ask for directions, and even charm a taxi driver in two languages, a superpower that's come in handy more than once.

Beyond the beaches and fiestas, I met a cast of expat characters worthy of their own sitcom. One friend, a master of homemade moonshine and a connoisseur of 103-proof Wild Turkey, would invite me to join him and his wife for hearty meals and even heartier laughs. As my island adventure drew to a close, he handed me a slip of paper with a name and number. "Call this person when you get stateside, they're expecting you." It was my fourth "gift horse" in a career full of surprises, and I was grateful for the friendship, the fun, and the sense that, on this wild ride, the next adventure was always just around the corner.

As soon as I landed back in the United States, I looked at the mysterious piece of paper, a contact, a name, and the promise of a new adventure. Little did I know, this was my golden ticket to a whirlwind assignment in Sines, Portugal, courtesy of a renowned EPC company, that *abbreviation* stands for "Engineering, Procurement, and Construction." The recruiter, with the efficiency of a secret agent, zipped through the terms and conditions, and before I could say "obrigado," I was on a plane bound for Lisbon, my mind racing with visions of castles, custard tarts, and maybe a little Port.

Upon arrival, a driver whisked me away to Sines, a coastal town two hours south of Lisbon. The drive itself was an adventure, imagine a jet-lagged American, wide-eyed and clutching a suitcase, barreling down winding roads while trying to decipher Portuguese road signs that looked like they'd been designed by Picasso on a caffeine binge.

In Sines, I was introduced to a lively band of expatriates, most of whom were in family status and had already survived several projects with the same EPC company. Our daily routine was a blend of camaraderie and comedy: we'd pile into car vans like a circus troupe, commute to the refinery, and, after a long day of wrangling pipes and processes, we'd reconvene at a pastry shop in the town square. This wasn't just any pastry shop, it doubled as a beer and wine bar, where laughter flowed as freely as the vinho verde. Every evening, we'd swap stories, some true, some suspiciously embellished, before heading out to conquer the local restaurants, one forkful at a time.

Now, here's where the real adventure began: I didn't speak a word of Portuguese beyond "obrigado." My attempts at communication were, at best, a slapstick routine. The local operators at the plant would greet me with friendly smiles and rapid-fire Portuguese, to which I'd respond with a hopeful grin and a lot of enthusiastic nodding. It was like playing charades, but with more oil stains and fewer points.

Desperate to bridge the gap, I dusted off my limited Spanish. To my relief (and their amusement), many of the Portuguese operators understood enough Spanish to turn our daily interactions into a delightful linguistic game. We'd mix Spanish,

Portuguese, and a generous helping of hand gestures, creating a new dialect I like to call "Portuñolish." Every successful conversation felt like winning a gold medal in the Olympics of Miscommunication. The humility of not knowing the language was balanced by the humanity of everyone's willingness to meet me halfway, and sometimes, all the way.

The Portuguese approach to workplace culture was a revelation. Forget the sterile, coffee-fueled meetings of my past. Here, the plant manager would host weekly lunches in the conference room, professionally catered and featuring not one, but two large bottles of wine. The first time I saw this, I thought I'd stumbled into a Mediterranean wedding by mistake. The atmosphere was relaxed, the conversation lively, and the wine, well, let's just say it made even the trickiest process diagrams seem a little less daunting. It was camaraderie in a bottle, and I learned quickly that in Portugal, productivity and pleasure are not mutually exclusive.

But the surprises didn't stop there. Each operating unit had its own operator shelter, complete with a refrigerator stocked with beer and wine, right alongside the lunches. At first, I thought this was a prank, surely, someone was testing the gullibility of the new American. But no, it was just another example of the Portuguese philosophy: work hard, relax harder. The humility of being the outsider was softened by the warmth and humor of my colleagues, who never missed a chance to toast to a job well done, or at least, a job attempted.

As the plant's operations stabilized, the client decided to recognize the key contributors. They made a list of preferred operators to stay on for the critical performance tests, and to my astonishment (and a little pride), I was one of the final three chosen. It was a humbling honor, proof that even a language-challenged, wine-loving American could find a place in the heart of a Portuguese refinery.

Before heading home, the client handed me the keys to a car and a seven-day vacation, an unexpected bonus that turned my work trip into a grand tour of Portugal. I explored Lisbon's winding streets, marveled at the fairy-tale palaces of Sintra, wandered the historic halls of Coimbra, and basked on the sun-drenched beaches of the Algarve. Each stop was a new adventure, filled with excitement, a dash of humility (especially when ordering food in my best Portuñolish), and plenty of lighthearted humor. I returned to the States with a suitcase full of memories, a heart full of gratitude, and a newfound appreciation for the magic that happens when you embrace the unknown with open arms and a sense of humor.

Moral of the story: Sometimes, the greatest adventures begin with a single word, "obrigado", and a willingness to laugh at yourself. In Portugal, I learned that humanity, humility, and humor are the true universal languages, and that every challenge is just another story waiting to be told.

After years of squinting at the world through a foggy windshield, I found myself drawn to Phoenix, Arizona, lured by the reputation of a renowned eye specialist, a veritable wizard of Radial Keratotomy. The promise of clear vision was too tempting to resist. With a mix of hope and nerves, I underwent the procedure, half-expecting to emerge with superhero sight or, at the very least, the ability to spot a hummingbird from a mile away.

The moment I stepped outside, the world exploded into high definition. Every leaf shimmered with dew, every color seemed to sing, and I swear I could see the individual grains of sand on the sidewalk. For a brief, glorious period, I experienced the world as others did, crisp, vibrant, and full of hidden details. It was as if life had handed me a backstage pass to its most intricate wonders. Of course, in true comedic fashion, this newfound clarity was destined to be short-lived. But as any adventurer knows, it's not the length of the journey, but the thrill of the ride that matters most.

During this time, my daughter flew in for a visit, bringing with her a suitcase full of laughter and the kind of warmth that only family can provide. We set out to explore the local sights, turning even the most mundane errands into mini-adventures. Whether we were marveling at the desert sunsets or getting lost in a maze of unfamiliar streets (thanks to my "improved" but still questionable sense of direction), every moment was a reminder of the joy that comes from simply being together. Her presence rekindled a sense of appreciation for the little things, shared meals, inside jokes, and the comfort of knowing someone's got your back, even if you're both hopelessly lost in a parking lot.

Inspired by her visit and the realization that life's greatest treasures are found in connection, I decided it was time to move back to Huntington Beach. The call of the ocean, the pull of family, and the promise of new beginnings proved irresistible. I packed up my belongings (and my still-sharp vision) and headed west, ready to embrace whatever adventures awaited.

Back in California, I found myself in a transitional phase, living with an old friend, waiting for the next big project to appear on the horizon. To keep busy (and to avoid going stir-crazy), I took on a series of odd jobs. One of the most memorable was cleaning restaurants between midnight and six in the morning. There's a certain humility in scrubbing floors while the rest of the world sleeps, but there's also a unique camaraderie among the night crew. We swapped stories, shared laughs, and learned to appreciate the quiet magic of a city at rest. Plus, I discovered that nothing builds character quite like wrestling with a stubborn mop at 3 a.m.

This short-lived chapter, though unconventional, offered unexpected gifts. It gave me time to reconnect with my daughter, to re-bond as much as time allowed, and to find comfort in the simple act of showing up for each other. We didn't need grand adventures or exotic destinations, just a willingness to be present, to listen, and to laugh at life's little absurdities. In the end, it was a reminder that adventure isn't always about scaling mountains or crossing oceans; sometimes, it's about finding joy, humility, and humanity in the everyday moments we share with those we love.

In November 1994, I found myself once again deep in reflection, wrestling with the sum of my life's choices up to that point, and let's just say, the scorecard wasn't exactly in my favor. I'd managed to carve out a promising new chapter as an expat, living the kind of gypsy life that would make even my younger, restless self proud. But something inside me was shifting. Maybe it was the echo of old regrets, or perhaps the quiet hope that the best stories were still waiting to be written.

Looking back, I couldn't help but chuckle at the zigzags and detours that had brought me here. My past was a patchwork of bold leaps, spectacular stumbles, and more than a few "what was I thinking?" moments. Yet, for all the missteps, there was a certain grace in surviving them, and, if I'm honest, in learning to laugh at myself along the way. Humility, I've discovered, is the best travel companion for a wandering soul.

So, standing at that crossroads, I made a quiet promise: from this point forward, I'd focus on building a career worthy of the second chance I'd been given. No more drifting on the winds of circumstance. Instead, I'd embrace my new life as a gypsy, albeit one with a slightly better sense of direction and a much greater appreciation for clean laundry.

The future, of course, remained as unpredictable as ever. But I was determined to meet it with open arms, a grateful heart, and just enough humor to keep things interesting. After all, if there's one thing the past has taught me, it's that the best adventures are the ones you never see coming, and that sometimes, the only way forward is to pack your bags, tip your hat to yesterday, and set out with hope (and maybe a spare pair of socks) for whatever comes next.

I soon found myself at the threshold of a new adventure, one that would test not just my technical skills, but my humility, resilience, and willingness to laugh at myself. The same EPC company that had already thrown me into the deep end once before now offered me a second assignment: help develop technical operating manuals for a massive grassroots refinery in Map Ta Phut, Rayong, Thailand. The catch? The writing team would be based in Houston, Texas, and I'd be one of the first seven writers hired for a team that would eventually grow to forty. It felt a bit like being picked for the first shuttle to Mars, exciting, daunting, and with no guarantee of return.

Luckily, my sister Kaye lived just forty minutes away in Tomball, Texas, and she graciously invited me to stay with her and her two adopted daughters while her husband was working overseas. I accepted, grateful for the family support and the chance to save most of my per diem money that would otherwise have vanished into the black hole of Houston rent and utilities.

On my first day at the office, I was greeted by a sight that sent a chill down my spine: desktop computers at every workstation. Now, I'd wrangled plenty of digital control systems in the plant, but this was different. These machines looked like they could launch a space shuttle, or, in my case, launch me straight out the door.

With a mix of honesty and humility, I approached my manager and confessed my lack of computer experience, naively assuming we'd be handwriting the technical manuals. He chuckled (a sound that was both reassuring and slightly ominous) and assured me I wasn't alone. Apparently, several others on the team were just as green, and the company had a crack squad of administrative assistants ready to save us from ourselves. My job, he said, was to focus on the technical content and let the admins handle the formatting and digital wizardry.

No sooner had I found my footing than the first real challenge arrived. Our team was short on hands-on experience with the Residual Fluid Catalytic Cracking Unit, a process as intimidating as its name. The project leadership, perhaps mistaking my nervous energy for expertise, asked if I could take the lead. I admitted, with integrity, that I had no direct experience, but if they could provide the engineering data, I'd give it my best shot. We agreed to keep my inexperience our little secret, especially from the client's Subject Matter Expert (SME). With my manager's support, I became the first team member assigned to develop the unit's operating manuals.

Determined not to let the team down, I embarked on a quest worthy of Indiana Jones, except instead of ancient relics, I was hunting for engineering books in Houston's technical bookstores. I devoured everything I could find, learning the ins and outs of the process until I could practically recite operating procedures in my sleep. The adventure was real, the stakes were high, and the only thing more intimidating than the technical jargon was the thought of getting called out.

But the real heroes of this story were the administrative assistants, a group of exceptionally talented women who possessed computer skills that bordered on the supernatural. Recognizing that my survival (and possibly the project's) depended on mastering these digital beasts, I swallowed my pride and confessed my fears. "They're going to fire me for sure," I joked one day, plopping myself down in their midst.

Instead of laughing me out of the building, they rallied around me, promising that no one would be let go on their watch. From that day forward, they became my mentors, cheerleaders, and occasional therapists. Every day, at least one would check in, offering tips, tricks, and the occasional pep talk. Thanks to their patience and encouragement, I went from computer-phobic to computer-competent in record time.

Motivated by a mix of gratitude and sheer terror, I bought my first personal laptop and installed the same Microsoft software we used at work. I became the office's unofficial early bird and night owl, arriving before anyone else and leaving long after the cleaning crew. My evenings were a blur of after-work drinks with colleagues, late-night writing sessions at my sister's house, and the kind of sleep deprivation that makes you question your life choices. But through it all, I kept my sense of humor, and my determination to succeed, intact.

Sometimes, the most profound lessons in life arrive not through formal training or grand gestures, but in the quiet, serendipitous encounters that catch us off guard. My story begins on an ordinary workday, with a simple request from the project director's administrator: a new team member was joining us, and I was asked to greet and help settle this individual into our bustling office.

When the elevator doors opened, I was greeted by a man who seemed to carry decades of stories in his gentle smile and twinkling eyes. He appeared to be in his seventies, at least twenty years older than anyone else on the floor. There was a moment of surprise (and, I'll admit, a fleeting curiosity about why someone with so much experience wasn't already enjoying retirement on a sunny beach somewhere). Yet his presence radiated warmth and a quiet confidence that immediately put me at ease.

With a sense of adventure, I guided him through the maze of cubicles, introducing him to colleagues, pointing out the best spots for coffee, and making sure he had everything he needed. I assured him that if he ever needed anything, directions to the supply closet, a lunch recommendation, or just a friendly chat, my door (well, cubicle) was always open. Then, with a smile, I returned to my own work, thinking little of the encounter beyond the satisfaction of having helped a newcomer feel welcome.

What I didn't realize was that this was the beginning of one of the most unique and rewarding mentorships of my career. As the weeks unfolded, I discovered that this "newcomer" was, in fact, a legend in the industry, a commissioning manager who had started up more petrochemical plants than I could count. He had a knack for appearing at just the right moment, especially when I found myself wrestling with writer's block or the kind of technical conundrum that makes you question your life choices.

Whenever I was stuck, he would materialize beside my desk, settle into the extra chair, and, without preamble, launch into a story from his vast reservoir of experience. Sometimes, he'd clap his hands together with the enthusiasm of a magician about to reveal a trick, and share an anecdote from forty years ago: a lesson learned, a mistake made, a triumph celebrated. He never offered direct advice or criticism; instead, his stories were like breadcrumbs, leading me gently toward the solution I needed.

More often than not, I'd find the answer hidden in his tale, as if he'd anticipated my struggle before I even voiced it.

There was adventure in every conversation, sometimes we'd end up at a little hamburger joint, swapping stories over greasy fries and laughing about the quirks of the industry. There was excitement in the way he made even the most mundane technical challenge feel like a puzzle worth solving. And there was humility, too: he never flaunted his expertise, never made me feel small for not knowing what he did. Instead, he treated me as a peer, a fellow traveler on the winding road of professional growth.

Other team members occasionally wondered why I spent so much time with this older gentleman. Some even teased me about my "office grandpa." But I knew better. His mentorship was a rare gift, one that blended wisdom, patience, and a lighthearted sense of humor. He became the best teacher I ever had, not just on that project, but throughout my entire career. His guidance was never heavy-handed; it was graceful, subtle, and always delivered with gratitude for the opportunity to share and connect.

Looking back, I realize that the true adventure wasn't just in the technical challenges we solved together, but in the humanity we shared, the laughter, the humility, the mutual respect. His mentorship was a reminder that sometimes the most valuable lessons come from the most unexpected places, and that grace and gratitude are the true hallmarks of a life well-lived.

So, if you ever find yourself lucky enough to cross paths with a mentor of the most unique kind, embrace the adventure. Listen to their stories, laugh at their jokes, and let their wisdom guide you, not just in your work, but in the way you approach life itself.

There are moments in life when opportunity arrives not with fanfare, but quietly, like a gift horse standing patiently at your door, waiting for you to recognize its true value. My own "gift horse" moment came during a pivotal chapter of my career, and it would become a story of adventure, humility, and the blessings that often hide within uncertainty.

It began with a simple, unassuming conversation. The client's subject matter expert (SME), a person whose respect I had quietly earned through diligence and integrity, approached me with a proposition. His company had just lost a shift supervisor at their project site in Thailand, a critical role, and one not easily filled. He confided that he'd been asked to recommend someone from our team, and, to my surprise, he expressed genuine admiration for my work. Then came the question that would change everything: Would I be interested in stepping into the role?

Adventure and excitement surged through me. The prospect of working on-site in Thailand was both daunting and exhilarating, a leap into the unknown, far from the comfort of my current routine. Yet, beneath the thrill, I felt a deep sense of humility. The SME, for all his confidence in me, likely didn't realize that my experience with the process was largely theoretical, I had developed the operating manuals but had little hands-on operational exposure in the process that I wrote. Still, I recognized the rare nature of this opportunity. Many colleagues would have jumped at the chance, and here it was, offered to me, unbidden, a true blessing in disguise.

As I considered the offer, I couldn't help but reflect on the metaphor of the gift horse. Sometimes, life presents us with opportunities that seem intimidating or imperfect on the surface. It's easy to focus on what we lack, or to second-guess our readiness. But wisdom, and a bit of humility, reminds us not to "look a gift horse in the mouth." Instead, we must recognize the potential for growth, adventure, and transformation that lies within.

Respect for my current commitments weighed heavily on me. I had never left a job unfinished, and I knew that accepting this new role would mean stepping away from my current responsibilities. Out of respect for my team and my own values, I told the SME that I would need to clarify the situation with my manager before making any decisions.

What happened next was another blessing in disguise. When I approached my manager, expecting a difficult conversation, I was met with encouragement and understanding. He was already aware of the offer and, rather than expressing disappointment, he congratulated me on a job well done. He urged me to accept the new opportunity, recognizing that sometimes the best way to honor your current work is to embrace the next adventure with gratitude and courage.

Looking back, I see that moment as a turning point, a convergence of adventure, humility, respect, and the quiet excitement that comes from stepping into the unknown. The "gift horse" was not just the job offer itself, but the chance to grow beyond my comfort zone, to earn the respect of new colleagues, and to discover strengths I hadn't yet realized.

In the end, the greatest blessings often arrive disguised as challenges. They ask us to trust in ourselves, to honor the support of those around us, and to accept the adventure that life offers, sometimes when we least expect it. And when that gift horse appears, it's up to us to climb into the saddle, hold on tight, and ride toward the next horizon.

Just as the project was winding down and the next big adventure loomed on the horizon, I received a phone call that would turn an ordinary week into something extraordinary. It was my son, Jeremy, calling out of the blue with a simple but thrilling proposal: "Dad, how about I come visit Houston for a few days?" The surprise in his voice was matched only by the delight in my heart. In a world where work and distance often conspire to keep families apart, this felt like a stroke of pure fortune, a reminder that sometimes, the universe throws you a bone just when you need it most.

Jeremy's visit was more than just a family reunion; it was an adventure in itself. He stayed at Aunt Kaye's house, where I was also temporarily living, a setup that could have been the premise for a sitcom: two grown men, a generous aunt, and a revolving door of family stories. Our days were filled with relaxed moments, laughter, and the kind of conversations that only happen when you're not watching the clock.

We talked about everything from the mysteries of adulthood to the best way to grill a steak, but the real excitement came when Jeremy shared his latest news: his employer was offering him a chance to join a startup operation in Minnesota. The opportunity was as unexpected as it was promising, a leap into the unknown that could open doors to greater responsibility and adventure. I couldn't help but feel a surge of pride as I encouraged him to seize it, knowing that fortune favors the bold (and sometimes, the slightly nervous).

Of course, no father-son bonding would be complete without a little friendly competition and some classic Texas flavor. I made it my mission to introduce Jeremy to the authentic taste of Texas BBQ, because if you haven't had brisket in Houston, have you really lived? We also squared off at the pool table, where the stakes were high (mostly bragging rights and who would buy the next round). Now that Jeremy was of legal drinking age, we capped off our evenings with a few beers at my favorite local pub. There's a special kind of humility that comes from being soundly beaten at pool by your own son, but I took it in stride.

As my departure for Thailand approached, life became a whirlwind of coordination and last-minute errands. I drove my old Bronco back to Huntington Beach, an adventure in itself, given the car's age and temperament, sold it to my older brother, and shipped my few remaining belongings overseas.

The timing was serendipitous: I happened to be in town just as Jeremy, his new girlfriend Ann, and her young daughter Karisa were preparing to relocate to the Twin Cities. Jeremy had made the leap, accepting his employer's offer and stepping into the role of startup specialist. I couldn't help but feel a mix of excitement and humility, watching my son embark on his own journey, knowing that every adventure starts with a single, sometimes uncertain, step.

Before I left for Thailand, my brother David hosted a farewell gathering that brought the whole family together. He fired up his legendary barbecue and prepared his famous tri-tip steak, a meal so good it could make you forget your worries (or at least put them on hold until dessert). The house was filled with laughter, stories, and the kind of warmth that only comes from being surrounded by people who know all your embarrassing childhood stories and love you anyway.

It was a wonderful occasion to reconnect with everyone, young and old, including my daughter Regina. As I looked around the room, I felt a deep sense of gratitude and pride, knowing that, no matter where life's adventures took us, family would always be the anchor that kept us grounded.

And so, with a full heart, a lighter suitcase, and a few new pool-table bruises to my ego, I set off for the next chapter, reminded that life's greatest fortunes often arrive disguised as surprise visits, shared meals, and the laughter of those we love.

Chapter 14
The Land of Smiles

Landing in Bangkok just before midnight on July 14, 1995, I felt like an explorer stepping into a new world. The city's humid air buzzed with possibility, and even though jet lag clung to me like a stubborn backpack, I was too excited to care. After a late-night meal at the Amari Watergate Hotel, I tried to sleep, but my mind was already racing ahead to the next day's adventure.

The following morning, my company whisked me away to the Amari Resort Hotel in Pattaya Beach, a place that would be my home for the next three months. As I entered the lobby, I was greeted by a hostess whose smile could have lit up the entire city. She welcomed me with such warmth and grace that I half-expected her to hand me a lei and a treasure map. The check-in process was so smooth and thoughtful that I wondered if they'd mistaken me for royalty. If only they knew I was just a humble oil patch veteran with a suitcase full of wrinkled shirts and a heart full of curiosity.

My employer, determined to make my transition as seamless as possible, provided me with a car and a driver. Each morning, my driver would pick me up, and each evening he'd return me safely to the hotel. Eager to immerse myself in Thai culture (and maybe impress the locals), I carried a Thai/English translation book everywhere, determined to master more than just "hello" and "thank you." Spoiler alert: I didn't get much further than "hello" and "thank you."

One morning, as we cruised toward the refinery, I was buried in my translation book, trying to figure out how to ask my driver about his favorite Thai food. Suddenly, thump, thump! The car jolted over something sizable. I looked up, wide-eyed, expecting my driver to react. Instead, he stared straight ahead, as calm as a monk in meditation. Only when he noticed my panicked expression did he turn and, with the emotional range of a poker champion, simply say, "Dog."

I was speechless. Had we really just run over a dog? My Western sensibilities screamed for us to stop, check, and do something! But my driver, unfazed, continued on as if nothing had happened. Later at the office, I shared the story, expecting gasps of horror. Instead, my colleagues explained that, according to local Buddhist beliefs, the dog's fate was a matter of karma, perhaps it was paying off some mischief from a previous life. It was a humbling lesson in cultural perspective, and I realized that sometimes the world's mysteries are best met with a little humility and an open mind.

When I arrived at my new assignment, the real adventure began. I was immediately tasked with providing classroom training to Thai operators on a process I had only recently taught myself. It was a classic case of "fake it till you make it", except I was determined to do more than fake it. The training manager briefed me on the group: these operators had already completed six months of hands-on training in South Africa, so they weren't exactly rookies. My job was to tailor the training to our new refinery's unique procedures and systems.

Armed with the operating manuals I'd painstakingly written back in Houston, I dove into the challenge. I developed test criteria, evaluated their understanding, and kept meticulous records, partly out of dedication, partly out of sheer terror that someone would discover my own learning curve was still in progress. Every classroom session was a blend of structured instruction, practical walkdowns, and the occasional moment of comic relief (like the time I accidentally asked for a "fried elephant" instead of "fried egg" in Thai).

What made the experience truly special was the humanity and camaraderie that developed. The operators, sensing my genuine effort and humility, responded with respect and good humor. We learned together, laughed at our mistakes, and celebrated each small victory, whether it was mastering a tricky process or finally pronouncing a Thai word correctly.

For People Like Me

During my time at the refinery, I found myself not just working, but truly living an adventure, one that brought together people from all corners of the world and turned colleagues into friends. The Thai engineers and my fellow expatriates became more than just coworkers; they were companions on a journey filled with discovery, laughter, and the occasional cultural misstep that made every day memorable.

One lunch break stands out as a delightful chapter in this adventure. I was at the local bank, waiting to transfer some money, when the wife of one of the Japanese expat engineers joined me. With a twinkle of curiosity in her eye, she asked what life was like for an unmarried foreigner in Pattaya, a city famous for its vibrant nightlife and the legendary Walking Street.

Her question caught me off guard, but I couldn't help but smile at her candor. I shared, with a bit of self-deprecating humor, how the Thai ladies at the outdoor bars found my hairy appearance endlessly amusing, even bestowing upon me the nickname "King Kong." She burst out laughing, and in that moment, any cultural barriers melted away, replaced by genuine camaraderie.

Evenings at the resort hotel were a blend of relaxation and gentle mischief. The lobby bar became our gathering place, a stage for supervisors, their spouses, and me, the lone bachelor, to unwind and share stories. The wives, ever the matchmakers, took a keen interest in my love life, determined to find me a suitable romantic partner among the many charming Thai women. Their efforts were as endearing as they were persistent, and I always responded with warmth and gratitude, assuring them that while I appreciated their concern, I was quite capable of finding a date when the time was right.

The teasing about my bachelor status became a running joke until one evening, the conversation took a playful turn. I confessed that there was a particular lady at the hotel who had caught my eye, her radiant smile and genuine kindness made her stand out in any crowd. With a mischievous grin, I challenged the group: "I'll bet $1,000 she wouldn't agree to go out with me." One of the wives immediately accepted, and laughter erupted as we shook hands to seal the bet.

The next morning, still groggy from our late-night escapades, I was jolted awake by a phone call. My betting partner announced her imminent arrival, and moments later, she burst into my room, waving a piece of paper, gleefully declaring that I owed her $1,000. The paper listed a name and phone numbers, proof, she claimed, that I'd lost the bet. We both laughed at the absurdity, and she reassured me that the wager was all in good fun.

After she left, I prepared for breakfast, still chuckling at the morning's events. As I walked down the hall, I encountered the lady I truly admired. We exchanged the traditional Thai greeting, and as I looked into her eyes, I saw only the same gentle warmth as before, no hint that she knew about the bet or my secret affection. It dawned on me that my friend had approached the wrong woman, and I couldn't help but laugh at the comic twist my love life had taken.

Over breakfast, I reflected on the humorous predicament: somewhere in the hotel, a lady believed I was interested in her, while the woman who truly held my admiration remained blissfully unaware. I worried that my true affection might be misunderstood, that I'd be seen as a "Butterfly," a flirt, rather than someone genuinely interested. Determined to set things right, I decided to address the situation with honesty and care.

After enjoying breakfast, I strolled into the main lobby of the hotel, feeling that familiar blend of anticipation and mild anxiety that comes with navigating the social jungle of expat life. Glancing toward the reception counter, I spotted a cluster of six ladies gathered in the corner, all of them beaming at me with the kind of enthusiasm usually reserved for lottery winners or long-lost relatives. Their collective energy was unmistakable, if smiles could talk, theirs would have been shouting, "Here he comes!"

Summoning my courage (and maybe a bit of that "fake it till you make it" bravado), I called for Khun Joy and asked if we could step aside for a private word.

I began, as honestly as I could, by explaining the situation: my friends, the ever-watchful wives of my colleagues, had been fretting about my status as a single man in Pattaya, as if I were a rare bird in need of careful matchmaking. I confided in Joy that there was one lady working at the hotel whom I was secretly interested in and hoped to invite to dinner. To my surprise, she responded immediately, saying she already knew about it, and then pointed to one of the beautiful ladies in the group who was smiling at me. I couldn't help but smile myself, partly at the mix-up, and partly at the sheer comedy of being the subject of such enthusiastic speculation.

Trying to keep things light, I clarified that my friends had, in their well-meaning efforts, approached the wrong lady. While her friend was indeed beautiful, I felt it was only fair to clear up the misunderstanding, after all, no one wants to be the accidental recipient of someone else's secret admirer. Khun Joy, ever the professional diplomat, reassured me with a gentle smile that she would explain the situation to her friend and that I needn't worry about it any further. I could almost hear the collective sigh of relief from the universe.

As our conversation continued, Joy explained that hotel policy strictly prohibited employees from dating guests. However, since I'd been living at the hotel for a couple of months, everyone was familiar with me and considered me a "nice guy", which, in hotel parlance, is just a notch above "harmless tourist." She added that if I revealed the identity of the woman I was interested in, she could discreetly speak with her and let me know if there was any mutual interest. It was all starting to feel like a scene from a romantic comedy, minus the dramatic soundtrack.

With a smile (and a heart pounding just a little faster), I asked Khun Joy if she would do that for me, and she agreed. Still smiling, I then confessed, perhaps a bit sheepishly, that it was her, Khun Joy herself, whom I wished to take to dinner. Her expression shifted in an instant, a mix of surprise and uncertainty flickering across her face. I could sense she wanted to decline, but was unsure how to respond.

Respecting her feelings, I gently asked her not to answer right away but to give it some thought, assuring her that I would ask again another time. With that, I walked away, realizing that I had "won" the bet after all, though, like my married friends, I had no intention of claiming any winnings. Sometimes, the real prize is simply having the courage to be honest, the compassion to respect another's feelings, and the good humor to laugh at yourself when life turns into a sitcom.

During that surprisingly remarkable chapter of my life, I had the privilege of witnessing Joy's journey from a respectful distance, a journey marked by unwavering dedication, resilience, and a quiet but powerful ambition. In the world of hospitality, where smiles are currency and patience is a superpower, Joy stood out not just for her work ethic but for the genuine warmth she brought to every interaction.

It was no surprise to anyone (except perhaps her, in her modesty) when she was first recognized as "Girl of the Month" and then, in a well-deserved crescendo, honored as "Girl of the Year." Her achievements didn't just earn her a flattering write-up in the local newspaper, they sparked admiration throughout her workplace, where her leadership potential was recognized by all who had the good fortune to work alongside her.

As a result of her exemplary performance, Joy was selected for the hotel's management training program, a prestigious opportunity that took her to the renowned Amari Watergate Hotel. There, she absorbed the finer points of hospitality with the same grace and diligence she brought to every task. When she returned to the Amari Resort Hotel in Pattaya, it was as a newly minted Guest Relations Manager, ready to lead with both heart and skill. I couldn't help but feel a surge of admiration (and, truth be told, a little awe) at how she navigated each new challenge with humility and a smile that could light up the entire lobby.

Meanwhile, I had moved into my assigned condo, quietly cheering her on from the sidelines. Building trust and friendship with Joy was a gradual process, one that required patience, sincerity, and a willingness to accept that sometimes the best things in life can't be rushed. When she finally agreed to join me for dinner, it felt like winning the lottery, if the lottery also came with butterflies in your stomach and the urgent need to Google "how not to mess up a first date in Thailand."

Wanting to honor Thai cultural customs (and avoid any accidental faux pas that might land me in the "awkward foreigner" hall of fame), I sought the advice of a Thai friend at work. With kindness and a twinkle of mischief, my friend explained the expectations and traditions I should observe. I took notes as if preparing for an exam, determined to show Joy and her family the respect they deserved.

When the evening of our dinner arrived, I picked Joy up at her grandmother's home, armed with a bouquet of flowers for Joy and a generous basket of food for her grandmother, a humble offering, but one given with heartfelt sincerity. To ensure Joy's comfort and safety (and perhaps to keep an eye on the "new guy"), her brother and cousin accompanied us to dinner. I like to think of them as my unofficial chaperones, ready to step in if I commit any major blunders. Once they were satisfied that Joy was in safe hands, they quietly departed, leaving us to enjoy our first evening together, a night filled with laughter, gentle conversation, and the kind of nervous excitement that only comes when two people are brave enough to take a chance on something new.

In the early days of my relationship with Joy, life felt like a delightful blend of uncertainty and possibility. Every evening, I made it my mission to pick her up from work, ensuring she had a proper dinner before escorting her home safely. It was a small gesture, but one rooted in respect and genuine care, a way to show her that, even in a world full of unpredictability, she could count on me for consistency and kindness.

Now, Joy was no stranger to independence, she zipped around on her trusty little motorbike like a pro. But she'd never driven a car before, and I saw an opportunity for a little adventure (and maybe a few laughs). One evening, I took her to a wide, open dirt lot, handed her the keys, and said, "Tonight, you're in the driver's seat, literally!" With a mix of excitement and nerves, she slid behind the wheel. I encouraged her to stomp on the accelerator, just to feel the car's power, and then to slam on the brakes, sending us sliding in the dirt. Her laughter echoed through the night, and for a moment, we were just two kids playing in a grown-up sandbox.

As our relationship grew, so did my admiration for her spirit. But I was also honest, with her and with myself. My work assignment was temporary, and the future was a big, intriguing question mark. I couldn't promise where I'd be next month, let alone next year. So, out of integrity and respect, I kept our relationship platonic, determined that if we ever parted ways, it would be with fond memories and no regrets. After all, nothing says "I care" quite like not making promises you can't keep (even if you're tempted to promise the moon).

Then came January 1996, and with it, a twist worthy of any romantic adventure. I decided to take a vacation to Bali, Indonesia, a place as full of intrigue as it is of beautiful beaches. Joy asked if she could join, and I couldn't resist the idea of sharing this adventure with her. We set off together, two travelers with open hearts and open minds.

Bali worked its magic on us. Between exploring temples, sampling exotic foods (and occasionally wondering if we'd just eaten something that could bite back), and getting lost in bustling markets, we found ourselves growing closer than ever. One night, under a sky full of stars, we shared our deepest secrets, honest, vulnerable, and unfiltered. There were no promises about the future, just a mutual understanding that what we had was real and that sometimes the best adventures are the ones you don't try to control.

After returning from Bali and settling back into work, I was met with a delightful surprise that spoke volumes about the bonds I'd formed. On my desk sat a large box, beautifully wrapped and topped with a card. The card's cover featured a big, grinning gorilla, a playful nod to an inside joke, and inside, it read, "to my baby brother," signed by my friends from Japan, the married couple whose wife had once asked me what it was like to be single in Pattaya.

Curiosity piqued, I opened the box to find a large stuffed black gorilla with a bright red bow around its neck. The sight made me burst out laughing, and as I looked up, I saw my co-workers gathered in the doorway, their faces lit with anticipation and shared joy. In that moment, the office was filled with laughter and warmth, a testament to the genuine friendships that had blossomed across cultures and continents. The gorilla wasn't just a gift; it was a symbol of camaraderie, a reminder that even in a professional setting, playful caring and thoughtful gestures can create lasting memories and a sense of belonging. To this day, I still have that gorilla, a cherished memento of the kindness and humor that defined that chapter of my life.

But life, as it often does, soon tested the strength of those bonds. Unexpectedly, I developed kidney stones and found myself hospitalized twice. During these challenging nights, Joy's devotion shone through. Despite her own exhaustion, she steadfastly refused to leave my side, choosing to sleep on the couch in my hospital room rather than return home. Her presence was a quiet act of love and solidarity, a reminder that true friendship and partnership are measured not just in grand gestures, but in the willingness to share discomfort and uncertainty.

During my second hospital stay, fate threw us another curveball: Joy herself fell ill, running a fever yet still insisting on staying with me. Witnessing her struggle, I felt a deep sense of humility and gratitude. It was my turn to care for her. Against medical advice, I checked myself out of the hospital, gently carried Joy home, and nursed her back to health. In those days, our roles reversed, she became the one in need, and I found purpose in offering her the same steadfast support she'd given me.

As our relationship deepened and we continued to date, I found that all the emotional defenses I had so carefully constructed, those bricks I thought were expertly shaped and securely cemented, began to crumble at my feet. It turns out, love has a way of sneaking past even the most fortified walls, especially when it arrives disguised as laughter, kindness, and the gentle touch of someone who truly cares.

The protective barrier I'd built around my heart, once my proudest DIY project, simply couldn't withstand the genuine connection growing between us. In those moments of vulnerability, I saw her not just as a companion, but as the very princess from my childhood dreams, the one I was destined to honor and protect above all else. Who knew that the journey to find her would require crossing the entire Pacific Ocean.

What I had never imagined, however, was that our separate paths, once so far apart, would finally converge so unexpectedly and perfectly. There she stood, not just as a partner, but as the missing piece I never knew I needed. Her compassion and warmth melted away my stubborn pride, and her laughter, always ready, always genuine, reminded me not to take myself too seriously. She had a knack for finding the humor in my quirks, and I learned that humility isn't about thinking less of yourself, but about being open to love, even when it arrives in the most surprising ways.

Through her, I discovered that true caring isn't measured by grand gestures, but by the small, everyday acts of kindness: a gentle word when I was frustrated, a patient ear when I rambled on about my day, and the way she'd slip her hand into mine as if to say, "I'm here, and you're safe." Her compassion was a quiet force, steady and unwavering, teaching me that real strength lies in vulnerability, and that the bravest thing you can do is let someone see your heart.

As the project reached its critical startup and performance phase, I found myself standing at a crossroads of both professional pride and personal vulnerability. Serving as shift supervisor, I was entrusted with overseeing three distinct areas of the plant, a responsibility that, if I'm honest, sometimes felt like juggling flaming torches while riding a unicycle. Yet, there was a quiet thrill in the challenge, and I approached each day with a mix of humility and enthusiasm, determined not to let my nerves show (at least not too much).

One of my most memorable assignments during this period was working side by side with the licensor's startup specialist in the residual catalytic cracking unit. Together, we faced a parade of operational challenges, some expected, others popping up like uninvited guests at a family reunion. There were moments of frustration, certainly, but also a deep sense of camaraderie as we tackled each issue, sometimes with a sigh, sometimes with a laugh, and always with a shared commitment to getting things right.

Our efforts, fueled by equal parts perseverance and caffeine, ultimately led to the successful completion of the performance test. That moment, when the unit finally met its operational standards, and we knew we'd set the stage for sustained commercial production, was both exhilarating and humbling. I may have done a little victory dance, behind closed doors, of course.

With commercial operations now running smoothly, my assignment drew to a close. I'd like to say I walked away with nothing but pride, but the truth is, there was a bittersweet sadness in leaving behind the team, the routine, and the sense of purpose that had anchored me for so long. Even more poignant was the personal transition that followed: Joy and I, after so much shared laughter and hope, prepared to say our farewells. We parted with a quiet, unspoken hope that destiny might one day bring us back together, and that the distance between us would prove only temporary. If life has taught me anything, it's that hope is a stubborn thing, it lingers, even when logic says it shouldn't.

Returning to Huntington Beach, I was fortunate, though perhaps a little surprised, to find myself with a substantial amount of savings from my time abroad. (Who knew that being too busy to spend money could be a financial strategy?) Recognizing that my future might hold more assignments in far-flung places, I decided to invest my earnings rather than let them languish in a low-interest account.

After some thoughtful discussions with my older brother and his wife, we agreed to pool our resources and purchase a house together. It was a practical arrangement, but also a deeply human one: my brother's family gained a comfortable home in a great neighborhood, and I secured a safe haven for my savings. Given my frequent absences, the partnership allowed both families to make the most of the opportunity, a win-win, as they say, though I suspect my brother's kids were mostly excited about having a new backyard.

In the months that followed our farewell, Joy and I did our best to bridge the miles between us. We spoke on the phone several times a week, sharing stories, worries, and the occasional bad joke. We even exchanged faxes, yes, faxes!, which, in retrospect, felt both quaint and oddly romantic. Those messages, filled with everyday details and words of encouragement, became a lifeline, helping us maintain our bond across the miles. Still, there were days when the distance felt impossibly wide, and I'd catch myself staring at the phone, willing it to ring.

Hoping to close that gap, Joy bravely visited the United States Embassy in Bangkok, twice, to apply for an entry visa. Both times, she was turned away. The embassy staff, with the bureaucratic compassion of a DMV clerk, informed her that a third rejection would mean waiting a full year before she could try again. Saddened by the setbacks and not wanting to risk further disappointment, I gently advised her to pause her efforts until we could find a better way forward. It was a difficult conversation, tinged with sadness, and the kind of humility that comes from realizing some things are simply out of your hands.

Determined not to let bureaucracy have the last word, I reached out to the United States Embassy in Washington, D.C., sharing our story with as much honesty and hope as I could muster. To my relief, and, I'll admit, a bit of surprise, they responded with a detailed set of instructions for applying for a fiancé visa. With renewed enthusiasm (and a healthy respect for paperwork), Joy and I worked together to complete the application, double-checking every form and signature. It wasn't glamorous, but it was a testament to our commitment, our resilience, and our belief that, with a little luck and a lot of patience, love might just find a way.

Just when I thought life had settled into a predictable rhythm, the universe decided to shake things up with a single, unexpected phone call from Joy. She sounded both amused and slightly bewildered as she explained that a friend of mine had shown up at her hotel, trying to track me down. He'd left a contact number and a simple message: "Call me." Now, I've learned to expect the unexpected, but I couldn't even have guessed what was coming next.

When I returned the call, my friend wasted no time. "I need your help on a project in Thailand," he said, his voice brimming with urgency and the kind of excitement that only comes from a plan that's half-baked and twice as ambitious as it should be. The project? Commissioning checks, tests, and supporting the startup of a deep catalytic cracker unit, right in the heart of Thailand, not far from my last assignment. It was the kind of opportunity that comes with a side order of adventure and a generous helping of uncertainty.

With a mix of honesty and humility, I admitted I'd never worked on a project quite like this before. But integrity demanded I give it my all, and the thrill of a new challenge was too tempting to resist. So, I accepted the lead position, packed my bags, and hopped on a plane, heart pounding with anticipation and a little bit of "what have I gotten myself into?"

Landing in Thailand, I was greeted at the airport by Joy and a couple of close family members. Their warm smiles and heartfelt welcome instantly reminded me of the humanity that makes every journey worthwhile. They whisked me away to Joy's hotel, where laughter, stories, and a few awkward attempts at speaking Thai set the tone for what would become an unforgettable chapter.

Now, my friend, let's call him "The Improviser", wasn't exactly a fan of detailed planning. His approach to project management was more "let's wing it and see what happens" than "let's stick to the schedule." That left me with the not-so-small task of developing daily work plans and managing communications with the client during our meetings. It was a crash course in humility, as I quickly learned that even the best-laid plans can unravel faster than a cheap suitcase in a monsoon.

Once commissioning was complete, the project transitioned to startup, and both of us were assigned to the night shift. The process technology was Chinese, and the day shift was run by a team of Chinese engineers who approached startup and performance testing with the precision of a Swiss watch, and the flexibility of a steel beam. Navigating the cultural and technical differences was an adventure in itself, filled with moments of confusion, camaraderie, and the occasional comic misunderstanding. But through it all, we found common ground in our shared commitment to getting the job done right.

Despite the challenges, the project was genuinely enjoyable and lasted about six months. There were days when everything went wrong, and nights when a small victory, like getting a stubborn valve to cooperate, felt like winning the lottery. The assignment came with some unexpected perks, too: a car, a per diem allowance, and the freedom to choose my own accommodation. Any leftover per diem was mine to keep, which made for some creative budgeting and a few extra nights out enjoying the local cuisine (and, let's be honest, the occasional street food gamble that didn't always end well).

But the real adventure wasn't just in the work. Amid the daily grind, I took a leap of faith in my personal life. With honesty and a heart full of hope, I officially proposed to Joy, presenting her with an engagement ring that sparkled almost as brightly as her smile. Together, we sought her family's permission to honor the traditional courtship customs of Thailand, a process that involved more negotiation, laughter, and heartfelt moments than any business deal I've ever struck.

In Thai culture, marriage is not just the union of two people, it's the weaving together of families, traditions, and generations. The dowry negotiation, a time-honored ritual, is a moment where respect, obligation, and love all come together in a dance as old as time itself.

On the day of our engagement, we gathered outside Joy's family home, the earth beneath us warm and grounding. Joy's Grandmother and Aunt Suk, the respected elders, took their places as the dignified arbiters of tradition. Joy, ever dutiful and poised, was tasked with being the interpreter, her role was to faithfully relay every word, every nuance, and every raised eyebrow between her family and me. I could tell she took this responsibility seriously.

The negotiation began with a spirited back-and-forth between Grandmother and Aunt Suk, their voices rising and falling like a well-rehearsed duet. I watched, fascinated, as numbers were tossed around with the same intensity as championship poker chips. After about ten minutes, Grandmother turned to Joy, who relayed the verdict: the dowry was set at 144,448 Thai Baht, about $5,750 USD. I did the math in my head, but in my heart, I knew that no number could ever truly measure Joy's worth. Still, I nodded with respect, understanding that this was about honoring tradition, not putting a price tag on love.

With a twinkle of intrigue, I asked Joy to double-check with Grandmother and Aunt Suk if they were sure about the "lucky numbers." This sparked another round of animated discussion, clearly, luck and numerology are not to be taken lightly in these matters! After a few more minutes, the elders reaffirmed their decision, and I sealed the agreement with a smile and a nod, feeling both honored and slightly relieved that I hadn't accidentally bid against myself.

Just as we were about to rise from our seats, Grandmother had one last, important message. She instructed Joy to translate her words with complete honesty: "If my granddaughter ever mistreats you, you must come directly to me. I won't hesitate to take a switch from the tree and give her a gentle reminder, just as I did when she was a child." The seriousness in her eyes was softened by the unmistakable glint of affection. I turned to Grandmother, gave her a warm smile, and, unable to resist, offered a playful wink. She winked right back, sealing our new family bond with a gesture that said, "We're in this together."

A man cannot expect to marry a young woman and have her be happy without honoring her desire for a family. From the very beginning, Joy made her wish clear: she dreamed of having just one child, a boy. I respected her wishes, and, in the spirit of adventure (and perhaps a dash of impatience), we didn't wait for the wedding ceremony to begin our journey toward parenthood. By the time my assignment wrapped up in June of 1997, Joy was already expecting our child, a little miracle that brought excitement and a sense of destiny to our lives.

During this whirlwind, we received the official approval for Joy's fiancé visa from the American Embassy in Bangkok, a milestone that felt like winning the lottery, only with more paperwork and fewer confetti cannons. I had hoped to honor her family's traditions with a wedding ceremony in Thailand, fulfilling my promise to her Grandmother and Aunt Suk, and upholding the agreement about the dowry. But Joy, ever the practical and compassionate partner, gently vetoed the idea. "Why spend money on a big ceremony," she reasoned, "when we could save it for our future?" Her logic was as sound as her heart was generous, so the dowry arrangements were put on hold until our marriage was formalized.

As our time in Thailand drew to a close, Joy insisted on maintaining her cherished tradition of making a financial offering to her Grandmother. This wasn't just a custom, it was a heartfelt expression of gratitude and respect for the woman who had played such a significant role in raising her. Before our departure, Joy asked if she could give Grandmother 10,000 Thai Baht (about $400 at the time). I agreed without hesitation, understanding how much this act meant to Joy and how it honored the bonds of family.

On our final day, while Joy visited with her aunt inside the house, Grandmother approached me quietly. With a grip that could rival a seasoned arm wrestler, she grasped my upper arm, smiled warmly, and gave me a knowing wink, a silent but powerful gesture that said, "You're family now, and I care for you deeply." Seizing the moment, I discreetly handed Grandmother a 10,000 Baht bill, returning her smile and winking back in our shared secret. Without missing a beat, she tucked the money into her brassiere and hurried away to hide her newfound treasure, as if she'd just won the family lottery.

Later, when it was time for Joy to present her own offering, Grandmother was genuinely surprised and shot me a quick look, seeking reassurance. I met her gaze with another wink, our secret code for "it's all good",, and she accepted Joy's gift with a grateful smile. For a while, I kept my own gesture private from Joy, wanting to quietly fulfill my promise to Grandmother and support her in a way that was both respectful and loving.

In that moment, surrounded by tradition, affection, and a little bit of mischief, I realized that love isn't just about grand gestures or formal ceremonies. Sometimes, it's about honoring the quiet wishes of those we care about, supporting each other's dreams, and finding joy in the small, secret acts of kindness that bind a family together. And if you can do it all with a wink and a smile, well, that's the real adventure.

Chapter 15
A Cohesive Life and Living "Sabai-Sabai"

When we arrived at LAX, we braced ourselves for the gauntlet of immigration and customs, where Joy's paperwork and our personal belongings were scrutinized with the intensity of a reality show judge deciding who gets to stay on the island. For a moment, I half-expected someone to leap out and accuse us of being an undercover duo from the underworld's most charming (and unsuspecting) tag team of international criminals.

But, to our relief, and perhaps the disappointment of any lurking drama, we made it through unscathed, passports stamped and dignity intact. With a mix of excitement and disbelief, we set off for our new home in Huntington Beach, hearts pounding with the thrill of a fresh start and the humble realization that sometimes the greatest adventures begin with a suitcase, a smile, and a little luck at the border.

Once we arrived at the house, Joy found herself instantly swept into a whirlwind of family, a scene that could have overwhelmed even the most seasoned diplomat. Imagine this: as you step inside, family members appear from every doorway, each eager to greet you with open arms. Their voices blend together in a joyful chorus of welcomes, friendly questions, and the occasional bit of well-meaning advice about thriving in California.

For many, such an enthusiastic reception might feel like being lovingly tossed into the deep end of a pool, but not for Joy. With her background in hotel guest relations and years of navigating the unpredictable tides of international travelers, she handled the moment with the grace of a seasoned captain steering through choppy waters. While others might have clung to the metaphorical life raft, Joy simply smiled, nodded, and sailed through the introductions as if she were cruising on a sunlit bay, calm, collected, and utterly unflappable.

There was adventure in every handshake, excitement in every new face, and a genuine sense of humanity in the way Joy listened to each story, no matter how many times she'd heard about "the time Uncle Mike caught the world's smallest fish." She met every question, no matter how awkward, with humility, never letting on that she'd already answered "Where are you from?" at least a dozen times that afternoon.

And, of course, there was humor. When someone inevitably mispronounced her name ("Wiparat?"), she just laughed and replied, "Please just call me Joy." Her lighthearted spirit set everyone at ease, turning what could have been an overwhelming introduction into a joyful celebration of new beginnings.

My relationship with Joy has always been built on a foundation of honesty and integrity. From the very beginning, I loved this woman, quirks, dreams, and all. We approached every decision together, never shying away from the tough conversations or the little adventures that life brought our way. When it came to the idea of a wedding, I initially hoped we might celebrate in Thailand, not just for us, but to honor my promise to her family. But Joy, ever the practical adventurer, had her own perspective: "Spending huge amounts of money on ceremonial weddings is a waste, it belongs in the bank!" she declared, with a twinkle in her eye that told me she meant business (and maybe a little mischief).

So, with a shared sense of excitement and a dash of humility, we tossed aside the notion of grand ballrooms, towering cakes, and a guest list longer than a Texas highway. Instead, we chose the path less traveled, a simple ceremony at the Orange County Courthouse. No witnesses, no fancy frills, just two people standing face-to-face, making an honest promise for whatever adventures lie ahead. It was as if we were saying, "Let's do this, side by side, come what may."

There was something deeply human and humbling about that moment. We didn't need a crowd to validate our commitment; the excitement was in the leap itself, the adventure of building a life together with nothing but love, trust, and a healthy sense of humor to guide us.

Our honeymoon was as unconventional as it was unforgettable. Instead of jetting off to a far-flung island, we decided to keep things simple and meaningful, focusing on family, adventure, and the places that shaped who we are. I wanted Joy to meet my older sister, Kaye, who lived in Texas, and I knew the feeling was mutual. So, we flew Kaye out to join us in Las Vegas, where Joy and I would spend a couple of days soaking in the neon lights, sharing laughter, and making memories that would last a lifetime.

From there, our little trio piled into the car and set off on a road trip that would take us through the heart of my own story. Our first stop was my hometown of Oildale, where I proudly showed Joy the old homestead. There's something special about sharing your roots with the person you love, watching Joy take in the sights, hearing Kaye's stories, and feeling the warmth of family all around us. Even as Joy battled morning sickness (which, let's be honest, added a whole new level of adventure to every pit stop), she never lost her radiant smile or her sense of humor. If there were an Olympic event for "gracefully surviving a road trip while queasy," Joy would have taken the gold.

Next, we drove through the majestic sequoia redwoods, a place so awe-inspiring it made even my tallest tales seem small by comparison. We craned our necks to see the treetops, snapped photos, and let the fresh forest air work its magic. Of course, there were a few moments when the winding roads and Joy's morning sickness teamed up for a surprise attack, but she handled it like a champ. Kaye and I did our best to keep the mood light, offering up ginger ale, crackers, and a steady stream of corny jokes. (Note to self: "Why did the tree get a promotion? Because it was outstanding in its field!" did not help with the nausea, but it did get a groan and a smile.)

From the redwoods, we made our way to California's wine country, where we sampled the local flavors, well, Kaye and I did, while Joy stuck to sparkling water and gave us her expert opinion on the best cheese pairings. It was a short trip, but every mile was filled with laughter, love, and the kind of small adventures that become cherished family legends. Before we wrapped up our journey, we stopped to spend a day with my younger sister, Patty. While driving along the California coastline, the ocean breeze in our hair and the promise of home just around the bend, we made one last stop for a walk on Santa Monica Pier.

Looking back, our honeymoon wasn't about luxury or extravagance. It was about compassion, supporting each other through the queasy moments and the joyful ones. It was about family, welcoming Joy into the fold and sharing the places and people that made me who I am. It was about adventure, embracing the unexpected, from scenic detours to impromptu sing-alongs. And above all, it was about fun, finding humor in the hiccups, delight in the detours, and gratitude in every shared experience.

It was time for me to focus on work and the practicalities of life. But, as life often does, it threw us a curveball: my brother David and his wife decided to separate and divorce. Suddenly, the house we shared became a puzzle to solve, think of it as a real-life game of Monopoly, except instead of hotels and railroads, we were negotiating bedrooms and who got custody of the good coffee maker. With humility and a bit of concern for everyone's well-being, I bought out their shares, making sure the transition was as smooth and fair as possible. Joy, still expecting our child, and I found ourselves not just newlyweds but partners in our own home, ready to face the future as a family, even if we sometimes felt like we were assembling furniture without the instructions (and with a few extra screws left over for good measure).

Soon after, I accepted an assignment with a Houston-based company as Production Superintendent on an old Bethlehem Jack-up Platform converted to a production platform. The product, crude oil, would be pumped through a hose that connected the platform to a Floating Storage & Offloading vessel (FSO), another name for a floating tank farm. This assignment would take me one hundred miles off the coast of Gabon, Africa.

On the platform, I would be the Person In Charge (PIC) and would oversee the operation, with the exception of the floating tank farm, which, as I quickly learned, no one is above the Captain of a Ship, even if it's floating on a turret. The job would take me away from home on a 28-day-on, 28-day-off rotation, which meant I spent as much time offshore as I did at home. Before I left for Gabon, I let my employer know that my wife was expecting to deliver our child in January or February. To their credit, they showed genuine concern and compassion, granting me extra time at home so I could help Joy recover and care for our newborn. It was a small gesture, but it meant the world to us, a reminder that even in a business built on steel and oil, there's room for humanity.

Looking back, those days were a whirlwind of change, challenge, and unexpected joy. We faced each new twist with humility, welcomed each other's families with open arms, and learned to laugh at ourselves when things didn't go as planned. Through it all, love and compassion were the glue that held us together, proof that no matter where life takes you, the best adventures are the ones you share with the people you love. And if you ever find yourself assembling furniture at midnight, just remember: sometimes the missing piece is simply a good laugh and a little patience.

As the days ticked down to the arrival of our child, the air in our home was electric with anticipation. Joy had a special wish: she wanted to choose our son's first name, knowing in her heart that this would be our only child together. Out of respect for her and mindful of my older children, I agreed without hesitation. She chose the name Jessada, a name that sparkled with meaning: "gift from God." I was touched by her thoughtfulness, and, true to my nature, I couldn't resist adding my own twist. "How about I pick his middle name?" I asked, grinning. Joy, ever gracious, agreed, and so our son became Jessada James, a name that, in America, carried a hint of legendary outlaw spirit. We laughed, deciding his nickname would be "JJ," a moniker as friendly and approachable as a boy could hope for.

The night before JJ's grand entrance, our home was filled with the comforting aroma of pizza and the sound of laughter as we watched TV with my brother Mike and his three sons. It was a scene straight out of a Norman Rockwell painting, if Rockwell had ever painted a family in pajamas, balancing pizza slices and remote controls. Around 6:00 p.m., Joy's water broke. She took a gentle shower, calm as ever (not really), while I scrambled to gather our things, feeling a mix of excitement and the kind of nervous energy usually reserved for astronauts before liftoff.

At the hospital, Joy was the picture of determination. She told the nurse she wanted a natural birth, no epidural. The nurse nodded, and we settled in for the long haul. My brother Mike and Kathy (my brother's wife) soon arrived, and the four of us gathered around Joy's bedside, playing cards and sharing stories, trying to keep the mood light. Joy's spirit was high, her laughter infectious, and for a while, it felt less like a hospital room and more like a family game night with a very special guest on the way.

As midnight approached, Joy reconsidered her earlier decision and asked for an epidural. "I've changed my mind," she said with a sheepish smile. "Turns out, natural is overrated." We all chuckled, and once she was comfortable, the card game resumed, punctuated by jokes and gentle encouragement. The hours slipped by, and around four in the morning, the room transformed into a flurry of activity as the nurses prepared for JJ's arrival.

In the quiet, magical hours before dawn, JJ was born, peacefully, beautifully, and with a sense of calm that seemed to radiate from him. The nurses cleaned him, then gave his tiny foot a gentle tweak, coaxing out his first cry, a sound that filled the room with relief and joy. They wrapped him up and placed him in my arms. I looked down at this new life, marveling at his serene, attentive gaze. He seemed to listen to my voice, his eyes wide with curiosity, as if he already knew he was deeply loved. In that moment, I felt a profound sense of wonder and connection, a memory etched forever in my heart.

When Joy was ready, I placed JJ in her arms. The bond between mother and child was immediate and unbreakable, a quiet, sacred moment that needed no words. We both knew our lives had changed forever, and as we gazed at our son, we felt the warmth of family, the humility of new beginnings, and the adventure of a future waiting to unfold.

Looking back, I can't help but smile at the blend of excitement, love, and gentle humor that colored those hours. From Joy's determined birth plan (and her equally determined change of heart), to the card games and laughter, to the awe of holding JJ for the first time, it was a story of humanity at its best, messy, beautiful, and filled with the kind of moments that remind us what it means to be a family.

During this challenging period, I found myself standing at the crossroads of multiple responsibilities, each one pulling at my heart in a different direction. My primary concern was supporting Joy through her recovery after childbirth, ensuring she regained her strength so I could return to my offshore assignment with peace of mind.

At the same time, my daughter Regina's birthday was approaching, just a week before my scheduled flight back to work. I felt a deep, genuine desire to celebrate her birthday with her, not only to honor the occasion but also to provide an opportunity for her to meet her new half-brother. In my heart, I hoped this gesture would help bridge the gap between the old and new chapters of our family.

Yet, as much as I tried to approach the situation with honesty and integrity, I underestimated how Regina might feel. I called her, my voice filled with hope and a father's love, eager to share this moment and invite her into our evolving family story. But as the conversation unfolded, I sensed a wall rising between us, a wall built from confusion, hurt, and the raw vulnerability that comes when life changes faster than our hearts can keep up.

She was not ready. The words she spoke were honest, but they landed with a weight I hadn't anticipated. There was pain in her voice, a mixture of sadness, perhaps even betrayal, and a longing for things to remain as they once were. I could hear the confusion and the hurt, and suddenly, I found myself at a loss for words. All the compassion I felt, all the love I wanted to express, seemed to tangle on my tongue. I wanted to reassure her, to tell her that my love for her was unchanged, that she would always be my daughter, no matter how our family grew or shifted. But in that moment, the right words escaped me.

The call ended abruptly, leaving a heavy silence in its wake. I sat there, phone in hand, feeling the sting of misunderstanding and the ache of warm regret. I realized, with humility, that my good intentions had collided with her very real emotions. I had hoped to bring us closer, but instead, I had unwittingly created distance, a gap that would last for several years.

During those years, I often reflected on that conversation. I replayed it in my mind, wishing I had listened more, spoken less, or simply told her how much she meant to me. There was regret, yes, but also a growing sense of compassion, for her, for myself, and for the imperfect ways we all navigate love and change. I learned that sometimes, even with the best intentions, we can hurt those we care about most. And in those moments, humility is found not in defending our actions, but in acknowledging the pain, accepting responsibility, and holding space for healing.

It was only years later, after time and reflection had softened the edges of our misunderstanding, that Regina and I agreed to reconnect. We tried to let go of past grievances and make an honest attempt to rebuild our relationship. Unfortunately for both of us, we never really seemed to let the past go. On one visit, I experienced an evening of listening to my daughter's protective nature toward her mother, which deepened my understanding that the past will never be forgotten nor forgiven, and no matter how hard we tried, I would never fully be a part of her life, and I had to let go. My door will always remain open for a change, but until then, I will not live a condemned life to a sad memory.

Looking back, I carry a sense of warm regret, not for loving too much, but for not always knowing how to show it in the ways that mattered most. Yet, I am grateful for the lessons learned: that honesty and integrity sometimes mean admitting our mistakes; that love is as much about listening as it is about speaking; and that compassion, even when it comes with confusion and loss for words, is the bridge that can lead us home again.

During a rare break at home, I got word that my offshore platform had suffered a major incident, a ruptured heater treater tube sparked a fire and forced a total shutdown. Thanks to the crew's quick thinking, the blaze was contained, but the Person in Charge (PIC) was promptly relieved. When I returned, I found myself in the hot seat, tasked with steering the team through repairs and a tense restart.

No sooner had we fired things up than a new problem surfaced: the outlet plate exchanger kept clogging with wax, even though the crude was supposed to be "clean." Instead of running at full throttle, we limped along, keeping safety and operational integrity front and center while engineering scrambled for a fix. It was a test of patience, teamwork, and creative problem-solving, sometimes the biggest adventure is just keeping things afloat when nothing goes as planned.

But the real challenge was endurance. With no relief in sight, I worked four straight months on that tiny platform. The walls felt like they were closing in, and by the time my replacement arrived, I'd lost nearly thirty pounds and looked like I'd been through a reality-show survival challenge. My wife took one look at me and said, "You're not going back." For once, I didn't argue. Sometimes, the bravest move is knowing when to step away. I left that job with more than just a lighter frame, I carried away a lesson in humility and self-care.

For People Like Me

It was at this time that I suggested we sell our home in Huntington Beach and move to Houston, the city where all my contracts seemed to originate. It seemed that being able to attend face-to-face interviews would outweigh those performed by phone. Soon enough, we were resituated in Houston, and I landed my next gig, which took me to Venezuela, where I commuted to a gas platform in the middle of Lake Maracaibo by boat. Instead of napping like the others, I chatted with the captain in Spanish and even took the helm myself, much to the amusement of the locals. It was a reminder that every new place brings its own surprises if you're open to them.

One quirky habit I picked up was sketching high-level process diagrams for every project. One evening, the commissioning manager spotted my drawing and, impressed, offered me a commissioning manager role in Kansas. But corporate red tape tangled things up, a third-party contract meant I couldn't take the job without a waiver. After a weekend of waiting, I was told my interview "wasn't up to standard." I knew better, called out the misrepresentation, and resigned on the spot. Sometimes, you just have to cut your losses and move forward with your head held high.

In September 1998, life handed me one of those unexpected invitations to adventure, a previous EPC company reached out with an offer to join a Tension Leg Platform (TLP) project. The journey began in Taranto, Italy, where the TLP's hull was being constructed at a bustling shipyard. Now, if you've never experienced an Italian shipyard, imagine a symphony of clanging metal, shouted instructions, and the ever-present aroma of espresso wafting through the air. It was a place where even the machinery seemed to gesticulate with passion.

But fate, with its mischievous sense of timing, soon threw a curveball: a strike brought work to a standstill. For most, this might have been a setback. For me, it was an open door to adventure. Suddenly, I had the rare chance to explore Italy, not as a tourist, but as a temporary local. The cuisine was nothing short of divine, and November brought the arrival of the new wines. Each evening, our team gathered in a charming hotel in the hill-country town of Martina Franca, where the restaurant owner would personally fill our glasses with the day's novella, or new wine. I developed a fondness for Italian wines that, to this day, makes me smile every time I see a bottle with a label I can't pronounce.

With the strike in full swing, a compadre and I seized the opportunity for a three-day road trip to Rome. We found a quaint hotel near the Vatican, perfect for two wide-eyed explorers eager to soak up as much history as possible. We spent an entire day wandering the Vatican's endless rooms, marveling at its art and architecture, and then ventured out to the Colosseum and other awe-inspiring relics of Rome's storied past. The highlight? Attending morning Mass inside the Vatican, delivered by the Pope himself, who walked down the aisle no more than half a dozen people away from where we stood. I'm not saying I caught the Pope's eye, but I did feel a little holier for the rest of the day.

Back at the shipyard, the technical challenges kept the adventure alive. The hull drawings were schematic rather than the detailed blueprints I was used to, making it a real puzzle to match piping systems that penetrated the compartment walls. Channeling my inner MacGyver (and perhaps a bit of Leonardo da Vinci), I created my own set of flow diagrams, clearly marking every point where a pipe crossed a compartment wall. These diagrams became a secret weapon for the team, making it easier for anyone to follow the labyrinth of piping throughout the hull.

One day, the client's project manager strolled by my desk and spotted my handiwork. He immediately recognized these weren't part of the official documentation and asked about their origin. When I explained that I'd developed them myself, he was genuinely surprised, and delighted. He asked if he could keep the set, and I gladly handed it over. The next day, he returned, requesting an official electronic copy for the project. There's a special kind of satisfaction in knowing your midnight doodles can become a project's secret sauce.

Once the hull was completed, it was loaded onto a specially designed ship (think: a barge with delusions of grandeur) and set sail for Ingleside, Texas, where the integration with the topsides would take place. Our Italian assignment ended, and it was time to head home.

But Italy wasn't quite done with me yet. On the flight from Bari to Rome, my compadre and I sat in separate aisles. I found myself next to an elderly man dressed in classic Italian street clothes, who struck up a lively conversation. He had a laugh that could fill a cathedral and a particular fondness for the jellybeans served by the stewardesses. When he learned I was from Houston, he lit up, exclaiming his love for cowboys and Indians. Curious, I asked about his background. With a twinkle in his eye, he revealed he was a bishop in the Catholic Church, en route to a special meeting with the Pope.

Now, I tend to give people the benefit of the doubt, especially those who share their jellybeans. After we landed, I reunited with my compadre, who was skeptical about my new friend's ecclesiastical credentials. But as we picked up our luggage, there was my acquaintance, now dressed in ceremonial robes and a red cap, surrounded by two other men in vibrant gowns wearing extraordinary-looking purple hats. He approached, shook my hand warmly, and said, "I truly enjoyed meeting you, the conversation we shared, and may the rest of your future be blessed," and then the entourage went on their way to the Vatican. My compadre was left shaking his head, saying he would never have believed it, and that I was truly blessed, and apologized for doubting me. Sometimes, the universe rewards you not just with adventure, but with a little wink and a nudge, as if to say, "Keep on doing whatever you're doing."

After the hull arrived at Ingleside and the team regrouped, I found myself in the middle of a classic workplace standoff: my manager and the client's project manager were locked in a battle of wills that could have made for a decent reality TV show. Their disagreements, while sometimes bordering on the theatrical, were a masterclass in how not to run a meeting. The tension in the room was so thick you could cut it with a butter knife, or, if you were feeling particularly adventurous, a welding torch.

But here's where truth and integrity come into play. I respected both men for their strengths, even if their communication styles were as compatible as oil and water. Instead of picking sides or hiding under my hard hat, I decided to do what any self-respecting problem-solver would: I approached my manager with a suggestion. "How about I serve as the direct liaison with the client's project manager?" I offered. "You can focus on the budget and schedule, and I'll handle the daily back-and-forth." To my relief (and maybe his), he agreed.

Almost overnight, the mood shifted. With a single point of contact, communication became smoother than a freshly greased bearing. Our team started anticipating the client's needs, staying ahead of the curve, and, dare I say, enjoying the process. It was proof that sometimes, the simplest solutions are the most effective, especially when you approach them with honesty and a willingness to take responsibility.

One afternoon, as we strolled across the fabrication yard, the client's project manager casually mentioned he'd be out the next day, off to Houston for dinner with an old Amoco colleague. When he dropped the name, I couldn't help but grin. "I know your colleague," I said. "He was my direct line manager when I was the PIC offshore Gabon." The look on his face was priceless, like he'd just discovered a long-lost cousin at a family reunion.

He launched into stories about this legendary figure, whose photo apparently hung in the company's Hall of Fame. I simply asked him to pass along my regards, knowing it would give them both a good chuckle. It was a reminder that in this industry, the world is smaller than you think, and you never know when your past will catch up with you, in a good way.

When it came time for sea trials, I was handed the reins to lead the combined team. Now, if you've never led a group of engineers, operators, and assorted specialists through a high-stakes trial, imagine herding cats, if the cats were unionized and had strong opinions about flange torque specs. But with a spirit of adventure (and a healthy dose of humor), we pulled together, tackled every challenge, and completed the trials with flying colors. The client was so pleased that they offered me a spot on the final commissioning offshore. As tempting as it was to keep the adventure going, I'd already committed to another assignment in Saudi Arabia. Sometimes, integrity means sticking to your word, even when the next chapter promises new excitement.

Looking back, these experiences taught me that truth and honesty aren't just lofty ideals, they're practical tools for building trust and getting things done. Integrity is the compass that keeps you on course, especially when the seas get rough. And adventure? Well, that's just the reward for showing up, saying yes, and being willing to laugh when things don't go exactly as planned.

After all, in the world of commissioning, every day brings a new story, and if you can walk away with a smile (and maybe a good story for the next yard walk), you're doing something right.

Throughout my career, I've always believed that the real magic happens at the intersection of relationships and opportunity. That philosophy paid off in early 2000, when a simple act of staying in touch with a former client's Project Manager opened the door to one of the most adventurous chapters of my professional life.

I was offered the role of Mechanical Engineering Design Lead for an expansion project on a renowned Drill Ship operating in the Gulf of Mexico. The assignment was anything but ordinary: I was tasked with overseeing the review, planning, and commissioning of a Well Test Facility capable of handling 18,000 barrels of oil per day. The project also included converting two massive crude oil storage tanks and managing the intricate offloading systems aboard the ship. At the time, the vessel was drilling a well nearly 6,500 feet beneath the surface, off the coast of Louisiana, a feat that still fills me with awe when I think back on it.

From the moment I set foot on the 1,000-foot-long ship, I felt like an explorer stepping into a world where technology and nature were locked in a delicate dance. The ship itself was a marvel, equipped with ten dynamic positioning thrusters that allowed it to glide across the Gulf at over twenty knots per hour. These thrusters could hold the ship's position with such precision that it felt as if we were anchored to an invisible point in the ocean, even as the waves and wind conspired to push us off course.

But the adventure wasn't just in the machinery, it was in the unpredictability of the sea. One unforgettable episode came when we received just two days' notice that a hurricane was barreling toward the eastern Gulf. The sense of urgency was palpable. In a coordinated ballet of engineering and seamanship, the crew secured the well, disengaged the risers, and prepared the ship for a rapid escape. I watched, humbled, as every member of the team, from the most seasoned operator to the greenest deckhand, moved with purpose and focus. There was no room for ego; only mutual respect and a shared commitment to safety and success.

We crossed the Gulf ahead of the storm, the ship slicing through the swells as thunderheads gathered on the horizon. The tension was real, but so was the camaraderie. In moments like these, you realize that adventure isn't just about the thrill, it's about trusting your team, adapting to the unknown, and finding humor even when the stakes are high. After the hurricane passed, we returned to our position and, in a testament to the crew's resilience and skill, resumed drilling operations within two days. Witnessing such efficiency and coordination was both inspiring and humbling. It reminded me that, no matter how advanced our technology becomes, it's the people, their grit, humility, and genuine curiosity, that make the impossible possible.

During this same offshore project, adventure didn't just knock at my door, it barged right in, suitcase in hand, and set up camp at home. My wife, Joy, found herself in the middle of a domestic crisis that would test anyone's mettle: the air conditioning unit decided to retire early, right in the middle of a heatwave, and our son JJ was still very young. Now, if there's one thing hotter than a Texas summer, it's a Texas summer without AC.

Joy, ever the quick thinker, called me on the ship to report the situation. I could practically feel the beads of sweat through the phone. Channeling her resourcefulness, she'd already cracked open the phone book (remember those?) and lined up five HVAC companies to inspect the system. I was impressed, she was running the house like a Fortune 500 CEO, all while navigating a new country and a new language.

Meanwhile, we had a portable air conditioner that could be set up in the master bedroom for temporary relief. Joy, never one to back down from a challenge, rolled up her sleeves and tried to install the unit herself. When it stubbornly refused to cooperate, she called me back, this time, her voice coming through the ship's speaker system, giving the whole crew front-row seats to our troubleshooting saga.

She explained everything she'd tried, and I, in my infinite wisdom (and from a safe, air-conditioned distance), started walking her through the usual suspects: "Open the compartment and try the reset button." She'd already done that, but pressed it again for good measure. Still nothing. "Check for an exterior reset button on the back." Nope. "How about the sides?" Nada. Finally, I asked, "Are you standing in front of the unit?" She replied yes, and I said, "Kick that son of a bitch." Without missing a beat, she shot back, "I already tried that." The crew in my office erupted in laughter, tears streaming down their faces. Who knew HVAC repair could double as stand-up comedy?

After Joy had orchestrated five independent repair companies to inspect the stubborn HVAC unit, we came to the inevitable conclusion: the system was outdated and needed to be replaced. She collected multiple quotes, and we discussed the options over the phone. While the lowest bid was tempting, I reminded her that the cheapest option isn't always the best, sometimes you get what you pay for, and sometimes you just get a headache.

Instead, I asked her which company representative gave her the strongest impression of honesty and integrity. In the end, Joy made the final decision about which company would install the new system. For someone who, at the time, spoke only limited English and had been living in the country for barely a year, this was an impressive feat. I was genuinely proud of her for handling the situation with such cleverness, humility, and a healthy dose of quick wit. If there had been an Olympic event for "Household Crisis Management," Joy would have taken home the gold, and probably negotiated a discount on the medal.

After returning home from my latest overseas assignment, I found myself in one of those rare, quiet moments with my wife, a moment ripe for philosophical mischief. We were sipping coffee, the Texas sun slanting through the window, when I decided to stir the pot with a question about Thailand's most celebrated monarch, King Rama V.

"Darling," I began, "I've always admired King Rama V for uniting Siam and ushering in a new era of progress. But there's one thing I can't quite wrap my head around. Before his reign, a man could have as many wives as he could afford to house. Then Rama V changed the law, one man, one wife. Yet the king himself had over a hundred wives! How did he pull that off without a palace revolt from the menfolk?"

She didn't miss a beat. With a sly smile and a twinkle in her eye, she replied, "Well, Rama V did so many wonderful things for Thailand that people chose to overlook that one little inconsistency. When you're that good, you get a pass, at least once."

I couldn't resist. "So, haven't I done many wonderful things for our kingdom, here and in Thailand?"

She smiled, playing along. "Yes, yes you have, honey," she said, nodding with mock solemnity. "You've done many great things."

With even less resistance, I said, "So, shouldn't I be allowed to have more than just one wife?"

She smiled that big, beautiful smile of hers, playing along. "Yes, yes, you should."

For a split second, I marveled at how easily this conversation was going in my favor. I was already mentally composing my acceptance speech for "Most Progressive Husband of the Year" when she leaned in, her smile growing even wider.

"But there's just one small problem," she added, her voice dropping to a conspiratorial whisper. "In your kingdom, there's only one woman to choose from. And if you're not careful, she's going to move to another kingdom!"

I burst out laughing, humbled and delighted by her quick wit. In that moment, I was reminded, yet again, that I'd truly married the right woman. She never fails to keep me grounded, whether I'm floating on the clouds of my own cleverness or just trying to negotiate for a second helping of dessert.

Our marriage, much like the reign of King Rama V, is a tapestry of adventure, compromise, and the occasional royal decree. We've navigated the wilds of Texas and the bustling streets of Bangkok, survived international moves, language mishaps, and more than a few cultural misunderstandings. Through it all, her humor and wisdom have been my compass.

If there's a lesson in all this, it's that every kingdom, no matter how small, runs best on laughter, humility, and a healthy respect for the queen's quick comebacks. And as for royal privileges? Well, let's just say I'm more than happy to be a one-queen man, especially when she's the one who keeps me on my toes and laughing every step of the way.

My next project swept me back to Ingleside, Texas, for the integration and commissioning of another TLP, a chapter that promised not just technical challenge, but a full-blown adventure. From the outset, the assignment was anything but ordinary. The project owner, perhaps with a mischievous glint in their eye, hired me to orchestrate the infamous "three-week looking-ahead" planning. My mission: to keep the project on track, anticipate obstacles before they reared their heads, and ensure the right activities happened at the right time. It was a bit like playing chess on a construction site, except the pieces were people, the board was a maze of steel and cables, and the clock was always ticking.

But the real twist? The client subcontracted my services through their commissioning subcontractor, which meant I was now in the peculiar position of driving the activities of the very company that signed my paychecks. To add another layer of intrigue, the subcontract's site manager, who also happened to be the owner, now reported to me. Imagine the tension: every day, I was the guy he paid, but also the guy telling him what to do. It was a workplace paradox worthy of a sitcom, and the air sometimes crackled with the kind of energy you only get when everyone's a little unsure who's really in charge.

As with all projects, the days were long, the challenges relentless, and the stakes high. But this one had an extra dash of drama. The owner, never missing a chance to remind me who signed my checks, would drop hints, sometimes subtle, sometimes not-so-subtle, that maybe, just maybe, I could cut his team a little slack. I'd smile, nod, and assure him that I was already working behind the scenes to help his crew resolve issues. After all, keeping the peace (and the schedule) required a delicate blend of humility, diplomacy, and the occasional well-timed joke.

Despite the underlying tension, there was a certain camaraderie that grew out of our shared predicament. The owner, for all his reminders about payroll, was quick to praise my work when things went right. In the end, we found a balance, he got the support he needed, I kept the project moving forward, and together we managed to turn a potentially combustible situation into a story worth retelling. If there's a lesson in all this, it's that a little humility, a sense of adventure, and the ability to laugh at yourself can turn even the trickiest project into a memorable ride.

It was during this project that I experienced one of those rare, unforgettable moments that life occasionally serves up, a moment that left me in genuine awe. I came home one evening, weary from the day's work, expecting the usual routine: maybe a quick bite from a takeout bag or a familiar booth at our favorite diner. Instead, I was greeted by the tantalizing aroma of a three-course meal, artfully arranged on our dining table as if we'd been transported to a five-star restaurant. For a split second, I wondered if I'd wandered into the wrong house, or if Joy had secretly hired a chef while I was away.

Now, let me be honest, Joy had never cooked before. Our family's culinary adventures typically involved drive-throughs, pizza boxes, or the age-old question, "What are you in the mood for tonight?" So, as I sat down, still in my work clothes and blinking in disbelief, I couldn't help but ask, "Where did you cater this from?"

That's when Joy, with a twinkle in her eye and a hint of mischief, began to tell me her secret. She confessed that every day, she'd been watching a television show featuring a chef with a contagious laugh and a flair for the dramatic. This chef would toss spices into his dishes with a flourish, punctuating each move with a booming "Bam!" Joy, ever the attentive student, had memorized every step, every ingredient, and every cooking temperature. She'd then venture out to the store, gather all the necessary supplies, and return home to recreate the magic in our own kitchen.

The result? It was nothing short of fabulous. Each bite was a revelation, a symphony of flavors that made me forget the stress of the day and left me grinning from ear to ear. I was both humbled and delighted, realizing that Joy had not only surprised me but had also discovered a new passion and talent right before my eyes. From that day forward, whatever "Mr. Bam" cooked on TV, that's what I had for dinner. And let me tell you, I never looked at a spice rack the same way again.

Following the last project, I embarked on what I thought would be another chapter in my career as a commissioning specialist, joining an EPC company for an expansion project in Hassi Berkine, Algeria. The assignment began with a sense of adventure that was both exhilarating and humbling. My introduction to the Sahara was a flight in a small, single-propeller plane, just the pilot, three passengers, and the endless expanse of desert below. As we soared above the rippling red dunes, I was struck by the stark beauty and isolation of the landscape. The sand stretched to the horizon in every direction, a reminder of both nature's grandeur and our own smallness within it. The flight itself felt like a rite of passage, intimate, slightly nerve-wracking, and unforgettable.

Upon landing, the adventure continued. The plane circled a solitary runway before touching down, and as I stepped onto the tarmac, a vehicle was already waiting to whisk me away to the project camp. There was a sense of camaraderie among the small group of expats, engineers, technicians, and support staff, each of us drawn together by the shared challenge of working in such a remote and demanding environment. The desert, with its harsh beauty and unforgiving climate, demanded respect and humility from all who ventured into its domain.

But the world changed overnight. The events of September 11, 2001, sent shockwaves across the globe, and even in the isolation of the Algerian desert, we felt the tremors. Suddenly, the sense of adventure was tinged with anxiety and concern. Rumors began to circulate, whispers that Algeria might harbor secret training camps linked to radical groups from the Middle East. The atmosphere at camp grew tense, the camaraderie now underscored by a quiet vigilance.

We were a handful of Americans in a vast, unfamiliar land, our nearest neighbors a nomadic family living off the refuse of a distant dump, and a small military camp whose loyalties were uncertain. The desert, once a symbol of freedom and possibility, now felt like a place of vulnerability and risk.

Recognizing the heightened danger, our employer called a meeting in the warehouse, a gathering that was both sobering and surreal. The company presented a master evacuation plan, the gravity of which was not lost on any of us. We were instructed to keep a knapsack packed at all times: two bottles of water, two rolls of toilet paper, a toothbrush and toothpaste, and a change of underwear. If the emergency horn sounded three consecutive blasts, we were to lock ourselves in our rooms, turn off the lights, and wait in silence for a familiar knock.

Wait until a familiar voice knocks at your door, and we would load into fully fueled trucks and make a desperate dash across the dunes, aiming for the safety of Tunisia, just over a hundred miles away. The plan was both a comfort and a stark reminder of our precarious situation, preparedness in the face of the unknown.

The days that followed were filled with a mix of emotions, adventure and excitement still lingered, but they were now accompanied by a deep concern for our safety and the well-being of those around us. There was a new depth to our interactions, a compassion that emerged as we checked in on one another, shared stories, and tried to keep spirits high despite the uncertainty. Humility became our constant companion; we were no longer just professionals on assignment, but human beings bound together by circumstance, each of us acutely aware of our own limitations and the fragility of our situation.

The evacuation plan, though daunting, was a testament to the company's commitment to our safety. Yet, the reality of the threat was never far from our minds. The day after the plan was presented, our employer offered flights home to anyone who felt uncomfortable with the escape strategy, assuring us that choosing to leave would not affect our standing with the company.

For many, including myself, at my wife's heartfelt request, this was a moment of reckoning. The decision to leave was not made lightly; it was shaped by concern for loved ones, a sense of responsibility, and the humility to recognize when adventure must yield to caution. Arranging flights home was itself an ordeal, as the aftermath of 9/11 brought temporary no-fly zones and logistical challenges, stretching our departure into a week-long exercise in patience and hope.

Looking back, that chapter in Algeria was more than just a professional milestone. It was a journey through excitement and fear, camaraderie and solitude, adventure and humility. It taught me that true courage is not just about facing danger, but about caring for those around you, making difficult choices with compassion, and accepting that sometimes, the bravest thing you can do is step back and protect what matters most.

Returning to Houston, I found myself swept into a new chapter as commissioning manager for a Floating Storage and Offloading (FSO) Conversion and Single Point Mooring (SPM) Turret project. The assignment itself sounded like something out of a maritime adventure novel: take a 357,000-deadweight-ton ULCC tanker, so massive it could double as a small island, and transform it into a floating oil fortress capable of handling 225,000 barrels a day and storing over two million barrels of oil. The final destination? Moored off the wild coast of Chad, Africa, tethered by a tower-yoke mooring system that looked like it belonged in a Bond film.

The real adventure began in Singapore's Jurong Shipyards, a place where the clang of steel and the scent of the sea mixed with the constant hum of possibility. My weeks were a blur of hard hats, blueprints, and the occasional "Where did I leave my coffee?" At least once a week, I'd cross the border into Malaysia's Pasir Gudang Shipyard. On those days, I discovered a secret perk: golf courses so lush and affordable that even my swing looked respectable. There's nothing like sinking a putt in the tropics to make you forget you spent the morning arguing with a stubborn valve.

Living in Singapore was its own kind of adventure. The city's two causeways made it easy to slip into Malaysia for a quick round of golf or a culinary escapade, while Thailand was just a short flight away, perfect for spontaneous family getaways. My company, perhaps sensing the need for creature comforts, set us up in a three-bedroom condo and handed over a company car with a credit card for gas. I like to think they were investing in my happiness (and, by extension, my productivity), but it's possible they just didn't want me showing up late because I was stuck hailing a cab in the rain.

The project itself was a whirlwind of deadlines, teamwork, and the occasional "How did that get approved?" But the real test came during the client's readiness audits. For a week, the shipyard buzzed with the energy of a reality-show finale. The Startup Manager and Deputy arrived, clipboards in hand, ready to poke holes in our plans. When the Deputy Startup Manager asked if I had a commissioning plan, I pointed him to a file cabinet stuffed with bound copies, my secret arsenal. He took one, we chatted, and he left with a handshake.

The next day, I braced myself for the grilling of a lifetime. Instead, I was excused with a smile: my plan was the only one accepted without a single comment. I didn't get a bonus, but the handshake was so enthusiastic I thought he might dislocate my shoulder. Sometimes, recognition comes in the form of a sore arm and a story to tell.

While I wrangled with engineers and inspectors, Joy was busy building a community. She and JJ quickly befriended the expatriate wives in our condo complex, turning shopping trips and lunches into mini-adventures. These outings became the heartbeat of our social life, a reminder that even in a city of millions, it's the small circles that make you feel at home. The friendships forged over shared meals and laughter became the glue that held us together, especially when the workdays stretched long and homesickness crept in.

JJ, meanwhile, thrived at his Montessori school, and his fourth birthday became the social event of the season. We threw a party that would make Willy Wonka jealous: finger foods, mountains of cake and ice cream, and a magician who wowed both kids and adults with tricks, balloon animals, and the kind of card tricks that left even the grown-ups scratching their heads. For one magical afternoon, the shipyard worries faded, replaced by the sound of children's laughter and the sight of adults trying (and failing) to guess how the rabbit got into the hat.

When the project wrapped up, we decided to make the most of our time abroad. First stop: Kuala Lumpur, where we dove into the city's vibrant culture, sampled street food that set our mouths on fire, and marveled at the Petronas Towers (which, for the record, are even taller when you're standing at the bottom with a camera that can't fit them in the frame).

Next, we headed to Phuket for some much-needed beach time, sun, sand, and the kind of relaxation that only comes after a year of hard work. Finally, we made our way to Bangkok, reconnecting with Thai relatives and sharing stories while enjoying the delights of delicious Thai food. By the time we returned to Houston, we were sun-kissed, well-fed, and grateful for the adventure that had brought us closer as a family.

Looking back, the Singapore shipyard saga was more than just a professional milestone, it was a tapestry of adventure, excitement, and fun. It was about finding humanity in the daily grind, humility in the face of challenges, and humor in the unexpected. Whether it was a handshake that meant more than a bonus, a birthday party that brought neighbors together, or a round of golf that turned a work trip into a mini-vacation, every moment was a reminder that life's greatest stories are written not just in boardrooms and shipyards, but in the laughter, friendships, and small acts of kindness that make the journey worthwhile.

After the dust of 9/11 settled, Algeria was once again "open for business", or at least, open for adventurous expats like me. I took on a new role as Commissioning Specialist at a remote gas project in Hassi R'Mel, where the only thing more elusive than the Algerian military (who were supposed to be guarding us) was a decent cup of coffee. After surviving the desert's heat, sand, and the occasional camel traffic jam, I was transferred to Krechba to develop startup procedures for two Mitsubishi CO_2 4-Stage Compressors. I like to think I left those compressors so well-prepared, they're still running on my good vibes.

No sooner had I unpacked my bags in Houston than I was off again, this time to Damietta, Egypt, for an LNG project. The twist? I was tasked with training an operations manager in commissioning, even though the existing team seemed to think "teamwork" was a spectator sport. My new trainee was open-minded and eager, and together we navigated the wild world of fractionation systems. We completed the job in four months, proving that with a little humility, a lot of patience, and a sense of humor, you can get just about anything done, even if you have to do it from behind the scenes.

Since 1992, I didn't just embark on a career as a freelance consultant, I set out on a wild, winding road trip through the world of commissioning and startup, with my life's GPS set to "adventure mode." Titles? Hierarchies? Please. I was more interested in three things: where the next assignment would take me, how long I'd be there, and, let's be honest, whether the compensation would fund my next escapade. This flexible, freewheeling mindset let me chase opportunities that matched my passions, not just my résumé.

But here's where the story gets interesting: after marrying Joy, I made a pact with myself to work only nine months out of the year. The other three? Reserved for what truly matters, family, fun, and the kind of memories you can't expense on a corporate card. After each assignment, we'd pack our bags and jet off to Thailand for a month, soaking up culture, laughter, and the occasional sunburn.

For several years, our family made it a tradition to escape to Colorado, trading the daily grind for the crisp mountain air, sparkling streams, and the endless playground of the Rockies. These trips were more than just vacations, they were our way of pressing pause on life, reconnecting with each other, and making memories that would last far longer than any souvenir.

One of our favorite rituals was visiting a special tree, tucked away in a quiet corner of the forest, where Joy and I had carved our initials and anniversary date. It was our secret landmark, a living testament to our journey together, and a spot that only she, JJ, and I could find. Every time we visited, it felt like we were adding another ring to the tree's story, and to our own.

The first year we brought Toby, our loyal (and occasionally mischievous) Shih Tzu companion, the adventure took on a new flavor. We pitched our family tent outside Lake City, ready for a night under the stars. As dusk settled and the mountain air grew chilly, Joy wrinkled her nose and declared, "Somebody here has stinky feet!" Instantly, the tent erupted in laughter and playful accusations. Fingers pointed in every direction, at each other, at the dog, even at the innocent sleeping bags. No one was safe from suspicion.

That's when inspiration struck. "Let's let Toby be the judge!" I announced, grinning. Toby, ever the good sport, was summoned for the ultimate sniff test. First, he inspected Joy's feet, nothing. Then mine, again, nothing. But when he got to JJ, Toby's reaction was priceless: he jerked his head away dramatically and let out a loud, theatrical "Whew!" The tent exploded with laughter. JJ, red-faced but giggling, became the good-natured target of our teasing for the rest of the trip, and, truth be told, for many camping trips to come.

It was a moment of pure, unscripted joy, the kind that only happens when you're surrounded by people (and pets) who love you, quirks and all. In that tent, under the Colorado stars, we weren't just a family; we were a team, united by affection, compassion, and a shared sense of fun. Life, as I saw it, was pretty grand, and I was determined to enjoy every mile, every laugh, and every "Whew!" along the way.

My lifelong passion for motorcycles was like a stubborn engine that just wouldn't quit. From my teenage years, the roar of a bike promised freedom, adventure, and a dash of rebellion. But as adulthood rolled on, so did responsibilities, bills, family, and the ever-watchful eye of practicality, embodied by Joy, my partner and the CFO of our household dreams.

It all began in 2001, when I first floated the idea of buying a Harley-Davidson. Joy, ever the voice of reason, gently reminded me that our financial priorities didn't include a two-wheeled midlife crisis. "Maybe someday," she said, with a smile that said, "not a chance." But the dream idled in the background, revving quietly every time I saw a Harley glide by.

Each year, like clockwork, I'd bring up the Harley. Each year, Joy would point to the budget, and I'd park my dream in the garage of "maybe next year." By 2005, my longing had grown louder than a Harley with straight pipes. I confessed to Joy that this wasn't just a passing fancy, I was haunted by the thought of reaching the end of my days without ever owning that legendary bike again. To my surprise, Joy looked at me, shrugged, and said, "Then why don't you go buy one?"

I nearly dropped my coffee. Was this a trick? A test? Or had she finally realized that a Harley was cheaper than therapy? Without waiting for her to change her mind, I raced to the dealership and bought a brand-new Harley-Davidson Road King Classic. It was love at first sight, chrome, leather, and the promise of open roads.

But this wasn't just any bike. Inspired by a vivid, almost mystical vision I'd had during a psilocybin-fueled adventure (don't tell the kids), I commissioned an artist to transform my Harley into a rolling work of art. The clouds in my vision had formed the shapes of four native forefathers, and I wanted that spirit captured on my bike. The artist painted these ancestral figures, along with a dreamcatcher, a lone wolf, and an eagle, symbols of heritage, freedom, and the wild journey of life. Every ride became a celebration of my roots and a reminder that sometimes, the best adventures begin with a dream and a little bit of stubbornness.

Having matured and gathered a lifetime's worth of lessons (at least to a certain degree!), I always encouraged Joy that our most important job as parents was to help JJ discover his passion in life. We knew he thrived in social circles, he was the kind of kid who could make friends with a lamppost, but he needed something more, something physical to balance out the muscles growing in his head from all that socializing and daydreaming.

Now, let's be honest: JJ wasn't destined to be the next football star. He didn't bounce a basketball so much as dodge it, and every time a ball flew his way, he'd turn his head as if it were a meteor on a collision course. So, what would fit his nature? Our first experiment was gymnastics. He learned a few moves, but it quickly became more of a playdate with friends than a pursuit of Olympic gold.

Then, one evening, as we all watched Jackie Chan flicks on TV, where Jackie, with a wink and a tumble, always managed to save the day, an idea sparked. "JJ, would you be interested in learning a martial art?" we asked, half-expecting a shrug. To our surprise, his eyes lit up like a kid who'd just found the golden ticket. "Yes!" he exclaimed, bouncing off the couch with excitement.

Cue the family debate: Taekwondo or ninja school? (For the record, I lobbied hard for ninja school, but Joy pointed out that we didn't need any more stealth missions to the cookie jar.) After some research and a few good-natured arguments, we enrolled JJ in Taekwondo.

What followed was nothing short of an adventure. Over eleven years, JJ transformed from a white-belt rookie, whose uniform was two sizes too big and whose kicks barely cleared the floor, into a junior instructor and eventually a third-degree black belt, with the skills (and bruises) to prove it. He was even qualified to test for his fourth-degree black belt, a feat that made me prouder than a dad at a Little League game, minus the embarrassing shouting from the sidelines (okay, maybe just a little shouting).

But the real magic wasn't just in the trophies or the perfectly tied belts. Martial arts taught JJ honor, respect, and the kind of humility that comes from getting knocked down and getting back up, sometimes with a little help from Mom and Dad, and sometimes with a sheepish grin and a "Did anyone see that?" The dojo became his second home, a place where he learned that true strength isn't about how hard you hit, but how hard you try, and how you treat others along the way.

The biggest surprise? The once-shy kid who used to hide behind his belt when called on in class suddenly found his voice. JJ joined the high school debate team, stepping onto a new kind of stage. Suddenly, the kid who once ducked from flying dodgeballs was competing at state and national tournaments for four years running. Something had shifted inside him, a quiet confidence, forged in the fires of both the dojo and the debate stage.

Through it all, we cheered him on, sometimes from the bleachers, sometimes from the kitchen table, always with hearts full of pride and a sense of awe at the adventure unfolding before us. There were moments of excitement (his first board break!), moments of compassion (helping a younger student tie their belt), and plenty of lighthearted humor (like the time he accidentally bowed to the janitor instead of the master).

Helping JJ find his passion wasn't just about martial arts, it was about supporting him, laughing with him, and sometimes picking him up (literally and figuratively) when he stumbled. It was a family adventure, filled with excitement, compassion, and the kind of joy that comes from watching someone you love discover what makes them come alive.

Looking back, these adventures, on two wheels and in the martial arts studio, were more than just hobbies. They were about chasing dreams, facing fears, and laughing at the bumps along the way. There were moments of excitement (the first ride on the open highway), humility (holding JJ's boards and getting kicked), and humanity (watching JJ bow to his instructors, then instruct and protect those much younger than himself).

Through it all, we had fun, from getting a new Harley to celebrating JJ's black belt and speech tournaments. Our family learned that the best stories come from living boldly, embracing adventure, showing heart, and finding humor when things go wrong.

My next project, in 2005, was an adventure as a systems completion coordinator in Sakhalin, Russia, which was a crash course in both project management and the fine art of office politics. Picture this: five project managers, five commissioning managers, five completions managers, and a startup management team, all with their own agendas, all convinced their priorities were the only ones that mattered. My job? To be the diplomatic glue holding this five-ring circus together, ensuring everyone marched (or at least stumbled) in the same direction.

I'd never considered myself a political animal, but Sakhalin changed that. Every day felt like a new episode of "Survivor: Corporate Edition." One manager would pull me aside, whispering that their task was a top priority. Minutes later, another would insist the opposite. I quickly learned that in this jungle, the startup manager's word was law, so I focused on that, hoping not to get voted off the island (or at least not before lunch).

Eighteen months between Houston, Japan, Korea, and Sakhalin taught me more about navigating internal politics than the rest of my career combined. I emerged with a new appreciation for humility, sometimes, the best you can do is keep your head down, your sense of humor up, and your coffee cup full. When the assignment ended, I moved on, a little wiser and a lot more diplomatic.

In March 2006, I found myself at the threshold of a new challenge, one that promised not just technical complexity, but a sense of adventure and a chance to revisit the very roots of my offshore career. I'd accepted an assignment as a project manager with a small but mighty engineering firm in Houston, Texas. This wasn't just any firm; these folks had a reputation for engineering wizardry, having designed the TLP Hull on my first TLC project and the offloading system for the legendary Drillship.

I was handed the reins to upgrade the UPS systems on two major offshore platforms in the Gulf of Mexico. Short-term projects, sure, but they demanded the kind of careful planning and attention to detail that keeps your adrenaline pumping and your coffee cup full. My role required boots-on-deck leadership. I traveled out to both platforms, ready to roll up my sleeves and make sure every upgrade was executed to the highest standards.

There's nothing quite like the thrill of landing on a helipad, the wind whipping around you, knowing you're about to dive into the heart of the action. But this trip was about to deliver more than just technical challenges, it was about to serve up a full-circle moment that would leave me both humbled and proud.

As the helicopter touched down on the first TLP, I was greeted by the Offshore Installation Manager (OIM) with a handshake that could have cracked a walnut. The hospitality was exceptional, but the real surprise came when I realized I knew this OIM. Years earlier, I'd trained this very person on the hull ballast systems back in Ingleside, Texas. Now, here they were, running the show, a testament to their growth, dedication, and the ripple effect of mentorship. I couldn't help but feel a surge of pride, mixed with a healthy dose of humility. After all, it's not every day you see someone you once taught rise to such heights.

The adventure didn't stop there. In the OIM's office, I spotted a shelf lined with the operating manuals and drawings I'd developed for the project years before. The OIM explained that whenever the team needed to conduct a turnaround or access the hull compartments, they relied on my guidelines and reference materials. I'll admit, my chest puffed up a bit, there's a special kind of honor in knowing your work stands the test of time (and the test of saltwater). It was humbling, too, realizing that my contributions would continue to guide the team for as long as the platform remained operational.

That visit wasn't just another day at the office, it was a milestone, a grand finale to my offshore career. As I left the platform, I couldn't help but chuckle at the journey: from rookie to mentor, from drawing up manuals to seeing them become the backbone of operations. And, of course, I made sure to leave the OIM with a bit of advice: "If you ever get lost in those manuals, just remember, page 42 is where I hid the secret to eternal platform happiness." (Okay, maybe not, but a little humor never hurts when you're surrounded by steel and sea.)

Of course, every hero's journey has its plot twist. Mine came in June 2007, courtesy of my wife, Joy. One evening, she hit me with a question that stopped me in my tracks: "When are you going to get a real job?" I nearly choked on my coffee. A real job? Wasn't I already living the dream? But Joy, ever the voice of reason, clarified: "A real job is one where you come home each night, on weekends, or at least every other weekend." Translation: less Indiana Jones, more Ward Cleaver. Her words made me reflect, maybe my work-life balance was a bit too heavy on the "work" and "life" parts, and not enough on the "balance."

I could have argued the perks of consulting, the income, the epic family trips, the stories that would make even Hemingway jealous. But I understood what Joy was really asking for: stability, presence, and a partner who'd be there to help navigate the wild ride of raising a teenager. As any parent knows, adolescence is its own kind of adventure, one that requires a steady hand on the wheel and a sense of humor when the GPS inevitably says, "Recalculating..."

Finding a "real job" wasn't going to be easy, especially without an engineering degree. But I promised Joy I'd try, with the caveat that miracles take time. Meanwhile, we decided to make the most of the present.

Some people have said that I'm lucky, a lucky man. Well, maybe I am, because in October 2007, just as the leaves were turning and the air was thick with the scent of possibility (and maybe a little pumpkin spice), I received a call that would set the stage for a new adventure. Another major EPC company was on the line, dangling the prospect of a commissioning specialist role for a Liquefied Natural Gas (LNG) project in Plainfield, Illinois. At the time, I knew as much about this company as I did about quantum physics, which is to say, not much. But a little research revealed they were titans in the tank-building world, with roots stretching back to the days when derricks were made of wood and men were made of, well, slightly tougher wood.

What really piqued my interest was discovering that this company had recently acquired a previous EPC company I'd worked with. It felt like the universe was nudging me forward, whispering, "Go on, this is your next chapter." The stars aligned: a reputable company, and they were offering me a direct-hire position that promised both challenge and reward. How could I say no?

First was a project that started in Plainfield, Illinois, with the design and preparation of commissioning documentation for a Regas LNG plant destined for Sabine Pass, Texas. Never one to waste a good road trip, I decided to make the drive from Houston to Plainfield an adventure in itself. Along the way, I reconnected with family, my Aunt Kenna and Uncle Bill welcomed me with open arms and a restful evening, while on another night, Cousins Marian and Bernard treated me to the kind of quality time that only family can provide. Even in the dead of a Midwest winter, I made sure to visit Uncle Julian, a man whose stories of valor (Silver Star recommendation, Special Forces Ranger training) could make even the most seasoned action hero blush.

That Christmas was truly one for the books. The apartment, usually a quiet and practical space, was transformed into a bustling winter den, air mattresses and sleeping bags sprawled across every inch of floor, creating a cozy nest for our hibernating "cubs." Joy and JJ had flown in, their arrival bringing a burst of energy and laughter. Jeremy and Ann made the trek from Bemidji, Minnesota, their car packed with three grandchildren, Karisa, Maddy, and Jake, each one radiating the kind of anticipation only the holidays can inspire.

The adventure began the moment everyone arrived. We bundled up and set out to build a snowman worthy of a Frosty audition. The kids dove into the snow with wild abandon, rolling and stacking until our creation stood tall and proud, its carrot nose slightly askew, scarf flapping in the wind. Even the adults couldn't resist joining in, their laughter echoing down the block as we debated the best way to keep Frosty's head from toppling off. There was humility in those moments, grown-ups rediscovering the simple joy of play, letting the world's worries melt away in the snow.

Inside, the spirit of togetherness continued. We explored Chicago's iconic sights, braving the winter chill for a glimpse of the city's twinkling lights and festive storefronts. Each outing was an adventure, whether we were marveling at the towering Christmas tree or navigating the labyrinth of holiday shoppers in search of the perfect last-minute gift. The excitement was palpable, and even when we got lost (which happened more than once), we found ourselves laughing at our own misadventures, grateful to be lost together.

But the heart of the holiday was the Christmas meal, a feast that brought everyone to the table, hungry and happy. My wife, who had become the protégé of "Mr. Bam," orchestrated the most beautiful Christmas dinner imaginable. The kitchen was her stage, and she moved with the confidence of a seasoned chef, tossing spices with a flourish and punctuating each move with her own signature "Bam!" The aroma of baked turkey filled the apartment, mingling with the scent of stuffing, mashed potatoes, and gravy simmering on the stove. There were green beans glistening with butter, cranberry sauce that wobbled just right, and rolls so soft they disappeared the moment they hit the table.

As we gathered around, plates piled high, the conversation flowed as freely as the gravy. There was a choice of pumpkin or apple pie for dessert, each slice a little piece of heaven, especially when topped with a generous dollop of whipped cream. The kids, faces smeared with pie and eyes sparkling with delight, declared it the best meal ever (though I suspect the promise of presents played a role in their enthusiasm). The adults, meanwhile, exchanged knowing glances, silently agreeing that the real magic was in the company, not just the food.

Christmas Eve was a riot of laughter and excitement. We all sat around the little mini decorated tree, sitting atop a small table in the corner, the floor a sea of wrapping paper and ribbons. The children tore into their gifts with the kind of unrestrained joy that makes the holidays unforgettable, their squeals of delight filling the room. Even the grown-ups got in on the fun, trading playful jabs about who had the best wrapping skills (spoiler: it wasn't me). There was humility in those moments, a recognition that the greatest gifts weren't the ones under the tree but the people gathered around it.

On Christmas Day, as we lingered over second helpings and swapped stories from years past, I was moved by the sparkle of laughter and the warmth of togetherness. The following day, Jeremy, Ann, and the grandkids packed up and headed home, but the glow of that Christmas lingered, a reminder that adventure, excitement, humanity, and humility are best experienced side by side, with a little warmhearted humor to tie it all together.

After the festivities, Joy and JJ returned home for school and work, and for the next two months, when I was not at work, I often found myself gazing out at the hill where the snowman we had built together slowly melted away. Each day, the snowman took on new, increasingly lopsided shapes, sometimes resembling a modern art sculpture, sometimes just a sad, slouching lump. Watching it shrink and sag, I couldn't help but feel a pang of loneliness settle in, as if the snowman and I were both quietly mourning the end of a joyful chapter.

There's a peculiar comfort in the way a melting snowman can mirror your own thoughts. I'd catch myself talking to it, well, not out loud (I haven't lost it yet), but in that way you talk to old memories. "Hang in there, buddy," I'd think, "we'll both see brighter days." There's humility in realizing that even the grandest snowman, built with laughter and love, is at the mercy of the sun. And there's humanity in knowing that, like me, it was just doing its best to hold it together until the next reunion.

Loneliness, I discovered, isn't always loud. Sometimes it's just the quiet ache of an empty house, the echo of laughter that lingers after everyone's gone, or the way you find yourself counting down the days until you're reunited with the people who make you feel whole. I'd dream of the future, picturing the next time we'd all be together, maybe building another snowman, maybe just sharing a meal and a story or two. In the meantime, I tried to keep my spirits up, reminding myself that even a snowman with a crooked grin can make you smile if you let it.

When Joy and JJ returned to Illinois, and I wrapped up that phase of the project, we took our time driving back to Houston. We squeezed in one more visit with my Uncle Julian before spending a night with my Aunt Helen and Uncle Lamoine in St. Louis, because in our family, you never pass up a chance for a good story and a warm meal. If there's one thing I've learned, it's that the best antidote to loneliness is a table full of relatives, a plate of something homemade, and a willingness to laugh at yourself (and occasionally, at your snowman's expense).

After returning to Texas and as the project was gaining momentum, Hurricane Ike struck in September 2008, halting progress and leading to extensive repairs. Commissioning a plant amid storm debris and flooding was a true test of resilience, but the adversity also opened new doors.

During the downtime, I learned of an opportunity for a FEED project in Cartagena, Colombia, which perfectly matched my refinery operations experience and allowed me to be home nightly. After a successful interview, I became commissioning manager, dedicating the next year to ensuring the operability and maintainability of every refinery unit. Although I pitched for a broader commissioning role, the client chose to self-perform, limiting us to engineering and construction. Sometimes you win the scope; sometimes you just gain a good story.

Momentum continued. While at a design review in Beaumont, I was asked to support an Oil Sands project, thanks to my expertise in systems completion. I soon transitioned to that team. Months later, the Cartagena client reversed course and requested my help to lead a team developing detailed pre-commissioning and commissioning procedures.

Just as we were building steam, another opportunity arose: managing all commissioning activities for a Gas Plant project in Natrium, West Virginia. For the next fifteen months, I split my time between the office and the site, completing six major projects back-to-back. By the time I returned to Houston, I felt I'd passed the ultimate test in flexibility, and was ready for a well-earned break, or at least a really good cup of coffee.

In the midst of a demanding period, balancing multiple projects, 2012 became a year marked by profound personal loss: it was then that my father passed away after a courageous two-year battle with cancer. Our relationship had always been close, but during those final years, our conversations grew even more frequent and meaningful. My family and I made several trips back to California to visit him, cherishing every opportunity to be together.

Between my father and me, there was a shared understanding that the worst fate would be to leave this world burdened by unresolved regrets. Determined not to let that happen, we made it a point to address any lingering differences, engaging in honest conversations that allowed us to find true closure and peace. That legacy of reconciliation and mutual understanding is something I hold dear to this day, a testament to the power of open hearts and the healing that comes from facing life's most difficult moments together.

Since 2012, the role with my employer evolved in ways I could never have fully anticipated. I found myself entrusted with greater leadership responsibilities within our commissioning organization, a privilege that brought both a deep sense of honor and a healthy dose of "am I really the grown-up in the room now?" humility. Stepping in to provide oversight for projects on short notice, I earned the trust of peers and management alike, which, let's be honest, is no small feat in a world where engineers can spot a missing comma from a mile away.

My promotion to assistant global commissioning and startup director was a milestone that filled me with pride, not just for the title, but for what it represented: the opportunity to develop and maintain global policies and procedures for all onshore and offshore projects. It was a role that demanded both vision and vigilance, and I took it on with a sense of accomplishment, knowing that every decision could ripple across continents (and occasionally, time zones that made my coffee habit legendary).

My days became a tapestry of proposal support, estimating, and guiding teams through the thorniest of challenges. Sometimes this meant global travel, collecting passport stamps like merit badges, sometimes it meant late nights, fueled by equal parts determination and caffeine. But always, it meant doing work I believed in, surrounded by people I respected and admired. In this new role, and since 2012, I provided oversight support to more than twenty different projects, a number that still makes me shake my head and wonder if I should have started a punch card for frequent flyer miles.

Through it all, I've tried to balance pride in what we accomplished with the humility to know that no one succeeds alone. Every late-night call, every last-minute pivot, and every shared laugh with colleagues reminded me that leadership is as much about listening as it is about leading. And if you can't find a little humor in the chaos, well, you're probably not reading the fine print on those global policies.

In 2019, during a casual chat with my manager, I floated the idea of semi-retirement: 24 hours a week, full benefits, and the freedom to contribute as long as I was needed. To my delight, corporate management approved my request in January 2020. I adopted a three-day work week, Tuesday through Thursday, with four-day weekends. I knew of no other employee with such a schedule, and I felt deeply honored and grateful.

Reflecting on nearly sixteen years with my employer, I am profoundly appreciative of the chance to collaborate with so many knowledgeable, kind, and gracious colleagues. Their support and mentorship have been instrumental in my professional growth and development. Because of these relationships, I have been able to participate in many of the industry's technological advancements and work on projects around the globe, making the world feel much smaller than it did when I first entered the petroleum industry.

On November 10, 2024, my birthday, I made the decision to fully retire after a long and fruitful career, 52 years of adventure, excitement, humility, and, above all, integrity. And if you're wondering, yes, I still encourage Joy to buy those lottery tickets. After all, you never know when the next adventure will begin.

Chapter 16
Retirement and Reflection

Much of my time these days is devoted to the humble, everyday tasks that keep our household humming along. Whether I'm tackling the infamous honey-do list (which, I'm convinced, grows longer every time I blink), getting lost in a woodworking project, or waging a valiant battle against the weeds in the garden, I find a quiet sense of purpose and satisfaction in each small act.

These routine chores and repairs aren't just about keeping the house standing (though that's a nice bonus). They're daily reminders of the importance of contributing to the well-being of our little kingdom. Each squeaky hinge silenced, each flower planted, is a small act of love, a way of saying, "I'm here, I care, and I'm doing my part."

Of course, Joy and I know the importance of stepping away from the daily grind. We make it a priority to escape now and then, whether it's a camping trip under a sky full of stars or a quiet afternoon at a local coffee shop. There's something magical about sipping a hot cup of coffee together, sharing stories, or simply enjoying the comfortable silence that comes from years of shared adventures. Sometimes, we'll treat ourselves to a glass of wine over dinner at a cozy restaurant, toasting to the simple joys of life and the fact that we still haven't burned down the kitchen.

During these moments, we talk about everything and nothing, our latest projects, memories from the past, or the curious behavior of the neighbor's cat. Sometimes, we just sit together, letting the world slow down around us. These shared experiences, whether filled with laughter or quiet reflection, deepen our bond and remind us that love is found in the little things: a gentle touch, a shared smile, or the warmth of a hand held across the table.

Retirement, for me, has been more than just a milestone, it's been a chance to reflect on the wild, winding journey that brought me here. I often think back to the pivotal moment when I chose to take a risk, to step through the door of opportunity and change the status quo of my life. Had I listened to the naysayers or let fear hold me back, I might have missed out on the adventures, the laughter, and the love that now fill my days.

So, as I tend the garden, chase down runaway socks, or share a quiet moment with Joy, I do so with a grateful heart. Every sunrise is a new adventure, every sunset a chance to reflect. And if you ever find yourself wondering whether to take that leap, remember: sometimes the greatest stories begin with a single, uncertain step, and a willingness to laugh at yourself along the way.

Nowadays, when greeted by others with a cheerful, "Good morning, how are you?" my instinctive response is, "Wonderful! Every day I wake up on the top side of the turf is a good day." I hold a deep belief that every new day is a true blessing, deserving to be treasured regardless of the circumstances we may face. Rising early is a cherished ritual for me; I find immense joy in stepping outside with the hope of witnessing another breathtaking sunrise as birds fill the morning air with their song.

These quiet moments at dawn serve as a powerful reminder of life's blessings and renew my sense of connection with nature. At the close of each day, as the sun sets and the sky is set ablaze with delicate pastel hues, I take time to reflect on the events that have unfolded and express gratitude. As I drift off to sleep, I do so with the hope that I will be fortunate enough to wake and witness another sunrise.

I feel truly fortunate to have traveled to five continents and visited more than thirty countries, where I either lived and worked with the local people or vacationed. The insight gained from visiting foreign lands, experiencing their culture, and getting to know the people firsthand far outweighs anything you read about or watch on television. It has been a blessing that I deeply appreciate. Each place I have visited, and every experience gained along the way, has enriched my perspective and contributed to the tapestry of my life's story.

While many other men sit around and dream of the fight, I dream about all the fun and excitement I've had in my life, such as the days when I used to ride my Harley. For example, I remember August 2007, when we loaded my Harley-Davidson onto a trailer and headed to my oldest son Jeremy's house in Bemidji, Minnesota. Jeremy, ever the independent rebel, had just bought a motorcycle (not a Harley, but we don't judge). Together, we set out on a father-and-son pilgrimage to the legendary Sturgis Motorcycle Rally in South Dakota, a week-long festival of roaring engines, scenic rides, and enough leather to outfit a small army.

The days were a blur of wind in our hair and the Black Hills rolling by, Mount Rushmore, the Badlands, Spearfish Canyon, and even a detour to Devils Post Pile in Wyoming. Nights were for concerts, barbecues, and swapping tall tales with fellow bikers at the Full Throttle Saloon, our home base complete with a couple of beds, a community shower, and 24-hour access to the kind of breakfast that sticks to your ribs (and your arteries).

Adventure, of course, loves company, and a good plot twist. On our way out of Bemidji, a bird dropped its prey (rat? rabbit? we'll never know) right in front of Jeremy, nearly turning our ride into a real-life game of Frogger. Later, we got lost in South Dakota for an hour, proving that even the best navigators sometimes need to ask for directions (or at least admit when they're lost). But we made it, and the rally was everything we hoped for, camaraderie, laughter, and enough bottles of beer to float a small boat.

The ride home was its own test of grit. We joined a pack of bikers on I-90, thundering east at 90 mph, racing the sunset and the creeping cold. By the time we crossed into Minnesota, the night air was so frigid I thought I'd turn into a popsicle on two wheels. We stopped a couple of times so I could thaw out, trying in vain to extract the slightest amount of heat from the bike's engine. At one point, I was pretty sure I was hugging that Harley closer than I ever hugged my high school sweetheart. Jeremy, being the compassionate son, tried to console me, but I quickly pointed out that I was only freezing to death, not dead yet, so he laughed, and we pressed on, determined to finish what we started.

Once we finally rolled into Jeremy's driveway, we toasted to our survival with a nightcap and a shared sense of triumph. I'm not saying we looked heroic, but if there had been a medal for "Most Likely to Survive a Midwestern Deep Freeze on a Motorcycle," we'd have been a shoo-in. No good father/son motorcycle road trip would be complete without a nostalgic souvenir; we each commemorated the trip with an FTS tattoo on our shoulders, a permanent reminder that sometimes, the best stories are the ones you wear on your sleeve (even if the artwork leaves a little to be desired).

The rally was such a hit, we brought the wives along in 2008 and 2010, reliving the magic and making new memories in the Black Hills. We partied so hard at the 2008 rally that all I can remember are two things: One, a girl named Johnnie, who every time we reminisce about that trip, we all laugh in unison and repeat her favorite saying, "Are you shitting me?" And two, we got hit by a tornadic hailstorm that totaled my truck and rental trailer, causing me to limp all the way from Sturgis to Houston.

In 2017, Jeremy and I weren't done chasing adventure. We towed our bikes to the home of my niece in Conway, Arkansas, where we spent the night (and dropped off the wives). The next day, we set off at dawn for Tennessee, where we met up with Jeremy's friend and tackled the legendary "Dragon Tail", a ride so twisty it could make a roller coaster jealous. After conquering the curves, we cruised to Maggie Valley, North Carolina, found a hotel, and set out to find a local bar. That night, we befriended the owners, swapped stories, and racked up a $350 tab (Pro tip: never let Jeremy mix drinks behind the bar unless you want to meet everyone in town).

The next morning, running on fumes and fighting a hangover that could slay a dragon, we mounted our bikes and rode back to Conway. It was grueling, but the promise of family and a hot meal kept us going. We made it, exhausted but exhilarated, closing another unforgettable chapter in our ongoing road trip saga.

Ah, but those were some fun times, and for sixteen glorious years, my Harley carried me on countless adventures, through rain, sun, and the occasional swarm of bugs. Eventually, I traded it in for a couple's camping trailer, marking the end of one era and the start of another. The Harley may have moved on, but the stories (and the bug stains) remain.

I consider myself truly blessed to have experienced the journey of marriage and having a family, as each relationship has offered invaluable lessons and revealed aspects of myself that I needed to learn and understand. Even through three failed marriages, I view these failures not as shortcomings but as essential experiences that contributed to my personal growth and development.

When I met Joy, it was as if the child was reborn in my heart. Suddenly, I was the kid on the playground again, just wanting to hold her hand and to be there for her, whether she needed a hand, a hug, or just someone to laugh at her jokes. And if anyone ever dumps sand in her hair, I'll put knots on their head, metaphorically, of course. (I'm a lover, not a fighter, but I do have a mean glare that's been known to wilt houseplants.)

I count myself incredibly lucky that life has blessed me with three beautiful, creative, and adventurous children, each one with a unique character who has contributed to building not only a successful career but families of their own. Between the three of them, they've managed to produce three grandchildren and, just to keep things lively, seven great-grandchildren.

While I cannot claim to have always played as integral a role in each of their lives as I might have wished, I recognize that this is not a reflection on them. Rather, it is the result of choices I made along the way, and I accept full responsibility for the outcomes that have followed from those decisions. There have been times when I was able to spend meaningful, quality moments with my loved ones, and other periods when those opportunities were far less frequent. The circumstances influencing these interactions have varied, sometimes bringing us closer together, and at other times creating distance, whether for better or worse.

Despite the ebb and flow of these connections, and regardless of whether these experiences were positive, negative, or simply neutral, I can state with all honesty and openness that my love for each of them remains unwavering. My affection endures, steadfast and forgiving, even as the nature and regularity of our relationships have shifted over the years.

In my younger years, I often misunderstood love, seeing it as a fleeting emotion tied closely to desire, personal need, or mere attraction. Now, I see love as something more modest, best defined by our actions toward others and our willingness to graciously accept the gestures and care offered to us. This exchange should never be taken for granted or exploited; instead, it must be grounded in mutual respect and genuine appreciation. There is no greater expression of love than the willingness to act for someone else without expecting anything in return, and equally, to accept their acts of kindness with humility and gratitude. This dynamic, built on respect and appreciation, truly embodies love at its finest.

In reflection on a life full of experiences with adventure, heartache, dedication, humility, humanity, and love, I offer only one piece of wisdom for consideration:

"Look to your parents and find the things about them that you love and cherish. Keep those things near and dear to your heart, forever. The things you don't like or disagree with, don't blame your parents for these things. Your parents are a product of their time and life, not yours. If you want these things to change, then change them in yourself. Break the chain, sometimes referred to as the sins of the father, by becoming a better person than your parents. Teach your children well, and ask them to do the same. In this manner, perhaps the future of humanity will improve, and someday, the world will live in harmony and peace."

I hold no regrets about who I am, what I have done, or what I have left undone. Regret, I feel, would diminish the value of my journey through this life. I believe each person is born for a reason, even if that reason remains elusive throughout their lifetime. I would be remiss not to admit that every action I have taken could have been improved upon, but I accept my life's path as it is, always striving to learn and grow from my experiences.

I am deeply grateful to still have my health, my wit, and my teeth. These blessings allow me to continue enjoying life and participating fully in each day's activities. The ability to remain sharp and physically well is something I do not take for granted, and I cherish the vitality that allows me to engage with my loved ones and pursue my interests. My intention is to live forever, although we all know how that story ends, just not when or why.

As for anyone who has taken the time to read my stories, you too have a story to be written and shared. Each person's journey starts with certain innate traits that become shaped by unique experiences, backgrounds, and decisions, whether they are the result of deliberate choices or unexpected events. Regardless of these differences, every individual possesses a narrative that holds meaning and value. The act of telling one's story is not limited by origin or temperament; it is an opportunity to reflect, connect, and contribute to a larger tapestry of human experience.

By sharing our stories, we acknowledge that every life is worthy of being remembered and understood. The details may vary, but the common thread is the significance of our experiences and the lessons they offer. Through the process of writing and sharing, we not only preserve our own histories but also encourage others to recognize the importance of their own journeys, reminding us all that every life has a story waiting to be told.

For People Like Me, if I can survive all the plot twists, pratfalls, and "what-was-I-thinking" moments life has thrown my way, and still have enough energy left to tell my story (and trust me, I'm not done yet), just imagine what's possible for you!

www.ingramcontent.com/pod-product-compliance
Lightning Source LLC
Chambersburg PA
CBHW050726010526
44107CB00009B/745